PRAISE FOR *TH*
OF PROJECT LE

CW00419553

Susanne Madsen's new book is a great guide for project managers looking to move from implementers to leaders. At every turn of the page, the evolving project leader will find stories, self assessments, and quizzes that will help solidify the learning and provide pathways for the application of new, stronger leadership skills to their projects. The emphasis on changing your mindset from of one of implementation to one of leadership is one that all project managers should take great effort to apply to their careers. **Dave Wakeman, Principal, Wakeman Consulting Group**

The Power of Project Leadership is a must-read for everyone in the project world who wants to up their game or be less stressed about delivery. Written with an energy and commitment borne out of personal experience, Susanne's book is packed with frameworks and reflective leadership exercises to challenge the way you work and has many stories from practitioners to inspire. Be brave, take a risk, get a copy and change your game! **Carole Osterweil, Director and Change Catalyst, OMQ Change Consulting**

Susanne's book clearly demonstrates the insights and tools to become an inspirational leader as well as an intelligent manager of projects. Teams want their leaders to be inspirational and the processes they use intelligently selected. Whether you are an experienced practitioner looking to reflect and hone your skills or setting out with a goal to become an inspirational leader of projects this book provides the insight to do so. Highly recommended. All my team have a copy. I'm that confident of the effect it will have on my business. **Paul Daniels, Managing Director, Leadership and Management Ltd**

Reading the book is like having a personal coach assess, tune and hone your transition from manager into leader. Susanne's coaching skills have created an incremental learning environment where the value of earlier exercises become even more apparent as the pages roll on. A must for postgraduate students and project professionals alike; I hope my students read it. **Dr Nicholas Lambrou, Principal Lecturer, University of Westminster**

In this great and inspiring book, Susanne has gathered the core elements and key insights to bring you the essence of project leadership. Not only will project managers find value in reading this book, but also those in a leadership role or who seek to evolve into one. Similar to her first book, it contains coaching questions that challenge you to think about yourself, assess your situation and commit to becoming the leader you wish to be. This book should be your personal development tool for this year! **Birger Kontek, Senior Change Manager and Vice President, Barclaycard Germany**

Key#1 is 'be authentic' and with this book Susanne has shown true authenticity by empowering her readers with stories, insights, tools and practical activities, along with a vision of what a project leader needs to be. *The Power of Project Leadership* is recommended reading for all project managers. **Peter Taylor, The Lazy Project Manager**

Susanne provides a refreshing approach to project leadership. A refined mix of insight and practice gives us all the opportunity to take a look in the mirror and choose to make some changes. This isn't a theoretical treatise, but rather a workshop manual that I wish had been available earlier on in my career. It would have saved me from a few scrapes! **Julian Bullen, Project Director, The Clarkson Alliance**

Susanne's book is a blueprint for moving from project management to project leadership and will, without a doubt, become a reference for those who are looking to take their leadership skills to the next level. The book is a true hands-on approach with each chapter chock-full of principles you can almost immediately cut-and-paste into your professional engagements. With tested ideas for professional development, avoiding common pitfalls, empowering your team, and engaging stakeholders, Susanne takes Project Managers by the hand and equips them with all they need to stop managing and start leading. **Cesar Abeid, PMP, founder of PM for the Masses podcast**

Susanne has produced a guide to enable the transition to project leadership that balances the right amount of theory, with relevant and insightful stories and sticky ideas from practitioners that are relevant and easy to understand. She also makes the reader reflect on one's own behaviors, barriers, drivers and motivations in a way that is not intrusive but sometimes confronting. This work will support the growth of project leaders worldwide and can only result in the delivery of more and more successful projects and programs and leaders. I commend this work as a must read to every project manager regardless of the type of project you are working on – it will help you now and in the future. **Deborah Hein, CEO, International Centre for Complex Project Management**

This excellent book takes you on the next vital step of your project career journey from manager to leader. Susanne's book is a well thought out and highly practical guide to how to break through the fear barrier of 'not wanting to let go of control' and moves you into learning how to 'inspire rather than perspire' – I highly recommend it. **Stephen Carver, FAPM, Cranfield School of Management**

I am delighted to see that the need for greater focus in leadership and communication has been captured in Susanne's new book *The Power of Project Leadership*. This book captures the importance of entrepreneurial spirit and correctly emphasizes the 'human aspect' whilst addressing the psychological and physiological issues in leadership development. Congratulations Susanne, your new book helps provide the 'keys' for future leadership development and will make an important contribution to the global complex project management community. **Stephen Hayes MBE, Founding MD of ICCPM and MD of Complexity Solutions**

Managing projects is exciting and fun. But there comes a moment in every project manager's career when you realize that there must be more than just bringing tasks to completion. This is the moment when you realize that you want to go from project manager to project leader, which is when you have to pick up *The Power of Project Leadership*. Susanne Madsen's book is an in-depth road map that shows you exactly how to re-invent yourself and go from managing your projects at the task level to leading them through vision and empowerment. **Cornelius Fichtner, PMP, Host of The Project Management Podcast**

The Power of Project Leadership

By the same author:

The Project Management Coaching Workbook

The Power of Project Leadership

7 Keys to Help You Transform from Project Manager to Project Leader

Susanne Madsen

KoganPage

LONDON PHILADELPHIA NEW DELHI

Publisher's note

Every possible effort has been made to ensure that the information contained in this book is accurate at the time of going to press, and the publishers and authors cannot accept responsibility for any errors or omissions, however caused. No responsibility for loss or damage occasioned to any person acting, or refraining from action, as a result of the material in this publication can be accepted by the editor, the publisher or any of the authors.

First published in Great Britain and the United States in 2015 by Kogan Page Limited

2nd Floor, 45 Gee Street	1518 Walnut Street, Suite 1100	4737/23 Ansari Road
London EC1V 3RS	Philadelphia PA 19102	Daryaganj
United Kingdom	USA	New Delhi 110002
www.koganpage.com		India

© Susanne Madsen, 2015

The right of Susanne Madsen to be identified as the author of this work has been asserted by her in accordance with the Copyright, Designs and Patents Act 1988.

ISBN   978 0 7494 7234 4
E-ISBN 978 0 7494 7235 1

British Library Cataloguing-in-Publication Data

A CIP record for this book is available from the British Library.

Library of Congress Cataloging-in-Publication Data

Madsen, Susanne.
    The power of project leadership : 7 keys to help you transform from project manager to project leader / Susanne Madsen.
        pages cm.
    ISBN 978-0-7494-7234-4 (paperback) – ISBN 978-0-7494-7235-1 (ebk)   1. Project management.
    2. Leadership.   I. Title.
    HD69.P75M325 2015
    658.4′092—dc23
                                                                    2014030002

Typeset by Amnet
Printed and bound by CPI Group (UK) Ltd, Croydon, CR0 4YY

The world needs your genius and it needs your leadership

CONTENTS

FOREWORD

This book is not about project management as most people understand the term. It is about the rapidly growing new specialism of project leadership in organizations. The world of project management is evolving rapidly in two fundamental ways. Firstly, it is moving away from a preoccupation with project planning and control tools as the keys to success, and towards the management of people and their performance. Secondly, it is moving away from a preoccupation with complex construction projects towards a wider appreciation of the diversity of projects that are mushrooming within organizations.

That was how the preface to *Project Leadership* by Briner, Geddes and Hastings began. Had the word *IT* replaced the word *construction* you could have skipped a couple of decades and imagined it had been written not for the nineties but for the noughties. But in the nineties this type of idea was largely ignored. I remember receiving with excitement and reading my first BoK (Body of Knowledge) only to find that only a couple of pages (at the end) had been dedicated to anything related to people and even then the references were to HR and not leadership. However, those early pioneers – Boddy, Buchannan, Gareis, etc – in the 'softer' side of projects, began a movement that it seems has taken forever to arrive.

There has been a slow revolution in project management, but improvements in the science (hard/tools) and art (soft/human) of project management have been constantly outpaced by increases in the speed, complexity and ambiguity of the business and organizational environment. As the world has become more uncertain and with the pace of change outstripping our ability to make sense of things, more and more projects have moved, in my language, from allowing us to 'paint by numbers' to leaving us 'lost in the fog'.

Projects in uncertainty mean change for people. And human beings are not really at their best when surprised by change or when they have it thrust upon them. Now, more than ever, we need guides to help us navigate the leadership challenges.

I had the pleasure of reading *The Power of Project Leadership* in a single sitting on a flight from London to Chicago (yes, I do still travel by moving my body, not just by sending a Cubot avatar in my place!). As I often do, I made notes in the margins using green erasable ink and turning down the page corners so I could go back though the interesting points and reread them. (Please don't try this on a Kindle.) By the end the manuscript was a mess with many, many corners turned down. This is a good thing.

What Susanne Madsen has achieved with *The Power of Project Leadership* is to bring together decades of know-how on the 'soft side' of programme and project leadership into an accessible structure. She has done this with a witty and amusing narrative and with clear signposts for the reader. As a reader you weave your way through short case stories, explore the underlying theories and develop some concrete actions and tools that you can apply immediately. Her overarching seven-step framework helps readers to position themselves on their learning and transformation journey.

As we look forward over the next two decades, what will the vision of project leadership be then? There are many future echoes in this book. The focus on innovation, the move away from influencing in hierarchies to influencing in networks, the move from the importance of processes to chains of apps and more.

Now, today, many of us share the vision of 'ZERO – Creating a world where every project succeeds'. This book is a significant building block in transforming the vision into reality.

Eddie Obeng

Pentacle

The Virtual Business School

Burke Lodge, Beaconsfield, UK

FOREWORD

Some time ago I was listening to a colleague who was delivering a lecture on 'Leadership'. He started by telling us that he had put 'Leadership' into a search engine and it came back with over a million references! He then went on to say – 'and I don't believe a word of it!' Were he to carry out this exercise today, I would hope that the search would provide a reference for Susanne's book *The Power of Project Leadership*. This is a different sort of book on leadership and to make the best use of it you have to allow it to stimulate your own thought processes and help you to use it as a tool for your own personal development. This is a book with words that you can believe!

Unlike many books in the world of Project Management, it does not provide a series of recipes for successful projects but it gives some interesting examples and good ideas that the wise listener can think about and develop for his or her own use. When I first looked through the book I was worried by the numbered lists – I am concerned that checklists inhibit original thinking. We do see a lot of these in our PM literature and it is too easy to tick items off without giving them full consideration. I hope that Susanne's book will persuade readers to add their own items and create their own checklists.

As Project Managers we have always been pre-occupied with the tools and techniques of our business, and for many people this is what they believe is Project Management. My own view is that to be effective as a Project Manager it is necessary to be a Leader – people are the key to success and understanding them is of critical importance. Where this book is so good is that it takes this point of view but makes it clear that before understanding others, you have to understand yourself. Working through the book will help you to find out about yourself.

Susanne has made a valuable contribution to the Project Management Library. I think that it will be especially useful for those project managers who find themselves in the world of complexity where leadership is a key competence to enable success. Project Leadership is indeed powerful and like all power must be used with wisdom.

I recommend Susanne's book to all who aspire to become true project leaders.

Mary McKinlay

Director and Trustee, APM

Vice-President of IPMA

Adjunct Professor of PM at SKEMA

ACKNOWLEDGEMENTS

I would like to thank Andy Taylor, Arnon Yaffe, Benoit Jolin, Colleen Garton, Dave Sawyer, Eileen Strider, Hala Saleh, Harlan Bridges, Julia Strain, Kevin Ciccotti, Liz Pearce, Michael Fleron, Morten Sorensen, Patrick Yengo, Paul Chapman, Paul Hodgkins, Penny Pullan, Peter Taylor, Rich Maltzman, Robert Kelly, Rod Willis, Sam Fleming, Steve Pikett and Thomas Juli for having contributed to this book with their stories and insights. I consider many of you as my colleagues although we may have never met or formally worked together. We live in a truly magnificent time where social media makes it possible to connect with like-minded individuals from across the world. I am truly grateful for the warmth and kindness you have shown and for being able to share your insights.

I am also grateful to Professor Eddie Obeng and Mary McKinlay for having written the forewords, as well as Ben Hughes, Cesar Abeid, Dave Wakeman, Julian Bullen and Nicholas Lambrou for their valuable feedback on the manuscript. Finally I would like to thank the many readers of my first book who continue to get in touch. Thank you for your support and encouragement. It means a lot.

Introduction

The world needs your genius and it needs your leadership

Thank you for picking up this book and for wanting to read it and learn from it. I am thrilled, not because you are reading my words, but because I feel your ambition and your desire and willingness to grow and learn. That is where all progress and success stems from – the desire to learn, adapt and improve. We all have different motives for why we want to progress. Some are driven by monetary rewards and recognition, others love to take on a new challenge, and others again are motivated by the opportunity to express their creativity or to contribute to a particular project or idea.

Irrespective of what your drivers are for wanting to grow professionally, there are positive outcomes: you feel more fulfilled and you contribute in some way or another to a cause greater than yourself, even if it isn't that apparent to you. It may be that you have a positive impact on people who work for you, maybe you help deliver a great new product or service, or you pave the way for future projects to be delivered in a smoother and more effective manner. There is a great need for all of these contributions and for many more.

You are probably as familiar with the statistics of failing projects as I am. A study by *The Economist* and the PMI (Project Management Institute) shows that only 56 per cent of strategic initiatives are successful[1] whereas according to other studies the success rate is far lower depending on sector. The House of Commons in the UK, for instance, has reported that only one-third of major government projects are delivered to time and budget.[2]

Projects fail because of unclear scope and success criteria, lack of strategic alignment, lack of buy-in and engagement from senior stakeholders, lack of change management skills, underestimation, inadequate risk management and poor resourcing. According to the PMI, organizations are losing an average of $109 million for every $1 billion spent on projects due to lack of focus on people, processes and outcomes.[3] And that is in spite of more tools and techniques being available to us that help us keep track of the many moving parts of a project. It also appears that project failure rates continue to be high during periods of economic uncertainty and increased competition. During such times we should be spending our resources carefully and delivering better-quality projects at a lower cost. Instead, it seems financial and human resources continue to be wasted on failing projects.

But why do projects continue to fail? An important aspect is the increased complexity of projects and the environments in which they are undertaken. Many factors contribute to this growing complexity – for example, social and technological change, growing global interdependency, increasing numbers of stakeholders and the need to communicate and coordinate cross-culturally. As the ICCPM (International Centre for Complex Project Management) writes in its report *Hitting a Moving Target*, 'It is clear that the situation has to be addressed radically and comprehensively. If we do what we've always done, we'll get what we've always got – and there are too many examples that prove what we've always got isn't good enough'.[4]

So your ambition and willingness to grow as a project manager and leader is highly appreciated. We need more people who can navigate complexity, who want to learn from past mistakes and who have a real desire to develop and become great leaders and ambassadors for better ways of doing projects. Imagine what a difference that would make. Imagine if all project managers and their teams were working towards a common goal of continuous improvement and experiential learning – and if they shared the same enthusiasm and understanding of how to go about delivering the best possible product to the customer with the least amount of resources. That would be a dream come true! But dreams and dream teams come about only when someone takes the lead and has the vision and insight to show the way. Unfortunately, people like that can be hard to come by.

How many people, for instance, do you know from your profession who are really passionate about making a difference? How many have an inspiring personality and are excellent at engaging and motivating others to contribute to an appealing and meaningful vision? And how many of them are highly respected and liked for their integrity, authenticity and always delivering on their promises? Not that many I would have thought. Some people are excellent at leading others through change, but they are few and far between.

According to PMI's research, over 80 per cent of high-performing organizations now report that the most important acquired skills for project managers to successfully manage complex projects are leadership skills.[5] Traditional dimensions of project management such as cost, schedule and performance are necessary but insufficient. The world is changing at a rapid pace, and the need for leaders is greater than ever before. We need leaders who can deal with ambiguity, take ownership of the vision, foster collaboration, gain buy-in and motivate the team to achieve the expected outcomes.

I assume that you are ambitious and that you want to generate results for your project and for your clients. I also assume that you want to grow and develop and be recognized in the process. To do so you have to optimize your ways and help others do the same. Thinking and behaving with a traditional project management mindset of control and compliance is not serving you. It is limiting your opportunities and it is contributing to project failure.

Given the right environment, the right mindset and the right support, I believe that all project managers have the potential to be great leaders. Being a leader is not something that is limited to CEOs of a large company. Anyone can be a leader within his or her field. Leadership is not a result of the job title you hold but of the attitudes and behaviours you possess. So get ready and embrace a new way of doing projects and get ready to lead. Stand up tall and sharpen your saw. The world needs your genius and it needs your leadership.

What you will get from this book

This book is for project managers, programme managers, project administrators, PMO staff, team leaders, department heads, line managers and anyone else who is involved in projects and programmes and would like to get better at leading and implementing change. The book is also suited to MBA students and professional trainers who would like to study or teach the topic of how to progress from project manager to leader.

The book will show you how to adapt to a world of increasing complexity, and how to reap the opportunities it presents by shifting your managerial mindset into one of project leadership. This shift will enable you not only to successfully deliver your projects but to do so in more fruitful and innovative ways. You will learn to address the most fundamental causes of project failure and to use the project you are currently working on to step up and lead. Studying this book will assist your transition into a confident, driven and focused project leader who adds real value; someone who continuously learns and improves and who delivers outstanding projects by motivating, engaging and inspiring everybody around them.

My aim with the book is not simply to inform you about project leadership, but to inspire you to take action and implement the ideas presented to you. I will do that by providing a set of simple and powerful exercises and by incorporating dozens of transformational stories and interviews with project leaders and project management professionals. Some of the project leaders who have contributed with their insights and stories include Rich Maltzman, author of *Green Project Management*; Peter Taylor, author of *The Lazy Project Manager*; Colleen Garton, author of *Fundamentals of Technology Project Management*; Thomas Juli, author of *Leadership Principles for Project Success*; Penny Pullan; and Kevin Ciccotti, to name just a few. Their stories and contributions are displayed in stand-alone boxes so that they can easily be distinguished from the main narrative of the book. Many have contributed with more than one topic, so you may see their name appear in more than one place. The full list of contributors can be found in the prelims.

Throughout the book I will support you as much as I can, and I will appeal to your logical side as well as your more creative and emotional side. You may be well aware of the things you need to do differently in order to step up, but somehow fail to do them. That is why I will engage your emotional side and also delve into behavioural theories. After all, your success as a project leader is not dependent on your knowledge alone, but on the manner in which you *implement* that knowledge. We could call that wisdom. Wisdom is the ability to discern and judge which aspects of your knowledge are right and applicable to a particular situation.

Project leaders are wise because they are able to relate their knowledge no matter the situation and because they put their knowledge into action. A large part of this book is geared toward helping you become a wise leader and to apply your knowledge. But the book does more than help *you* to develop; it also helps you to help others. A big part of being a leader is to develop other people's potential and enable them to perform and contribute. This book will assist you in doing so. For each insight, tool or strategy you come across, first apply it to yourself, then apply it to the people you work with.

With this objective in mind, please be warned that I may challenge your existing beliefs and behaviours, and that oftentimes I will ask more questions than I will provide answers. Asking the right set of questions is in many cases more powerful than simply providing the right set of answers. And besides, there may not always be a 'right' set of answers. In a complex world of fast technological, social and economic change, there are very few absolutes. I hope I have your permission to ask these probing questions and to challenge you to expand your comfort zone and to take on a new set of beliefs and habits.

Just get stuck in – by Dave Sawyer

My advice to project managers is to always be learning and to just get stuck in. Make mistakes, admit them, move on and get better. Don't cover up your mistakes, because everyone will become aware of it. Talk through problems and ask loads of questions. Be honest about what you do/don't understand and ask for help. Only idiots don't ask for help when they need it. In the early days, I felt overwhelmed by everything, but now I'm a lot calmer because I know that I can do it. To get there you just need to be patient and remember that it won't happen overnight. Keep learning and get a good mentor. When I left college, I thought, 'Well, that's it for learning'. How wrong I was! After another 20-plus years, I have professional qualifications, a master's degree and I have read literally thousands of articles on management, project management, leadership and strategy. I take great delight in reading all sorts of materials that I can apply to real life. It also means that I can set a good example and give people the support and opportunities that I had. Taking the MSc in project management really changed the playing field for me. It taught me to think critically and to ask questions designed to give the brain a good workout. What's also great is that the managers at work started to notice a big change in how I was working. As a result I now have bigger budgets, more staff and I'm certainly doing things much better than I was before.

– Dave Sawyer, Project Manager, UK Government

I realized that I needed to clone myself – by Arnon Yaffe

I have always been a people person and good at leading teams, but I was doing it intuitively, unaware. My AHA moment came when I realized what I needed to do in order to advance my career. I was a senior PM in a small 30-people consulting firm. I realized that if I wanted to grow then I must bring up a new generation of PMs that will enable us to take on more projects and grow the business. In other words, I needed to 'clone' myself. I knew I could train my colleagues in hard skills, but I also knew that it would take more than hard skills to become an effective PM. At the time I didn't know what the missing piece was, I just knew I couldn't do it on my own. Back then I wasn't aware that coaching existed, so eventually I brought in a consultant who specialized in training salespeople to teach us soft skills. I attended the classes myself and from that point on my life became an endless chain of AHA moments. The company grew rapidly; I became COO and then Co-CEO of the then 150-people firm. But it didn't stop there. . . I fell in love with coaching and decided to become a mentor and personal coach. It completely transformed my life.

– Arnon Yaffe, Project Leadership Consultant and Coach

The four chapters

The book comprises the following four chapters:

Chapter 1 – The world is changing and so must you

The book starts off explaining the differences between management and leadership and why a pure management approach is not enough to successfully deliver projects. We look at the ways in which our society is becoming increasingly complex, interconnected and competitive and how it is impacting both the project management profession and how you work. We discuss the most fundamental causes of project management failure and enable you to determine your own project management style and positioning in relation to these failures. Towards the end we introduce the 7 keys to project leadership and explain how they can help you add more value, serve your client and deliver better projects.

Chapter 2 – Your hidden drivers

The second chapter of the book is an introspective that takes a closer look at your own sources of motivation and the beliefs you hold about your capabilities as a project manager and leader. The purpose of this section is to help you gain insight into some of the beliefs and working patterns that may be holding you back and to assist you in replacing them with something more conducive. We also examine your goals and aspirations and the underlying

FIGURE 0.1 The four parts of the book

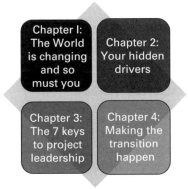

reasons that drive you to achieving them. This part of the book prepares you and ensures that you have the right frame of mind before we move into the formal discussion of project leadership strategies.

Chapter 3 – The 7 keys to project leadership

Chapter 3 is the main body of the book where we discuss the 7 essential keys to project leadership. The 7 keys encompass the complete set of capabilities, skills, attitudes and behaviours that you need in order to become an effective project leader and break free from past mistakes. The 7 keys are:

1 Be authentic.
2 Lead with vision.
3 Improve and innovate.
4 Empower the team.
5 Get close to your stakeholders.
6 Establish a solid foundation.
7 Work with intent.

Chapter 4 – Making the transformation happen

In the last part of the book, we look at specific actions you can take to embed the 7 keys and sustain your transformation. I provide you with a set of tools that will help you let go of the old ways that are not serving you and embrace the new. These tools will help you feel more confident and assist you in stepping up and doing whatever it takes to become an authentic and impactful project leader. They will facilitate your transformation and enable you to contribute with all that you have to become a great role model for others to follow.

Website and bonus material

The book is supported by additional material that has been collated for your benefit on the supporting website at www.powerofprojectleadership.com. The site contains more detail about the interviews that have been conducted for the book. It also provides you with inspirational videos, worksheets, background material and recommended resources that will help you and encourage you to transform from project manager to project leader. I will remind you of this extra material and encourage you to use it as we move through the book.

What motivated me to write this book?

My passion for project leadership, and helping project managers become leaders, stems from my own transformational experiences and from the many stories and AHA moments I have witnessed as a coach. My defining moment happened about 10 years into my career as a project manager. I was working hard and I was working long hours running a business-critical multiyear project. I wanted to do a good job, and at the time I thought that meant knowing it all, doing it all and micromanaging the team. Unfortunately, that led to stress and exhaustion and very poor leadership on my part. I was good at interfacing with stakeholders, but less successful when it came to creating a collaborative, fully empowered team. I also didn't feel that I had sufficient knowledge of the client's business to effectively question the requirements or the strategy of the initiative. I spent most of my time dealing with urgent issues and was constantly on my back foot. I was under a lot of pressure, and I didn't feel that I had anyone to delegate to. But more important, I wasn't leveraging the human potential of the team, let alone my own.

Around the same time I attended a five-day leadership course – an experience that had a profound effect on me. What changed me the most weren't the many assessments and discussions that shed light on my personal leadership style, but the one-to-one coaching that I received as part of the course.

During this coaching I realized that I had the power to change my reality and that if I wanted to become a more fulfilled project manager (meaning more at ease, more effective and less overworked) then I could absolutely do so.

As simple as it sounds, this was a true light-bulb moment for me, which kicked off a chain of events. Firstly, I started studying and experimenting with what it meant to become a better manager and leader; secondly, I decided to become a coach; and thirdly, it inspired me to write my first book, *The Project Management Coaching Workbook*. I was so fired up that I worked evenings and weekends coaching project managers on top of my day job as a programme manager.

I now work full-time as a project leadership coach helping people overcome the many challenges they face in a project environment. By making a few essential adjustments, they are able not only to overcome them but also to dramatically increase their performance and well-being. Enabling more project managers to step up and lead is crucial if we want to address the reasons why so many projects fail. The world is full of managers who are good at complying and upholding standards, but if we want to deliver better projects we have to start doing things differently. We have to think broader, deeper and further, and we have to be comfortable standing out and taking the lead.

My vision and desire is to see more project managers transform into great project leaders who improve and innovate, who partner with their clients with a view to delivering what they really need – tactically and strategically – and who maximize human potential by motivating and inspiring everyone around them. My mission is to assist you with this transformation, to see you become a valuable mentor to others and to be part of a new culture in the workplace. When that happens, everybody benefits – the team, the client, the organization, society and you, the project manager, or *leader* should I say!

Notes

1 The Economist Intelligence Unit (2013) Why Good Strategies Fail: Lessons for the C-Suite, sponsored by the Project Management Institute (PMI), http://www .pmi.org/~/media/PDF/Publications/WhyGoodStrategiesFail_Report_EIU_PMI. ashx and http://www.pmi.org/en/About-Us/Press-Releases/New-Research-Why-Good-Strategies-Fail-Lessons-for-the-C-Suite.aspx

2 House of Commons (2012) Assurance for major projects, Fourteenth Report of Session 2012–13, http://www.publications.parliament.uk/pa/cm201213/ cmselect/cmpubacc/384/384.pdf

3 PMI (2014) *PMI's Pulse of the Profession In-Depth Report, The High Cost of Low Performance 2014*, Project Management Institute (PMI)

4 ICCPM (2013) *Hitting a Moving Target: Complex Project and Programme Delivery in an Uncertain World*, International Centre for Complex Project Management (ICCPM)

5 PMI (2014) *PMI's Pulse of the Profession In-Depth Report, Navigating Complexity*, Project Management Institute (PMI) http://www.pmi.org/~/media/PDF/Business-Solutions/Navigating_Complexity.ashx

The world is changing and so must you

IN THIS CHAPTER YOU WILL LEARN

- What the differences are between management and leadership
- What the three most fundamental mistakes are that projects managers make
- How technological, social, cultural and economic change is affecting you and what you can do to work with it rather than against it
- How the 7 keys to project leadership can help you break free from the management trap

Management versus leadership

In recent years there has been much debate on how to characterize management versus leadership. *Management* is said to be the discipline that specializes on maintaining the status quo, conforming to standards and organizing and directing individuals around the boundaries that have been set to achieve the task. These boundaries relate to time, money, quality, equipment, human resources and anything else that involves achieving that assignment. If you are a good manager it means that you are good at producing a set of products and services in a predictable way, day after day, on budget and to consistent quality. It is a discipline that requires you to be rational and logical and make use of certain skills and methods.

Leadership on the other hand is concerned with setting goals, making improvements to existing ways of working and motivating and leading the team to reaching this new direction. It is characterized by certain behaviours such as sharing an inspiring vision, producing useful change, leading by example, empowering others and creating the most conducive environment for team success. Leadership is not about the specific skills you possess but about how you approach an assignment and how you relate to others.

One of the main differences between management and leadership is the way in which the two disciplines motivate people and teams to achieve objectives. Managers rely on their authority and on task-related boundaries to get work done. Leaders, on the other hand, influence, inspire and appeal to people at an individual level. They strive to get the best out of people by aligning each person's individual objectives to those of the project and organization.

Another way of illustrating the differences between management and leadership is that managers are effective at chopping down trees according to a set schedule, whereas leaders will climb to the top of the trees and may declare that they are not even in the right forest! In other words, managers are concerned with doing things right, leaders with doing the right things. Figure 1.1 illustrates the main differences.

As we move into the heart of this book, we will explore the differences between management and leadership in more depth and you will come to understand how these two disciplines can be combined to create the best possible conditions for you, your client and your team. Project leaders make use of both disciplines, but as you grow and develop in your career, you will likely come to rely on leadership over and above management.

It is worth emphasizing that in contrast to project management, leadership is not a destination you reach – for instance, through a specific type

FIGURE 1.1 Management versus leadership

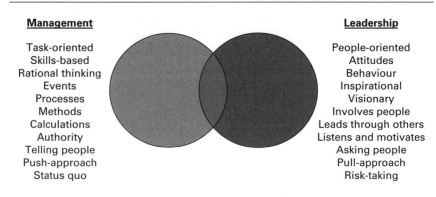

Management	Leadership
Task-oriented	People-oriented
Skills-based	Attitudes
Rational thinking	Behaviour
Events	Inspirational
Processes	Visionary
Methods	Involves people
Calculations	Leads through others
Authority	Listens and motivates
Telling people	Asking people
Push-approach	Pull-approach
Status quo	Risk-taking

of job – as it is related to the attitudes and behaviours you display more than the skills you possess. In that sense it is possible for someone in a project management role to be perceived as a *leader* due to the behaviours the person exhibits, and it is equally possible for someone in a CEO role to be perceived as a *non*-leader. Leadership is not attained through a job title but through a continuous journey of introspection, observation and development.

The more-for-less culture is upon us

Traditionally, a good project manager was someone who was logical and rational and effective at dealing with events, tasks and processes. It was someone who would work to the client's brief and use his or her authority to deliver the desired outputs. Often, this type of project manager would study best practices and company procedures so that the individual could play by the rules and ensure that the standards were upheld. By understanding how the firm operated, the project manager could blend in, adopt the company culture and ensure that his or her team would continue to contribute to the way things had always been done.

But this approach no longer works. We cannot rely on the old ways of delivering projects, as the world is becoming increasingly complex and competitive with a growing need for adaptability, innovation and better use of human resources. As one executive put it, 'If a project manager just follows orders he is not much use to me'.[1]

The global economic crisis that dominated the world from 2008–2013 has affected us in more ways than we could have expected and is one of the factors that have made the world a more competitive place. Many sectors and businesses felt the pinch, and the squeeze on revenues forced many to downsize. The competition for roles intensified, and there was increased scrutiny around the types of projects that got approved for implementation. Only the most critical projects got kicked off – often on a reduced budget.

In many ways, this scenario still exists. Most people think we go back to normal as soon as an economic crisis is over, but in reality that never happens.[2] Whereas the economy moves in cycles of ebb and flow, things are never the same. Every time the economy takes a jolt, we downsize and are forced to look for new and better ways of doing business. When the economy bounces back, the jobs aren't added back into the economy at the exact same places where they disappeared. Instead, jobs are created

FIGURE 1.2 Old versus new world: from compliance to adaptability

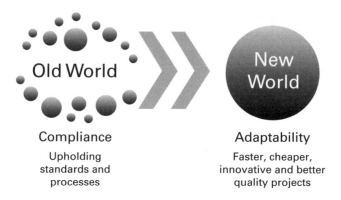

Compliance

Upholding
standards and
processes

Adaptability

Faster, cheaper,
innovative and better
quality projects

in new areas, performing new activities. Old working patterns have been replaced by something new.

What that means for project managers is that we have to adjust to the changing economic climate. Not only do we need to up our game in order to both be considered for a job and keep it, we also need to look for new ways we can deliver the same outcomes and benefits to our clients with fewer resources. Essentially, the more-for-less culture is upon us with a demand for faster, cheaper and better-quality projects, a quest that is not without challenges. It requires that we continuously question, innovate, take risks and change the practices that are no longer serving us. As Tim Harford, an economist and author of *Adapt*, argues, success in our complex world comes down to how quickly we can learn from past mistakes, adapt and adjust.

When budgets and resources are cut, our first reaction is often one of resistance. We may feel that we have to compromise and that quality of the end deliverable is affected. We also have to spend more time justifying our projects and their expenditure, including cost of staff, software, materials, training, equipment and product features. Everything is being questioned, which can be very trying. We feel that the negatives are far bigger than the positives; hence we resist. In his best-selling little book on change, *Who Moved My Cheese?*, Dr Spencer Johnson writes 'the more important your cheese is to you, the more you want to hold on to it' and 'the quicker you let go of old cheese, the sooner you find new cheese'. 'Cheese' represents the outdated habits and benefits that we take for granted. The more attached we are to them, the more painful it is to change. The trick, however, is to accept that things will never be the same. We have to adapt and change.

Each new financial crisis shakes things up – by Colleen Garton

During each economic crisis companies are forced to take a look at where they can be more efficient. It can be a painful process but it also halts complacency and wasteful business practices in their tracks. During the dotcom boom years, many organizations did not even have experienced project managers. They let anyone manage projects or just let technical folks manage themselves.

The crash changed all that. Project management became a real profession. Processes and best practices were no longer things to be sneered at with a 'We don't need that nonsense here' attitude. Each new financial crisis that comes along shakes things up: people lose their jobs, money gets tight, and employee perks are lost. However, it is also like hitting an efficiency 'reset' button. Organizations are forced to be more efficient, to make better business decisions, to think before they spend or act. This is not a bad thing.

– Colleen Garton, author of *Fundamentals of Technology Project Management* and *Managing Without Walls*

Less is definitely more – by Benoit Jolin

My recent experience has led me to believe that two factors are contributing to a change in what executives expect from project management. (1) Urgency and the need to deliver tangible results in shorter and shorter time frames, often due to investor/shareholder pressures for rapid returns and an increasingly competitive landscape, and (2) return on capital as we expect more from each dollar invested. As a result, what we are seeing is a growing distaste for unnecessary ceremony and planning, and a growing appetite for lean project management principles: early project de-risking through test and learn methods, fast failure models, high fidelity demos or prototypes, etc. It's about keeping it real (read: data driven decision-making) and focusing outcomes over outputs (read: useful, usable and tangible results). Less is definitely more today, and wasteful procedure is making way for more experimentation.

– Benoit Jolin, Head of Global Supplier Experience, Expedia Inc

Project managers must understand financial and economic drivers – by Morten Sorensen

It is true that today's expectations of rapid delivery, fast benefit realization and faster than ever response times to changes are driving project management practices. There is less appetite for time-consuming upfront design, detailed planning and related project management planning documentation. There is furthermore a trend of increased expectations of more senior project management roles. They must to a higher degree be competent in areas such as financial, business and customer services/solutions. Factors such as market gains, economic value and rapid return on investments are becoming bigger drivers for business requirements and benefits realization. Project managers are increasingly being expected to relate to these aspects of the client's environment.

– Morten Sorensen, Area VP, Global Client Services at Verizon Enterprise Solutions

Everything is wanted 'faster, cheaper, better' – by Sam Fleming

Everything is wanted 'faster, cheaper, better', which is the mantra of most executive leadership teams. Companies are now fully bought into the 'Single Customer View' within their technology estates, and only invest in expensive solutions if they lead to cheaper projects of the future and a better all-round view of their customers so that communication is tailored and opportunities are gained. So the challenge for project managers seems increasingly to encourage the business to ask for the right level of requirements and foster them into adopting standard functionality, moving away from costly customizations.

– Sam Fleming, Head of Project Delivery, British Gas Plc

The more-for-less culture means that project managers must become more financially aware right from inception of a project through to its delivery and to the realization of the ultimate benefits. We have to be more focused on business value and see our primary role as delivering sustainable value to the company – not just completing projects on time and on budget. This means that we have to help senior managers and customers select the projects that make the most economic and strategic sense by creating a business case where every benefit is related back to a dollar figure or to corporate strategy. In addition we have to challenge each part of the project lifecycle, the inputs and outputs and the development methods we use, so that we can better understand how to work smarter. We must critically assess which new technologies and working practices we can employ, which extra benefits we can deliver – and very important – how we can better utilize the human potential of our projects.

Evaluating project processes and technology is not enough. What will really get us somewhere is the optimization of human capital across our global and multicultural teams. The team is the project's biggest asset, and this is where we find one of the largest opportunities for development. As Forrester Research writes, 'The new breed of project managers must have higher levels of team-building, collaboration, and people skills, and stay well attuned to the rhythms and needs of their teams. . . Empathy and the ability to connect are critical'.[3]

But the need to understand and work with human behaviour extends far beyond the immediate project team. It relates to everyone involved in the change process – including the project's stakeholders and the end users. Projects bring about change, which invariably upsets the way people are used to doing things. If project managers ignore the emotional and psychological side of the project, they will likely come across resistance and lack of buy-in, which in turn undermines the change process. Many change initiatives produce a suboptimal outcome because of this failure to engage the team and stakeholders at a deeper level. Traditionally, project managers operate at the surface, where they are predominantly concerned with the delivery of a product or an outcome through the completion of tangible actions, tasks and activities. It is much more uncommon to consider the values and beliefs of those involved and to deal with human behaviour, fear and resistance to change.

We don't need more followers; we need leaders!

Economic challenge is only one of many factors affecting the project management profession. In its report *Hitting a Moving Target – Complex Project and Programme Delivery in an Uncertain World*, the ICCPM argues that projects and programmes are becoming more and more complex due to technological innovation, globalization, new economic models, growing interdependency, regulatory requirements, stakeholder activism, cross-cultural complexity, limited global resources and sustainability. It also argues that there is a demand for more sophisticated and flexible leaders who possess greater technical competencies alongside social, commercial and relationship skills coupled with determination and courage.

The ICCPM writes that:

> The time has come to reorient our perspective; from a solely linear, 'inside the box' focus to a holistic view that includes the linear, but also enables us to think and act from a point of higher leverage, thus ensuring that we have the information and capability to steer projects dynamically in times of high complexity, ambiguity and rapid change. On the ground, we must be aware of what's going on outside as well as inside the project; be able to acknowledge and integrate multiple, often competing, interests; be flexible enough to respond; and if necessary, change direction without apology.[4]

That may initially strike you as a dramatic and daunting situation, but although it does require you to step up and sharpen your saw, it also opens up huge opportunities for your personal and professional growth in addition to the benefits it brings to the team, the organization, the customer and the wider society. Learning from past mistakes and making an adjustment to how *you* think and behave may be the single biggest factor that can help improve project delivery. If you take on the challenge and adapt, you are likely to stand out as a leader and a survivor. As Charles Darwin said, 'It is not the strongest of the species that survive, nor the most intelligent, but the one most responsive to change'.

In order to change your working patterns – and your mindset – you need to accept that you will have to do things differently going forward. You will not get better results by continuing to do what you have always done. It is a sad truth that many people know intellectually what they need to do, but are still not doing it. For that reason I will encourage you to take lots of action, as you will get results only by starting to do things differently. In addition, Chapter 2 is dedicated to helping you understand your beliefs and 'why' you do what you do. When you understand your beliefs and your sources of motivation, you can begin to change the decisions you make and in turn the action you take.

To get better results, you have to start taking the initiative and help define new and better ways in which your team and organization can work. In order for that to happen, you need to think unconventionally, learn and adjust as you go along, and have the insight and vision to put in place better

FIGURE 1.3 Understanding your beliefs helps you change your and others' working patterns

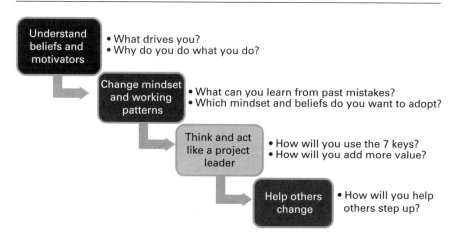

practices. That means that you have to have the ability to break away from what you have been taught and sometimes use uncommon sense, as common sense is likely to lead you back to where you already were. But it is not enough that *you* personally do it; you need to engage and empower everybody around you to do so too.

In doing that, one of the challenges you are likely to come up against is that many people have been taught to think inside the box, to conform and to follow. Throughout school we are being educated to deliver to well-defined assignments and to stick to the topic. As a result we have become good at complying and looking to others for direction, as opposed to setting it ourselves. Going through an economic downturn does not help. At a time when we need to innovate and change, we often feel paralyzed and afraid of taking risks, as it could cost us our job. We are reluctant to put our neck out and lead the way, even if it's the right thing to do. But our society doesn't need more followers; it needs leaders. It is time to show courage and authenticity.

Are you ready to move forward and start thinking like a project leader? I hope so, because what you are about to learn next is how to avoid three of the most fundamental mistakes that project managers make. Please don't feel that I am being disrespectful to my fellow project management colleagues by pointing out these fundamental shortcomings. I am the first to put my hand up and admit that I used to fall into the exact same traps. For years I managed a large programme of work, which almost led to burnout because I was working harder and harder, not smarter. I worked excessively long hours trying to get it all done. I was micromanaging the team and felt I needed to know it all and do it all. I wasn't accessing the genius of the team and I wasn't being as proactive as I should have been. Let me illustrate these project management faults as simply as I can with the sole purpose of preventing you from also making them.

The three most fundamental mistakes project managers make

The project managers I coach and train have a lot in common. Most of them have had some form of training in project management methods, and some are even certified, for instance with PMP®, PRINCE2®, APMP® or IPMA®. Generally they want to do a good job and deliver their projects successfully so that they can get the recognition and career growth that they desire. But many are struggling to do just that. They work long hours and are getting through a lot of activities, but they don't necessarily feel in control. Their projects are slipping, their clients are unhappy and their teams are demotivated. They have so much on their plate that something has to give. Often it is the most urgent requests that get their attention. At the bottom of the pile are activities that they never get around to, such as learning about their client's business, spending more quality time with the team, identifying new and better ways of doing things, addressing barriers to change, mitigating risks and ensuring that the team is ultimately delivering what the client wants and needs. They are simply too busy to be on top of it all and are falling prey to three of the most common traps in project management:

1 They manage tasks, events and processes at the expense of leading people.
2 They are reactive and focus on the urgent rather than the important.
3 They believe they have to know it all and do it all instead of looking to the team for solutions and innovative ideas.

Mistake #1: Managing tasks and events at the expense of leading people

The most common mistake project managers make is that they are more concerned with tasks and events than with people and the human impact

FIGURE 1.4 The three most fundamental project management mistakes

of change – often unknowingly. Many project managers come from a technical background and have a rational, logical and analytical way of thinking. It means that they are good at analysing facts, calculating duration, coordinating activities and making rational decisions. They are task-focused and concerned with how to get things done. They see their primary role as delivering what the customer has asked for within the agreed parameters of time, cost and quality. They are less concerned with *why* their customer needs the product and in which ways it affects their business and the people who develop it and use it. Their strength is in executing and following someone else's vision and specification – rather than helping to define it.

When it comes to dealing with the team and managing people, many project managers rely on their logical and rational mindset. They assess the work that needs to get done and the skills required to do it, and allocate work to team members accordingly. They view their relationship with the team as one based on authority and expect the members to carry out their job, by and large because they receive a salary for it.

There is nothing wrong with being logical and task-oriented. As project managers, we need those skills, especially when planning and estimating a large project. The issue arises when this is the *only* style in the toolbox, which is then being used to also manage people and communicate with customers. Building high-performing teams and great customer relationships and ensuring that the project actually delivers what the customer needs cannot be achieved solely through logic. It requires creativity, empathy, risk-taking, vision and, most important, the ability to connect with people at a very personal level.

Mistake #2: Being reactive and focusing on the urgent rather than the important

The second big mistake that many project managers make is that they are too concerned with urgent matters that need to be resolved in the here and now as opposed to being proactive and dealing with the long term. These urgent matters could relate to anything from technology, resources, requirements, finances and defects to people-related issues. It's human nature to respond to queries and issues, and it makes us feel good because we are taking action and being seen to do something. Oftentimes we are even *seeking* the urgent, for instance when we frequently check our e-mail to see if anything pressing has arrived. It is a culture and a mindset that some have adopted more than others.

Whereas it can be essential to deal with an important issue as it arises, many urgent requests simply aren't important. Oftentimes they aren't the best use of our time and they keep us away from the larger and more strategic aspects of the project that are fundamental to success. We may feel that we are responding to the more-for-less culture by working harder and by putting out more fires, but what we are doing could be the exact opposite.

EXERCISE   The urgent versus the important

Please take some time to consider the first exercise. It's essential that you carefully consider the insightful questions presented to you, as self-awareness is the first step to transformation. Please write down all your observations and learning in a separate notebook specifically dedicated to your professional development.

- Take a step back and ask yourself how much you recognize from the preceding scenario. How often do you leave the office with a feeling that you didn't get to address the most important and strategic aspects of the project because you were too busy dealing with short-term issues?

- What are the implications of operating like that?

- If you were given three hours more at work each day, which important activities would you like to spend that time on?

By busying ourselves and attending to urgent short-term requests, we operate at a surface level. We never get to address the root causes and free ourselves up to thinking smarter thoughts: questioning, innovating and developing human capital, including our own.

Mistake #3: Believing that we have to know all the answers

The third big mistake project managers make is that they believe they have to know all the answers. This helps them make decisions, communicate with clients, approve work and stay in control of the project. As a result they are often involved in very detailed conversations and in the decisions that help shape *how* the work is to be carried out by their teams. Whereas this approach works well for individual contributors and on a small project, it's a lot less effective on projects where there is a reliance on a team or where there is an element of complexity. Feeling that we have to know it all puts a huge amount of pressure on the project manager's shoulders and forces us to be involved in almost all conversations across the project. Not only is it exhausting and inefficient, it also disengages the team, as it is not being sufficiently involved in defining the work it is meant to carry out.

Wanting to know and control the details invariably means that project managers default to telling others what to do. This in itself is very disempowering, but it also results in the project being cut off from its best thinking – that of its team members. A far better option is to be the *enabler*, someone who asks the right questions and who challenges the team to think its best thoughts and do its best work. Instead of telling people what you know, help them learn what they need to know. In the Forrester report, Mary Gerush writes, 'Next-generation project managers let go of control and delegate responsibility to the team. They position themselves as facilitators and removers of roadblocks, and they eliminate distractions, enabling the team to perform its job'.[5]

I learnt how to get things done through others – by Penny Pullan

Project managers tend to get overloaded and then think that the solution is to go flat out doing all the work themselves and jettison all the important things like stakeholder engagement and communication as nice to have but not enough time for! I personally fell into this trap years ago, when I was less experienced and given a big chance to take on a major project. The project in question was already late, hadn't delivered anything and I was the third project manager. In short, it was failing. Those of you who are more experienced than I was then will see many danger signals, but for me, it was my first big chance. I relished the opportunity to deliver something big. The project team's motivation was rock bottom after all the delay, changes in project manager and lack of delivery, and within a couple of weeks starting, all of the rest of the team had resigned. All of a sudden, I was both project manager and project team! There was so much work to do that I stopped communicating with stakeholders, bar sending out hundreds of e-mails each day, and put my head down to get everything done. Needless to say, overload followed. The project delivered a good product just before the deadline, but it wasn't fun. I had put the doing of the project work (by me as it turns out) above the need to influence others to get things done.

A few years after this poisonous project, the lessons I'd learned so painfully about getting things done through others were bearing fruit. By this time, I was programme manager for a global endeavor involving the United Nations, government ministers and directors of multinational companies as key stakeholders. As before, when I joined, the programme was running late and hadn't yet delivered. This time, within six months, we'd delivered the key product. Did I say that only 50 per cent of my time was allocated to this global programme? What a difference! So what was it that made the difference? By then, I knew how to get things done through others, even those who were much more senior than me and in different organizations and even based on different continents. My transformation had begun by learning lessons from the overload and frustration of my earlier project. I had modeled what I saw the very best project managers doing and found what worked. I was also lucky enough to have a coach and mentor and had developed very strong facilitation skills over the years.

– Penny Pullan, co-author and editor of several project
management books

> **Happy project teams are not those with the least problems to solve, but those that are best empowered to solve problems – by Colleen Garton**
>
> *Many project managers go wrong because they direct too much of the 'how' rather than assigning the 'what' and letting each person figure out the 'how' on their own. A leader's role is to develop and grow strong teams so the strengths of the organization are multiplied by the number of people employed by it. If the leader tries to make all the decisions and direct every single action, the employees' strengths will never be developed or utilized. It is waste of good talent. Another typical mistake is that project managers take a reactive approach to management rather than a proactive approach. Risk, contingency and mitigation planning is never wasted time. It enables plans to be put into action quickly and efficiently in the event of a problem and helps avoid frenzied firefighting and panic. Taking a reactive approach results in a stressed-out manager and team every time a problem is encountered – which is almost every day on a project team! Happy project teams are not those with the least problems to solve; they are the teams that are best empowered to solve problems (even catastrophic ones) calmly and methodically.*
>
> – Colleen Garton, author of *Fundamentals of Technology Project Management* and *Managing Without Walls*

The Project Leadership Matrix™ and your modus operandi

Let us examine the three fundamental project management mistakes – and the differences between management and leadership – in a bit more detail. We will do that by looking at *The Project Leadership Matrix™*, which is illustrated in Figure 1.5. On the horizontal axis we have *task* focus on the left-hand side and *people* focus on the right-hand side. On the vertical axis we have *reactive* towards the bottom and *proactive* towards the top.

FIGURE 1.5   The Project Leadership Matrix™

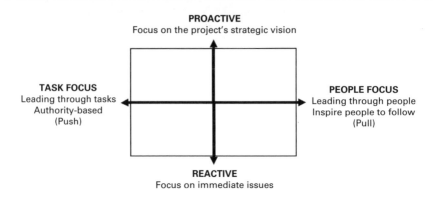

People who operate on the left-hand side of the matrix – who lead through tasks – predominantly have a rational and logical mindset and are focused on skills, events and processes. They make use of their logic and authority when assigning work and will often tell their team members what to do. We could say that this approach to managing people is a *push* approach.

On the contrary, people who operate on the right-hand side of the matrix have a natural tendency to focus on people. They don't rely on their authority, but appeal to people by finding out what motivates each person at an individual level. People-focused leaders involve team members in the decisions that affect them and show them how they fit into the overall vision. They don't just tell people what to do, but inspire them by painting an appealing picture of the project's objectives that they would like them to contribute to. We can call this a *pull* approach. They pull people with them like a magnet instead of pushing, or forcing them.

If you are in doubt where on this scale you operate, think about how easy or difficult you find it to approach a person who doesn't report to you. In matrix organizations, where team members don't have an organizational reporting line to the project manager, we cannot rely on our authority to allocate work. This is a situation that task-oriented project managers find challenging – not least when the team member they need to interface with is in a senior position and has a lot of experience. In such situations we need to make use of our people and influencing skills and of our understanding of human behaviour rather than relying on authority.

Let's examine the dimensions of the vertical axis, *reactive* versus *proactive*. People who operate in a reactive manner – towards the bottom of the matrix – are drawn to immediate issues that crop up. Even if they arrive at work with a clear intention of what they need to achieve, they may not achieve it because something urgent or unexpected comes up and derails them. They spend their time following the flow of events rather than defining it and are constantly on a back foot.

At the other end of the scale – towards the top of the matrix – we find people with a proactive mindset. People who operate here are concerned with the project's strategic vision and they take steps every single day to create a successful future for the project. They set their own agenda to the benefit of the project, the client and the team. They don't make knee-jerk decisions and only firefight when a true crisis emerges that cannot wait and that no one else can deal with. In that situation they will strive to address the root causes and put in place measures to ensure that the issue doesn't reoccur.

EXERCISE   Where in The Project Leadership Matrix™ are you positioned?

- Look at The Project Leadership Matrix™ and determine where you operate most of the time. Do you have a natural preference for tasks or people?

- Do you rely on your authority over people, or do you inspire and influence people at an individual level?

- Are you good at attending to important activities that lead to success of your project, or do you often get sidetracked and interrupted?

Although most of us operate in all four quadrants depending on the situation, we have a tendency to spend the majority of our time in one of them. Most of the project managers who are not getting the results they want operate in quadrant number II (indicated by a circle with a cross in Figure 1.6). They spend too much time firefighting and dealing with events and tasks that urgently need to be resolved. They are good at getting things done but will never be successful at implementing a strategic change initiative as long as they operate from this space. The biggest sign that something is wrong is the lack of clear direction and the number of project issues that crop up – interpersonal or otherwise. Oftentimes projects are kicked off before they are fully defined, roles and responsibilities are unclear, team members are not equipped to do the job, stakeholders are not engaged,

FIGURE 1.6 The ideal positioning of Project Leadership

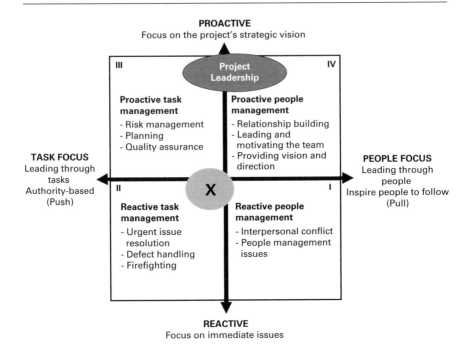

requirements are too vague and objectives aren't aligned to corporate strategy. Ultimately the project fails to deliver the expected benefits – or if it does deliver them, it's a long and arduous road to getting there.

Project managers who get *outstanding* results tend to operate in the top part of the matrix – in between quadrant III and quadrant IV. They are proactive and focused on the project's long-term strategy and they are partly oriented towards tasks and partly towards people. As you can see in Figure 1.6, this area is marked with an oval shape called *Project Leadership*.

Project leaders must continue to be mindful of the task side of the project and will not be effective if they operate exclusively in quadrant IV. People who operate exclusively in quadrant IV have great ideas and are good at inspiring people, but will often have no concrete plans or operational strategies to back up their vision. It's also worth noting that even project leaders spend time in quadrant II from time to time. But because they have set up the project correctly from the outset and have spent a significant amount of time building a great team, the time required to put out fires is greatly reduced and is not a strategy they rely on to get results.

Many project managers find if difficult to break out of the reactive and task-oriented pattern. They don't see how they can free up time and energy to proactively deal with people and the strategic side of the project. They are caught in the management trap and find it hard to shift their overreliance on control and rational thinking to a more people-oriented approach of trust and openness. After all, most of us are trained in mastering the detail and in thinking logically rather than building relationships and leading people. In addition, the more-for-less culture and the emphasis on reducing expenditure aren't helping. In many cases it may be increasing the workload and forcing people into a reactive and task-oriented mode.

But no matter why we find ourselves in these situations, there will always be ways around them by thinking creatively and by knowing that we have a choice. We may not be able to change external factors, such as limited budgets, reduced workforces and a reactive company culture, but we *can* control how we respond to them, what we choose to focus on and how we influence people around us. I was almost at the point of giving up my job as a project manager in financial services because I found it to be too exhausting. Little did I know that my working patterns were self-imposed and not the fault of the industry, the company, the project, the client or my manager. It is easy to feel victimized and look for someone to blame outside of ourselves. But the reality is that *we* hold the answer and the key to working more effectively, getting better results, feeling more energized and working with people to deliver better projects. Had I left my job I would have found the exact same problems elsewhere. Instead I started examining what *I* could do to change the situation. I started looking at how I could work smarter rather than harder.

Delegate, prioritize and focus on what's important – by Peter Taylor

While working with a particularly demanding team of people, the project I was managing some years ago hit a problem. There was an aggressive deadline, and there was a quite aggressive steering committee. The deadline loomed towards us but the technical challenges seemed never-ending. As quickly as one was resolved another (if not more) seemed to take its place. The working days got longer and the toll of all this pressure began to cause serious stress faults in the project team. In the midst of all this fractious harmony, we hit the problem. If the team had been at full efficiency and working as one, I am sure we would have spotted the cause earlier and resolved the issue quickly and quietly. As it was, we didn't do either. The cause went unresolved and the effects seemed to spiral ever towards being out of control completely. Rapid-response meetings were convened, and everybody was trying to resolve the issue. Unfortunately this meant that people stopped doing their day jobs, which resulted in further delays threatening the project.

Just when I honestly thought it was all going to implode, I had one of those 'eureka' moments. I can't say it was planned and I can't say it was done in a positive or creative spirit. It was done in a moment when I just had had enough. I ordered various parts of my project team off to various parts of the company offices to 'go and do their jobs and get us back on track'. Inadvertently I gave a number of people the authority to stop worrying about the problem and to concentrate once more on their scheduled tasks. In addition I was left with one fairly junior technical guy and, for the want of anything else to do, told him to head off to the IT department and find someone who could help think this problem through. And what did I do? Well, I was the one who went to the pub. I admit it, I just needed to escape the pressure and think. I had fallen into the trap of becoming subjective in all the chaos and panic, and I know now I should have remained above everything and objective in my view.

What happened then were three things. Firstly, I had a very nice steak pie, chips and peas with a pint of beer. Secondly, the junior technical guy just so happened to talk to the right person. And thirdly, the issue was initially worked around and later resolved through some third-party intervention. I was lucky. The crisis passed and the project staggered on for a while and eventually delivered, later than expected, but nevertheless it did deliver. But it did teach me an important lesson – filter what you should deal with, delegate everything you can, prioritize what is left and then focus on what is important. In this case I did none of these things and was lucky to get the result I did.

– Peter Taylor, author of *The Lazy Project Manager*

Moving towards project leadership

Moving away from a purely transactional way of managing projects – where you rely on control and authority – and towards a leadership approach will help you add more value, navigate complexity and deliver better projects. It will help you focus on the strategic outlook of the project, inspire and motivate the team and build a culture of continuous improvement. It will also help you foster the right set of attitudes, such as integrity, honesty, trust and accountability.

We will discuss the 7 keys in full in Chapter 3, but let's briefly look at what they are.

FIGURE 1.7 The 7 keys to project leadership

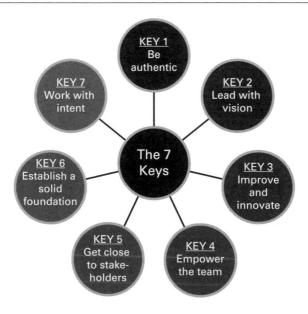

Key #1. Be authentic

The first of the 7 keys is to be authentic. This means that you instinctively know what is right and what is wrong and that you lead and make decisions accordingly. It means that you have a strong sense of purpose because you understand your role and how it adds value to your client, your team and to you. When you are authentic, there is harmony among what you think, feel, say and do. You have an honest approach to your work and you shy away from playing favourites or engaging in dishonest politics. Instead you seek to deliver on your promises, protect your team and stand up for what you believe is right.

Key #2. Lead with vision

Leading with vision means that you partner with your client and take joint responsibility for delivering the project's ultimate goals and objectives. You begin with the end in mind and work with your team and client to fully comprehend the project's strategic objectives and benefits. But you are also concerned with *how* to achieve these benefits and how to win people over and avoid resistance. When you lead with vision, you are not just focused on delivering the project's tangible outputs or capabilities. You are also focused on the *benefits* that these capabilities provide as well as how your team and the end users are impacted by them.

Key #3. Improve and innovate

The third key to project leadership is to continuously improve and innovate. This is about stepping back from the project, observing it from different angles and assessing which parts are working and which are not – and then having the courage to do something about it in collaboration with the team. When you improve and innovate, you empower people around you to think creatively and to come up with new and better ways of doing things. This is a process that requires courage, energy and clear sight, as it is much easier to maintain the status quo than to question it and improve upon it. It requires you to gain the trust and participation of your team and to be willing to take risks and step outside of your comfort zone for the sake of doing the right thing.

Key #4. Empower the team

Your ability to empower the team to deliver its best work is integral to project leadership. The team is the project's biggest asset, and how well you use this asset will depend on your ability to tap into each person's strengths and desires. When I say 'asset', I don't mean something that can be owned, but something that is valuable and worth looking after. To build a high-performing team you have to build rapport with each team member and understand what makes each person tick. This entails listening to people's needs and concerns and acting as an inspirational mentor and guide. But creating a high-performing team is also about challenging people, address-ing poor performance and establishing clear agreements around what is expected. To do that you will have to make use of both your supportive yin side as well as your challenging yang side.

Key #5. Get close to your stakeholders

Your primary concern as a project leader should be to serve your clients and to help fulfil their strategic objectives – not in the sense that you will take everything they say for gospel, but in that your ultimate goal is to provide them with the products and services that they need. In order to do that you will have to build excellent relationships with your customers and get to know their business drivers and objectives intimately. This will enable you to fully partner with them and help deliver the expected benefits. You will also have to be excellent at keeping your clients informed of progress and at gaining their buy-in and acceptance for solutions and the way forward. This involves the courage to ask for help and guidance when required and the ability to talk openly about risks and issues that need resolving.

Key #6. Establish a solid foundation

To step into the project leadership space, it's important that you understand the most powerful project management techniques and that you know when to use them. Projects must be planned before they are executed, and risks, issues and change requests must be formally logged and dealt with. Although this may sound obvious, many project managers fall down by not mastering the fundamentals. Mastering this key is also about the ability to produce a solid business case, realistic estimates, key performance indicators and honest project reporting. This key is not about getting lost in the detail of tools and techniques. It's about using the processes that add value; no more and no less.

Key #7. Work with intent

The last of the 7 keys is to work with intent. This means that in order to become an effective project leader who leads with vision, improves and inno-vates, empowers the team and builds strong relationships with clients, you have to be excellent at prioritizing and at optimizing your time in the best possible manner. The trick is to consistently put the important over the urgent and to focus on those aspects that yield the biggest results. This requires that you overcome procrastination, limit time waste, reduce multitasking and don't let excuses, fear or self-doubt get in your way. It also requires you to use delegation as an effective tool to train and grow others, and thereby free yourself up to keep an eye on the bigger picture and on the client.

As you can see, the 7 keys cover the full spectrum of project leadership – from how you lead yourself and others, and how you add value by defining the vision and delivering the project's strategic outcomes, to how you make best use of project management techniques and consistently focus on that which is most important.

As you move towards project leadership and begin to implement the 7 keys, you must be willing to take risks and stand up for what you believe is right. You must have the courage to challenge the status quo even when it is not the most popular thing to do. And you must keep your eye on the long term and be brave enough to take a hit today for the sake of tomorrow. Project leadership is about doing what is right for the project, the team and the client. In that sense it is a selfless discipline where the purpose is *not* to enhance your ego or position. Personal success is a positive side benefit of project leadership, not the main purpose.

How to spot a project leader – by Sam Fleming

Soft skills are critical in defining project leaders and high-performing individuals. Key elements are always around people skills, emotional intelligence, calm, non-aggressive ways of handling conflict and negotiations – and ultimately, having the confidence to challenge the status quo and look for the most effective and efficient ways of delivery. The other critical ability is the propensity to learn and the desire to coach others. Every great leader has this inherent trait, which allows constant progress and higher patterns of thinking. Finally, they must be able to effectively address the human impacts of change (far beyond systems and process) and put themselves in the shoes of customers, employees, executives and, ultimately, the shareholders to embed change and make it a success at every level.

– Sam Fleming, Head of Project Delivery, British Gas Plc

Outstanding project leaders perceive themselves as the project CEO – by Arnon Yaffe

Outstanding project leaders perceive themselves as the project CEO. They have a high level of self-awareness and are extremely attentive to everyone in the project ecosystem. They are true to their values and lead by example. Outstanding project leaders aim to excel both in interpersonal skills and professional/technical knowledge of their trade without excusing one trait for the sake of the other. They know that it is a never-ending process of ongoing improvement and will not fall victim of arrogance. They inspire people to excel and perceive themselves as a facilitator for their growth.

– Arnon Yaffe, Project Leadership Consultant and Coach

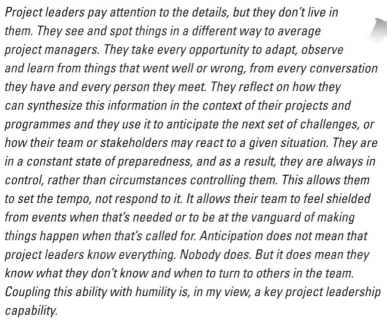

What differentiates project leaders from the pack is the power of anticipation – by Paul Hodgkins

Project leaders pay attention to the details, but they don't live in them. They see and spot things in a different way to average project managers. They take every opportunity to adapt, observe and learn from things that went well or wrong, from every conversation they have and every person they meet. They reflect on how they can synthesize this information in the context of their projects and programmes and they use it to anticipate the next set of challenges, or how their team or stakeholders may react to a given situation. They are in a constant state of preparedness, and as a result, they are always in control, rather than circumstances controlling them. This allows them to set the tempo, not respond to it. It allows their team to feel shielded from events when that's needed or to be at the vanguard of making things happen when that's called for. Anticipation does not mean that project leaders know everything. Nobody does. But it does mean they know what they don't know and when to turn to others in the team. Coupling this ability with humility is, in my view, a key project leadership capability.

Project leadership is about having belief and confidence in yourself as a project manager and leader. If you remain authentic and true to yourself, if you can adapt and anticipate, then even if you do get something wrong, you are much more likely to be forgiven. Leadership in projects is about learning from every element and dimension of projects and recognizing that in a given situation or with a given set of challenges, it is not a failure of leadership to know, that at that moment in time, you are not the best person to move things forward. 'Passing the ball' to a team member is not giving away responsibility. Taking it and knowing when to make the 'right pass' is also an attribute that sets apart project leaders.

– Paul Hodgkins, Executive Director,
Paul Hodgkins Project Consultancy

How to embed the new behaviour

How to embed the learning

- Use The Project Leadership Matrix™ to determine your typical operating style as a project manager.

- Assess the situations in which you tend to be reactive and firefight and what the underlying reasons and triggers are.

- Assess the extent to which you have a task-oriented and authority-based approach to people; i.e., do you predominantly relate to people from a rational standpoint as opposed to a more personal and empathetic standpoint?

- Consider the extent to which you prefer to control the detail of a project and tell people what to do and how to do it. What is the impact of operating in this way?

- List as many benefits as you can of stepping into the project leadership space and how it will help you to better manage projects in light of increasing complexity.

- Go to www.powerofprojectleadership.com to download worksheets and further resources for this book.

Checklist: Do you master the learning?

- You acknowledge that the world is becoming increasingly complex and that it has a profound impact on the project management profession. You accept that you need to adapt, grow and learn.

- You are able to assess in which part of The Project Leadership Matrix™ you operate most of the time, what it is costing you and what it would take to change it.

- You have a clear understanding of the behaviours you need to stop in order to become a more effective project manager and leader.

Before we start our detailed discussion in Chapter 3 of the 7 keys to project leadership, we will take some time in Chapter 2 to look at the underlying reasons and drivers that help explain why you operate the way you do. We will also discuss which habits and beliefs you need to modify in order to break free from the old ways of working and step into project leadership.

Notes

1 Interview with Steve Pikett, February 2014

2 Tim Harford, Author of *Adapt*, APM conference 2013

3 Gerush, M (2009) *Define, Hire and Develop Your Next-Generation Project Managers*, Forrester Research

4 ICCPM (2013) *Hitting a Moving Target: Complex Project and Programme Delivery in an Uncertain World*, International Centre for Complex Project Management (ICCPM)

5 Gerush, M (2009) *Define, Hire and Develop Your Next Generation Project Managers*, Forrester Research

Your hidden drivers

> **IN THIS CHAPTER YOU WILL LEARN**
>
> - How you can change your mindset to overcome some of the challenges you currently face as a project manager
> - What the six basic human needs are and how they impact the choices you make
> - What your own sources of motivation are and how you can best make use of them to develop your project leadership skills

Your biggest challenges

I am assuming that you have a genuine desire to grow and develop and that you would like to get to the next level of your career. I am also assuming that you have experienced many successes in your life and that you have had to overcome many obstacles to get to where you are today. You are a driven individual and you are exceptionally resourceful. Some of the obstacles you have come across seemed big and at times insurmountable, but you found a way around them, and as soon as you did they ceased to exist. They vanished as quickly as they appeared.

Other obstacles may have just emerged – for instance, if you have recently stepped into a new role or taken on a new project – and others still may be long-standing and harder to tackle. They require more courage and insight for you to overcome. But irrespective of where you are on your journey, there will be aspects of your job that challenge you and frustrate you more than others, aspects that you haven't got your head around yet. Life is a continual learning process of challenges and opportunities that require us to make decisions and to act in order to move on. That is how

FIGURE 2.1   Project management challenges

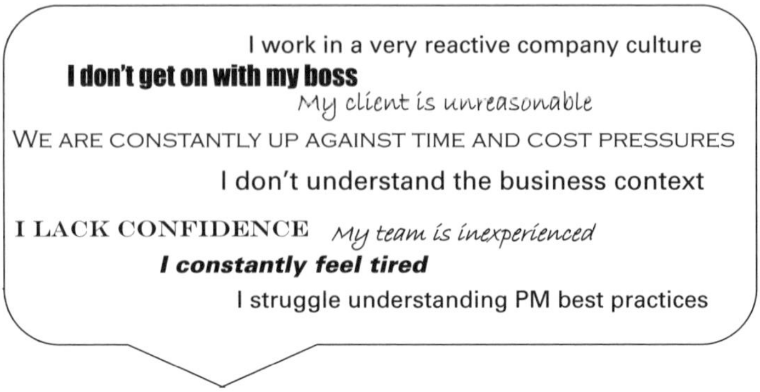

I work in a very reactive company culture
I don't get on with my boss
My client is unreasonable
WE ARE CONSTANTLY UP AGAINST TIME AND COST PRESSURES
I don't understand the business context
I LACK CONFIDENCE   My team is inexperienced
I constantly feel tired
I struggle understanding PM best practices

we develop and grow. But of course this can be easier said than done. Whereas we are often aware of the activities, situations and people who stress us or consume our time and energy, we are not always clear about the reasons for it, or how to go about changing it. It isn't easy to observe our own behaviour, habits and beliefs, and we rarely invest the time it takes to do so.

But even if you find it unfamiliar to examine the things that challenge you and explore their root causes, it is important to do so. These challenges consume your energy and, instead of building you up, they drag you down. They limit your performance and slow down your professional growth. The objective of this chapter is to help you understand and address these challenges and to provide you with some strategies and new beliefs that will help you take on the mindset of a successful leader. In order to do that, we will examine the basic needs that govern us all and the ways in which you go about meeting these needs. Having this understanding will provide you with some fundamental insights into how you can better lead yourself, which in turn will help you to better lead others.

EXERCISE   Examine your biggest project challenges

To get the most from this exercise, make sure you are not in a rush and that you have at least 10 minutes to spare to examine your working patterns. The questions may not be easy to answer at first, but they can make all the difference in becoming a project leader or not. If you don't feel that you are in the right space at this moment, simply skim the questions and come back and complete the exercise as soon as you can.

1 Take hold of pen and paper and write down the types of situations, tasks, people and activities that cause you the most worry and frustration in your job right now. This could relate to anything from budgeting or planning to interfacing with certain people such as your boss, a poor performer or the project sponsor. It may also be that you find specific situations uncomfortable – for instance, when you have to present to the steering committee – or that it is the long working hours and constant deadlines that you find the most stressful. Write down whatever comes to mind. If nothing tends to worry you or frustrate you, simply write down the types of activities that you enjoy the least.

2 Look at the challenges you just identified. In which ways would you say they are impacting your daily work and your ability to do a good job and add value to your client and your team? Do these challenges affect other people's perception of you? Does it mean that you are spending your time ineffectively? Does it negatively impact your well-being and your stress levels, or does it ultimately limit your career progression? Write down your thoughts.

3 We are going to go a little further with this. Don't feel embarrassed or be too proud to admit that certain elements of your job are nagging you. What is important is that you recognize it and that you actively start to turn it around. Project leaders come across many things that annoy them, but they feel empowered and are confident enough to do something about it. They don't let obstacles deter them. On the contrary, they have formed a habit of turning them into opportunities and making the most of any given situation. With a bit of practise and conscious attention, you can do the same.

4 The next step is to group the challenges you identified and to spot any common denominators among them. How many of the items you wrote down relate to people, for instance, either interfacing with your clients and stakeholders or your team? How many relate to lack of specific abilities, such as how to kick off a project or knowledge about your client's business? And how many are concerned with operating under time pressure, or related to how you feel about yourself, such as low confidence? Group them in a way that makes the most sense to you.

I would like you to keep in mind these challenges and concerns as we progress through the book. My hope is that you will have addressed them by the time you finish the material and that you will have replaced them with more powerful and effective project leadership strategies.

From the above exercise it should be clear that some of the items you find challenging stem from not having the right leadership strategy or your lack of a particular skill. How many of your challenges, for instance, could be resolved if you were generally better at dealing with conflict, leading the team and interfacing with people? And which of your challenges would diminish if you invested the necessary time to understand a particular strategy or knew the ins and outs of your clients' business better?

If we relate this back to The Project Leadership Matrix™, you will see that with the right focus between tasks and people, and by spending your time proactively, your concerns should reduce dramatically. Take a minute to consider how your challenges would reduce if you stepped into the project leadership space with your full commitment. Stepping into the leadership space requires you to focus on that which really matters. But first and foremost, it requires you to understand and remove the beliefs and working practices that are constraining you. This part of the book helps you to do just that.

Emotional intelligence, emotional intelligence, emotional intelligence – by Sam Fleming

My first inkling was about five years ago when I worked for a company that executed a huge outsourcing of its IT department. As senior managers, we spent over a week with occupational physiologists who taught us a number of techniques for handling our own emotions through this huge business change. More recently I took those learnings further through a senior management training programme and actually sat in a room and wept as I realized how our background and life events create the person we are today in a professional environment. I realized that I had been behaving and communicating with certain people based on old mind traps. (One example was that I'd swapped from proving myself to my father to proving myself to my manager. No wonder my manager was confused as to my behaviours; he wasn't my dad, and he had already accepted me!) The Monday after the programme, I walked to the office doors and stopped. I smiled. In my head I mimed putting a package down by the front door. That package contained all the behavioural history of my past that had leached into my professional 'being' but no longer had a place. I felt weightless, at peace and most of all. . . set free. That package is still metaphorically there by those doors today.

I believe the key to great leadership (be it of a project or an operation) is the ability to be adept at the awareness of ourselves and the awareness of others. This is a higher level of awareness where we can interpret the emotional state we are in and the emotional state of the individual or audience we are engaging with. Words themselves make up only a tiny percentage of what we take from a 'conversation'. Tone of voice, body language and intent are what we really 'take away' from an encounter. When we get it right, we have a connection that spans the boundaries of stress and short-term tasks. If project managers can embrace some emotional intelligence and direct that into their teams, it unlocks a human behaviour that is positively beautiful to behold; it drives an entire culture of consideration, respect, honest conversation, personal power, negotiation (without overassertion), recognition and awareness of how we use ourselves and others for ultimate outcomes.

As a first step, people should learn to recognize their feelings at any moment in time. If we are feeling tired, low, de-energized, irritated, angry, stressed, then our mind and mouth are likely to start operating from a less 'emotionally intelligent' place. Then we interpret others incorrectly, often layering on our own mind-talk over the top. This impairs our responses and is often very apparent to the other person. Learning to recognize our mood and how to get out of it is key. We're unlikely to be able to stand in front of our team and motivate them on a Monday morning if we have just had someone directing a good dollop of road rage at us. Being able to understand ourselves and use varying techniques to get the best out of others and challenging situations is essential if people want to climb the career ladder.

— Sam Fleming, Head of Project Delivery, British Gas Plc

Is your mindset serving you?

At the most fundamental level, the quality of your personal and professional life is determined by the quality of your *beliefs*. Your beliefs shape your attitudes, which in turn affect the actions and the results that you get, or don't get. As Henry Ford said, 'Whether you think you can or can't,

FIGURE 2.2   How large a percentage of your thoughts are negative?

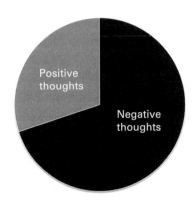

either way you are right'. In that sense, your beliefs shape your decisions, your outcomes and your reality. The scary part is that the large majority of our thoughts and beliefs in a day are believed to be negative.[1] That means that we are undeniably our own worst enemy in that we subconsciously limit ourselves and self-sabotage as a result of our unhelpful thought patterns. These thoughts and beliefs stem from our upbringing and from our life experiences. Unfortunately it's not uncommon that as we grow up we are being made aware of the things we *can't* do as opposed to the things we *can* do. One of the essential ingredients in transforming into a leader is to replace the beliefs, attitudes and behaviours that are not serving us with something more empowering.

But what are beliefs? Beliefs are something we accept as being true or real. They are firmly held opinions or convictions about what we think we can and cannot do. They play a large role in how we interpret the world around us and serve as a kind of lens through which we look. The things we see, experience, think and feel are all adjusted through this lens to fit with our beliefs. Our version of reality is therefore a creation of our beliefs. If we believe that opportunity is everywhere, that is what we will see. Likewise, if we believe that running a project is stressful and that people are hard work, then that is what we will experience. The problem is that most people are not consciously aware of what their beliefs are and of how they impact their behaviour. All they experience is a stressful or annoying situation; they don't necessarily see how their own beliefs and attitudes are contributing to that situation.

FIGURE 2.3 Our values and beliefs inform our attitudes and actions and ultimately determine the results we get or don't get

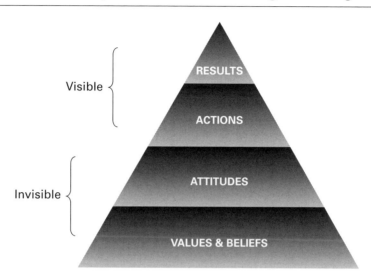

In her book *The Influential Leader,* Rebel Brown explains that over 95 per cent of our decisions and actions are driven by our unconscious mind and that our conscious mind never even gets involved. She states that whereas our unconscious mind takes in 11 million bits of data per second, mainly from our eyes, ears and feelings, only a very small percentage – 126 bits per second – is selected and presented to our conscious mind.[2] This means that we are not as logical and rational as we might think we are, as we are in many ways slaves to our unconscious mind. It is our unconscious mind, and the beliefs we hold about the world, that filters out the data and decides which part is being passed on to our conscious mind and which part is being withheld. If we want to change our reality, and the results we generate, we have to change our beliefs so that a different set of data will start to come through to us.

Beliefs are incredibly powerful. A positive and empowering belief system will carry us a long way, and when we master it, there is very little that can stop us in our tracks. Some of the studies that have been carried out come from educational circles where teachers and groups of pupils have falsely been led to believe that they were significantly more accomplished than the rest of the class. The results of these studies consistently prove that the students who (falsely) believed that they were more accomplished ended up with increased self-esteem and higher grades than their peers.[3] The shape and quality of our beliefs inform our actions, which in turn determine whether we are moving further towards or away from the things we want, and at what speed.

The easiest way to start identifying the beliefs and attitudes that are not serving you is to look at the results you produce, or lack of. The results and outcomes always reveal the underlying beliefs. Some of the challenges and obstacles you identified earlier are evidence of such results, which originate from the deeply rooted beliefs you hold. For example, you may logically *know* what it takes to become more assertive, but not be able to act in an assertive manner because you believe that assertiveness is equal to aggressiveness – which is bad. You will not be able to change and become more assertive until you have dealt with the underlying belief that assertiveness and aggressiveness are the same thing.

EXERCISE Is your mindset serving you?

Consider the following questions in respect to the areas of your career where you feel limited, unsure or unqualified. Note that limiting beliefs often show up in sentences where you use words such as 'I can't', 'I don't', 'I'm not' or 'I shouldn't'.

1 What do you feel you are not very good at? What makes you think so?

2 What is your least favourite work-related activity? Which aspects make you dislike it?

3 What do you believe about your successes, your abilities as a project manager and your role as a leader?

4 What are some of the stories you are telling yourself? Do you deserve to be successful? Do you feel that you are good enough, skilled enough and the right gender and age? Do you tell yourself that you are destined to be a great leader – or not?

5 In which positive and negative ways are these stories and beliefs impacting you? Are they moving you further towards or away from the things you want?

Make a note of the beliefs that negatively affect your performance and that you would like to replace with something more empowering.

The beliefs that are not serving you are like weeds in a garden. They keep growing, and if you don't remove them they will quickly grow tall and overshadow the flowers. Your job is to regularly pull up the weeds and to replace them with the seeds that you want. There are different ways in which you can shred the limiting beliefs that you hold. One of them is to adopt an evidence-based way of thinking. Evidence-based thinking is rooted on the knowledge that there is a certain way to do something, which has proved to be effective for other people, and that by taking the very same action it will be effective for you too. A good example of this is to model someone who has already achieved the things that you would like, whether material or immaterial. In this state of evidence-based thinking there is no room for limiting beliefs, because success is the result of logical and analytical steps rather than unfounded assumptions and emotions.

Another example of evidence-based thinking is when people believe that their ability to be a project leader depends on how skilled they are, something they know they can develop over time with the right amount of support and practise. They therefore know that they absolutely can become a successful and impactful project leader if they are willing to put in the right amount of time and effort. This is an empowering way of thinking because it puts individuals fully in control of the outcome. They know that their actions alone determine the result.

A more rigid and less effective way of thinking is when people believe what authority figures tell them, such as a boss or a parent, without challenging it, or when someone believes that different things are true for different people. They think that those who are successful are different to themselves and that they could never personally be as successful. They believe that successful leaders are more skilled, have more experience, have the right age and are more confident. They see these qualities as special advantages that explain why they personally could never be as good as those successful leaders.

In the next exercise we will look at some of the reasons for your beliefs and habits and where they come from. We are not going to go too deep with this exercise, but it does merit a couple of minutes of your time.

EXERCISE   Where do your beliefs and habits come from?

1   Look at each of the beliefs that you previously identified and that in some way or another are limiting you professionally. Where would you say that each of them stem from? Are they beliefs you have acquired

during your upbringing, your schooling or maybe from a specific boss or employer?

2   Examine some of your habits and ways in which you operate. If you tend to be very rational and task-oriented (or conversely very people-focused), where does this preference stem from? Can it be explained by natural ability, or would you say it is learnt behaviour as a result of the environments you have lived and worked in?

3   Similarly, if you have a tendency to firefight and get drawn to urgent issues, where does this behaviour originate from? Is it due to a belief that we are adding value as long as we are being seen to do something? Is it driven by a fear of saying no, or have you simply adopted the company culture without questioning it?

What did this exercise bring up for you? Imagine what it would look like and feel like if you could shed all of the beliefs that limit you.

The empowering mindset

Now I would like you to stand up for a moment and shake out your body. Literally! The quickest way to change your state of mind is to change your physical state. So please stand up and stretch for a moment. Stand tall and strong and take a deep breath. Raise your chin and move your shoulders back. Then lift your sternum and your chest until you feel powerful and strong in your body. I want you to shake off the negative state I just brought you in when we examined your limiting beliefs and the mindset that is not serving you. Now it is time to look forward and start replacing these beliefs with something more empowering.

In order to let go of the habits and beliefs that limit you, you have to change from the inside out. You have to take control of your internal world and thoughts so that they can influence your outer reality in a way that serves you. In other words, you need to make sure that your focus and your attitudes are as favourable and empowering as possible, so that you can increase the amount of control you have over the results you generate. As Anthony Robbins says, it is your decisions about what to focus on, what things mean to you, and what you are going to do about them that determine your ultimate destiny. It is not what is happening to you now or what

FIGURE 2.4 Your focus and the meaning you assign to events determine your actions and your results

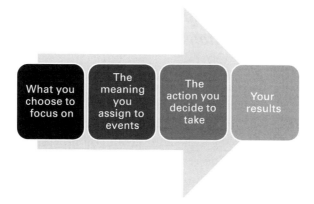

has happened in your past that determines who you become.[4] The key is to foster a positive mindset, being aware of how you respond to situations and taking action and pursuing your goals without hesitation or self-doubt.

Some people mistakenly think that having a positive mindset is the same as being in denial and ignoring the negatives by sweeping them under the carpet. But positivism should not be confused with optimism. A positive and empowering mindset is one where we clearly see situations the way they are; the positives along with the negatives. But instead of reacting emotionally to the negative aspects and letting them control and frighten us, we balance out the situation. We carefully assess the opportunities that the situation presents, and ascertain what we can do to move forward in the most constructive manner. Let's examine what some of these empowering beliefs look like.

I am in control and I choose my own responses

The most empowering belief you can adapt is to know that *you* are in control – whether consciously or unconsciously – and that you always have a choice. You choose your own beliefs, you choose what you want to focus on and you choose the decisions and the actions that you take. This is a very powerful and mature belief system because it means that you take full responsibility for your actions without having to deflect blame onto others. It is true that you may not have full control over everything that happens around you, but you *can* control the meaning you assign to external events and how to react to them. If, for instance, you work in a very busy, competitive and reactive environment, you can either see this as a reason to emulate the behaviour, or instead you can define your own way of working based on what you know will generate the best results.

I have faith that the right things will come to me as a result of my actions

Part of having a positive and empowering mindset is to trust that as long as you do what can reasonably be expected of you, then the right things will happen. There is no need to worry unnecessarily that things might not work out or to imagine what failure looks like. In fact, focusing too much on the things that you *don't* want is likely to derail you because you attract the things that you focus on. This relates back to the filter between your unconscious and your conscious mind. It is your beliefs that determine your reality. If you believe you will fail, chances are that you will. Your only concern should be to take constructive action towards your project leadership goals, stay focused and have faith that the right things will happen as a result. If you encounter a risk, by all means mitigate it, but then let go of it. Spending time worrying about the things you cannot control is lost energy. Empower yourself by being proactive and by focusing on the right strategy and trust that success will follow.

I see the opportunity in every situation

A great way to set yourself up for success is to make sure that you don't get discouraged or distracted by the issues or obstacles that you come across. We all encounter issues, but the difference between successful people and those who are not is the way in which they deal with the unforeseen. As Albert Bandura said, 'People with high assurance in their capabilities approach difficult tasks as challenges to be mastered rather than as threats to be avoided'.[5] When something unexpected happens, make sure you don't use it as an excuse to do nothing or to backtrack. Instead, ask yourself *how* you can move forward in spite of the issues and which new opportunities have opened up as a result. Your job is to focus on the opportunity and the way forward rather than the obstacle itself.

Let's look at an example. Let's assume that your company unexpectedly had to downsize and that you were losing your job. How would you react? What would your focus be, what meaning would you assign to this event and what actions would you take as a result? Would you panic and say to yourself that this is terrible/I'm a failure/how could they do it/it's their fault? Or would you say to yourself that this is their loss/I'm better off somewhere else/this is an opportunity to learn and do something new? Would you let this unforeseen situation paralyze you, or would you focus on the opportunity it presents and decide how to best move forward? The point is that although you can't control external events, you *can* control how you react to them. All it takes is mindful practice.

I believe in myself and I am my own best cheerleader

In order to act, behave and be perceived as a leader, you first have to believe in yourself. You will not come across as trustworthy, impactful and inspiring if you do not have a strong regard for yourself. You have to feel that you are *worthy* of achieving the things that you dream of, and you have to have absolute faith that as long as you take the necessary action, then you can be every bit as successful as everybody else. It is this undeniable belief in yourself and being willing to back yourself all the way that fuels your motivation and moves you to action. Note that this belief in yourself is not about being arrogant, putting yourself above the team or compromising collaboration. It simply means that you feel worthy of being called a leader. Feel this worth in every cell of your body and don't leave the house in the morning until you feel comfortable and certain that you will succeed.

There is no such thing as failure; only opportunities to grow and learn

An empowering mindset is also one in which we don't let fear of failure hold us back. If you are afraid of stepping up and showing yourself as a leader out of fear that you are not good enough – or that others might laugh at you – then you won't get very far. You need to alter your view of failure into something constructive and allow yourself to *feel the fear and do it anyway*. Your failures provide the opportunity to learn and grow and will genuinely move you forward as long as you take on board the lessons. And besides, what is the worst that can happen? Wouldn't it be better to have a setback and to learn from it rather than never to have tried? When you change your thinking pattern into one that doesn't see failure, you take away an enormous chunk of negative energy and worry. You free yourself up to pursue that which is truly important – your progress and the successful delivery of your project.

When I decided to become an entrepreneur and an independent project leadership coach, I faced a huge amount of fear. I had been an employee for 17 years and never before run my own business. Would I be good enough?

Would people want to work with me and would I be able to make money? It took me many months to come to terms with this fear and to not let it control me. I did as much as I could to prepare for my new venture, but at the end of the day I had to have faith that as long as I did what had proved to work for other successful entrepreneurs, I would be successful too. And then I reframed the situation and started to build up a new set of beliefs. I began to see and study all the great entrepreneurs around me and stopped focusing on failure. In fact I began to see my business as an experiment that I would learn from, in one way or another, even if one day I were to go back into employment.

I am fully committed to doing what it takes

We have probably all come across people who are dreamers. They keep talking about their big plans but rarely get around to implementing them. An empowering mindset is one where we are focused and committed and where we consistently take action that moves us closer to the things we want. There is no space for doubt or procrastination. Becoming a project leader who adds value in everything that you do may not be achieved in a matter of days. It will take much longer and will require you to be fully committed to doing whatever it takes and to learn and refine your approach. Sure,

FIGURE 2.5 Characteristics of a positive and empowering mindset

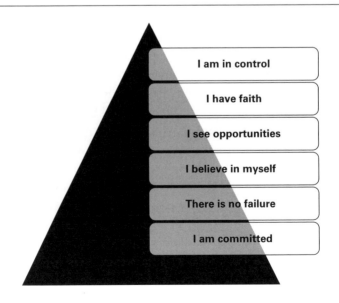

there will be times when you lose sight of the overall goal, but your drive, commitment and positive frame of mind will quickly get you back on track. At the end of the day it is your grit that will keep you going.

Interestingly, Psychology Professor Angela Lee Duckworth has proved that *grit* is the most significant predictor of success – irrespective of the industry or job role you are in. She explains that grit is about stamina and having passion and perseverance for long-term goals. It is about sticking with your future, day in day out, not just for the week or for the month but for years and working really hard to make that future a reality.[6]

All successful people have needed to rely on their determination to get to where they wanted. Thomas Edison attempted to invent the light bulb 999 times before he finally succeeded. And Colonel Sanders, the founder of KFC, traveled to four different states and had his recipe rejected hundreds of times before he found someone who accepted it. The key is to be willing to have setbacks and be wrong and to start over again with lessons learned.

EXERCISE   The Empowering Mindset

1   To what extent do you possess the characteristics of a positive and empowering mindset?

2   Which of the characteristics do you need to start working with and embed as new behaviours?

3   What if you raised your standards and committed to being excellent in everything that you do?

4   How can you use the strengths you already possess to back yourself and feel 100 per cent certain that you will succeed as a project leader?

Changing a mindset that is deeply ingrained can take a while and will happen only if you are serious about looking inward, observing yourself and understanding why you think and behave the way you do. You can embark on that journey by taking time out at the end of each day or week to examine the situations you found yourself in. Which situations did you find stressful, what did you enjoy and how did you react to these situations?

When something comes up that pushes your buttons or makes you feel unsure, it is important to explore the underlying reasons instead of brushing over them. It may not be easy to look your fears and limitations in the eyes and to be honest about the aspects that control or frighten you. But it is necessary in order to become an authentic and impactful leader. People go to great lengths to avoid the things they fear or find unpleasant – more so than the things they desire. Wanting to avoid pain and discomfort is human nature, but once you understand that, you can start to work with it and take control.

Understanding your big why

We have spent some time looking at the challenges you face and the beliefs you hold. Now we will seek to increase your level of motivation so that it will be quicker for you to transform and sustain your enthusiasm as a project leader. We will do that by identifying your hidden drivers and motivators and by clarifying what you will gain by stepping into the leadership space. You may be motivated to make a change because you would like to put your current challenges behind you. But why else might you want to step up and become a project leader? What motivates you to achieve that ambition? Is it the desire for money and recognition that is driving you? Is it the fact that you would like to contribute to society through the projects you are leading and delivering? Is it the fact that project leadership is an exciting challenge that you feel up for? Or is it more a question of wanting to grow professionally within your field or maybe building a high-performing team? What is it that drives you? What is your big why?

Many people have their mind set on something without quite knowing why. They progress along a path without asking themselves what they will find at the end and why they want it. If you don't understand why you want something, you may not be able to sustain your motivation for achieving it. What's more, once you get there, it may not fulfil you in the way you had imagined and you hurry along in pursuit of something else. Understanding what you want and why you want it is crucial in order to progress and feel that your accomplishments are worthwhile.

I would like you to spend some time imagining how it would feel to be a project leader and which of your desires it is likely to satisfy. Imagine yourself two years from now. What will you be, do and have as a project leader in two years' time that you don't have today? In which ways will it make better use of your strengths and the qualities that other people compliment you for? How would you be more fulfilled if you stepped up, added more value for your customers and became a role model for others to follow?

The six human needs

It may well be that you are not used to thinking about what you want, why you want it and what your core needs are – and this book is by no means an attempt to teach you psychology dressed up as project management. But in order to help facilitate a real and long-lasting transformation, it is important that you first look inward and understand what it is that drives you. To give you a bit more context and insight into the needs that likely govern you, let's examine the six basic human needs as taught by personal development experts Anthony Robbins and Chloe Madanes.[7] Not only will these six needs help you to better understand yourself, they will also help you to better understand the people you lead.

Robbins and Madanes state that human behaviour is motivated by the fulfilment of six human needs that go beyond desires and wants. Everybody has these six needs, but the order in which we prioritize them varies from person to person. Whichever needs are the most dominant will determine the choices we make and the action we take, as they are the underlying drivers for achievement. Although these six needs persist throughout life, their relative priority may vary from situation to situation and can change over

FIGURE 2.6 The six human needs

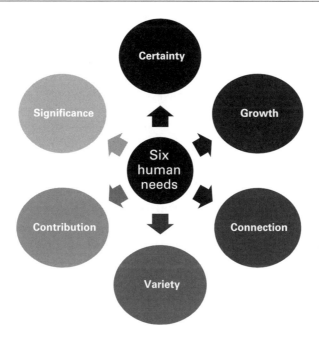

time. The six human needs are *Certainty, Variety, Significance, Connection, Growth* and *Contribution*.

1. Certainty

We all have a need for certainty, safety, stability and predictability in our lives. We like to feel secure in our jobs, in our homes and in our relationships, and we want assurances that our basic needs are being met. Some people pursue this need for certainty by striving to control all aspects of their lives, including the projects they run and the people who work for them. They want to be as certain as possible that things work out the way they planned and that people do as expected and complete their assignments by the agreed deadline. When we lack certainty we tend to panic and get stressed. When things get too certain, however, we feel bored and demotivated.

2. Variety

Another human need – which opposes the first one – is the need for variety and uncertainty. At the same time as we want certainty, we also crave change, excitement and new stimuli. Variety makes us feel alive and engaged. Many project managers work in change management because of the inherent variety it provides. Projects are temporary by nature, and the uncertainty is for the most part tolerable because we know when the project is expected to end and what might happen afterwards. Too much uncertainty, however, will bring us fear, while not enough will cause boredom. So the first two needs are pieces of the same pie. If your need for certainty is 70 per cent, your need for variety will be only 30 per cent. People with a big need for variety may come across as risk-takers and may also seek out conflict and crisis situations to make them feel alive.

3. Significance

Deep down, we all need to feel important, unique and special. We want our life and our work to have meaning, importance and significance. Imagine how uncomfortable it would be to work on a project that is not needed and no one cares about. We can fulfil our need for significance and importance in many ways. One vehicle is by becoming a high achiever or by having many people report to us because it makes us feel important, special and wanted. That may also show up as being overly competitive and performance driven. Another, rather poor way to get this need satisfied is to put other people down and to elevate ourselves so that we feel we are better than others. We can also signal our uniqueness and difference through particular clothes or unusual hobbies.

4. Connection

Everybody strives for a level of connection and affiliation with people around them and wants to feel part of a larger community. We want to be cared for and we want a feeling of closeness or union with like-minded people – be it friends, family, colleagues, members of a club or an online community. The need for connection is based on blending in and wanting to be similar to others in the group and is therefore the opposite of significance. If we are 100 per cent connected and part of a team, a project or a culture, we are likely to be encroaching on our need for significance and uniqueness, and vice versa. Many project managers feel this conflict in that they want to be part of the team community, but at the same token they need to differentiate themselves and stand out as the leader of the pack.

5. Growth

As human beings we all have a need to grow and expand in our personal and professional lives. Many people's goal is to reach a certain position, a financial target or a particular lifestyle, but when they get there, they become stagnant and unhappy because they are no longer growing. They have reached a plateau, and although there are no apparent reasons for why they need to learn and develop, they have an intrinsic desire for doing so. People are most happy when they feel they are making progress. We all need something to strive for, something that will challenge us to grow and expand emotionally, spiritually, physically, financially and intellectually.

6. Contribution

The sixth human need is the desire to make a difference and to contribute to a greater good. This is the need to help, serve and support someone or something bigger than ourselves in a meaningful way. As human beings we have a desire to contribute something of value, whether that is manifested through community, family, society or the project work that we do. Some projects have a very worthy cause and may help to make the world a better place to live, or at least they will have an impact on someone or something else. But when we are head-down managing the detail, we may not always see it. Very few people are mindful of how this aspect can help fulfil one of their most basic needs.

According to Robbins and Madanes, the way to lasting satisfaction and fulfilment is through the last two needs: a) the need to continuously grow and b) the need to contribute beyond ourselves. If we attempt to reach fulfilment through certainty, variety and significance alone, we will fall short. The problem with a high reliance on certainty is that no matter how much we seek to control our surroundings, we will never be able to gain complete certainty, as we live in a world of constant change. The issue with significance is that no matter where we look, we will always be able to find someone who is more significant than us, which may cause distress.

My need for certainty and significance was holding me back – by Kevin Ciccotti

When I look back on my previous career and think of how I was living and working, I can clearly see that what drove me – the need for certainty and significance. And the cost to me personally was considerable. My need for certainty would cause me to seek 'safe' situations, or situations I could control in one way or another. There were so many times I felt I wanted to push myself, challenge myself to try something radically different or out of my comfort zone, and I wouldn't. In addition, my need for significance had me comparing myself with others in multiple situations. And of course in my own mind, I never measured up. I always seemed to come up short. There were other drawbacks to this high need for significance as well. Because the fear of losing status is so strong, I found myself not taking on challenges or new activities unless I knew I could succeed. Failure was not an option. In my own mind, any perceived failure would result in the immediate loss of my job, my reputation and my self-esteem – or worse.

So what changed for me? The first thing was that I realized it was all my own doing; my own thoughts and actions were keeping me from having the impact that I truly wanted to have on my company, team, family and friends – and on the world. What I finally realized was that the pain of staying where I was had become greater than the fear of changing. It's called reaching the threshold level of pain.

Today, I am very clear about my needs and my strategies for meeting them. My top two needs are contribution and love/connection. I wake up every day asking the question, 'How can I contribute to the people in my life today? My clients? My family? My team at work?' Living in alignment with my core values allows me to contribute on a higher level than I've ever done before.

— Kevin Ciccotti, Certified Professional Coach, Owner, Human Factor Formula Inc

My client was held back by old beliefs – by Kevin Ciccotti

I was working with a client who is a division leader for a major US corporation (we'll call him Sam). He was having issues with engaging his team and really getting them to buy in to his leadership. About two months into our coaching engagement, I was with him on a site visit, when we met his boss in the hallway. His boss said, 'Hey, Sam, I wanted to tell you what a great job you did in that meeting this morning. The senior leadership team was very impressed with your delivery, and I was pleased to see how well you handled them'. As I watched Sam taking in this feedback, I noticed his face go almost completely blank, as though he had no frame of reference for what was being said.

When we got to his office, I immediately took that as my cue. I asked him what he experienced as he was receiving that feedback. After a few questions, I realized that his past had created powerful beliefs in him. We spent some time challenging those old beliefs, and focused specifically on his sense of significance. Here's why: I discovered that Sam had been a football player his whole life, and even played in college. And the deeply imbedded beliefs for him were that feedback was always about what you were doing wrong versus what you're doing right. His need for significance was being met by the fact that he was never good enough. (Note that your needs can be met in positive or negative ways.) Consequently, Sam had little or no reference to receiving positive input, and as a result he was also uncomfortable giving any.

We worked on creating a reversal of his old patterns. I had him focus on actively noticing when he was doing things right and also noticing

the same with his team, then being sure to acknowledge those with positive feedback (internally for himself, and externally for his team). Today, his leadership style has completely changed. He now seeks out the positive in himself and others, acknowledges accomplishments and has a whole new level of appreciation for his team. That has translated into deeper connections, more trust and improved performance across the board for him and his team.

— Kevin Ciccotti, Certified Professional Coach, Owner,
Human Factor Formula Inc

EXERCISE The six human needs

Examine the six human needs and ascertain which of them you value the most and how you go about meeting them. The more conscious you become about the needs that drive you, the easier it will be to make changes that will benefit you and support your ambitions.

1   Which of the six human needs do you value the most?

2   What are the ways (good and bad) in which you meet and balance these conflicting needs?

3   To what extent does your need for certainty lead you to exercise control over people, information and decisions on your project? And to what extent does it hold you back from doing something new because you are unsure about the outcome?

4   How is your need for variety being satisfied on a daily basis? Is there a possibility that you are drawn to firefighting and conflict because it makes you feel alive?

5   In which ways is your need for significance affecting your work? Do you see it as a way to gain recognition and respect? Do you sometimes elevate yourself in conversations or talk down to others? Or maybe you have been a victim of someone doing that to you.

6   To what extent do you seek to fulfil your need for connection through your work? Is it important to you that you are being seen as a team player and to feel accepted by the group?

7 How can you use your profession to satisfy your need to grow and to contribute to a cause bigger than yourself?

8 In which ways will becoming a project leader help you to better fulfil your needs?

When I examine the six human needs at a personal level, it becomes clear how they help explain my own passion for project delivery, coaching, speaking and writing books. These activities satisfy my needs for certainty, variety, significance, connection, growth and contribution to perfection! But that is not the way it has always been. There was a time when I was working hard as a project and programme manager, delivering great benefits to my clients, and still didn't feel fulfilled. That is when I started to study and learn about coaching and began to incorporate it into my day job. All of a sudden I found a way to deeply connect with others and a way that enabled me to grow and contribute to a worthy cause – being other people's development. It was a magical realization. In addition I began to speak and write about project management and leadership, which made me feel that what I was doing was truly rewarding and worthwhile.

People often think that in order to become more satisfied at work they need to change their lives in dramatic ways, giving up their job and devoting themselves fully to their hobby. But more often than not we can easily become more driven and passionate in our jobs by increasing our levels of contribution and by amplifying those aspects that give us the most meaning and purpose. As a project manager you can do that by starting to make more use of your strengths – or by finding a role where you can use your project management skills to deliver a project with a truly worthy cause. You can also volunteer your time to manage a pet project or an initiative that is close to your heart. Other options are to start mentoring more junior colleagues, teach or join an online community. There are infinite ways in which you can increase the synergy between your personal needs, wants and desires and those of the project and organization you work for.

The best strategy for lasting job satisfaction and sustained drive is to recognize that your work is part of your purpose and to look at ways in which *all* of your needs can be met by the work you do. As someone who wants to transform from project manager to project leader, your incentives need to be compelling enough to facilitate and sustain the change. In fact it would be impossible to operate as a project leader without also embodying a strong sense of purpose and drive. True leaders are not just doing a job. They are doing a purposeful job that fulfils all of their needs, including the need for growth and contribution.

I recently coached a project manager who was bored and unhappy in his job. He said that it contained no stretch or development opportunity and that he was working at only 60 per cent of his capacity. He wanted to progress into a more senior position, and knew that he had to find a new job in order to do so. But in spite of logically knowing that he needed to move on, he said that he wasn't going to. He valued the security and his manager's support of him too much. He knew that he could earn the same amount, or more, in another role but was still reluctant to change jobs. The project manager felt torn between his need for certainty and his need for growth and variety. It was only when we had an in-depth conversation about his fears that he realized how much he had allowed his need for certainty and stability to control his choices. The week after our coaching session, he decided to move on and found a new job that was much more suited to his level of ambition.

Is your need for certainty holding you back, and does it cause you to be overly controlling of the project and your team? Becoming aware of the needs that drive you – and seeking to fulfil them in more constructive ways – is an important step on your road to project leadership. As we will discuss in key number one, great leaders have an in-depth understanding of their values and beliefs and lead according to these values. Leadership is not about emulating others or following a specific set of rules. It's about finding your own way and being who *you* are whilst serving your client and bringing your team with you.

How to embed the new behaviour

How to embed the learning

- Start observing your beliefs and the things that you say to yourself on a daily basis. Become aware of the thought patterns that limit you and gradually start to replace them with more empowering and positive beliefs.

- Begin to build the habit of thinking strong and empowering thoughts. Be supportive of yourself and practise seeing the opportunities in every situation. Read inspiring books and surround yourself with positive people.

- Imagine yourself in two, three or five years' time. What type of project leader would you like to become, and what motivates you to achieve that ambition? See it, feel it and smell it and make it tangible by creating a dream board or a passion poster that captures your vision.

- Consider which of the six human needs impact you the most, and how these needs will be fulfilled as you move towards project leadership. Assess the ways in which you can better fulfil your needs for growth and contribution through your job.

- Go to www.powerofprojectleadership.com for further resources that will inspire you and help you embed an empowering mindset. It contains links to books, podcasts, YouTube videos and TED talks amongst others. Check it out!

Checklist: Do you master the learning?

- You are aware of the beliefs that tend to limit you and you are actively working to replace them with something more empowering.

- You know what your biggest and deepest motivators are and you are seeking to increase the ways in which you grow and contribute through your profession.

- You have a good understanding of what you will gain from becoming a project leader and the ways in which it will fulfil you.

- For the most part you have a positive and empowering mindset, you have faith in yourself and you are fully committed to transforming from project manager to project leader.

Notes

1 Marano, H E [accessed February 2014] *Psychology Today* [Online] http://www.psychologytoday.com/articles/200308/depression-doing-the-thinking

2 Brown, R (2013) *The Influential Leader: Using the Technology of Our Minds to Create Excellence in Yourself and Your Teams*

3 Duquesne University [accessed February 2014] Center for Teaching Excellence [online] http://www.duq.edu/about/centers-and-institutes/center-for-teaching-excellence/teaching-and-learning/pygmalion and Paul, Annie Murphy [accessed February 2014] *Time*, How to Use the "Pygmalion" Effect [Online] http://ideas.time.com/2013/04/01/how-to-use-the-pygmalion-effect/

4 Robbins, A (2006) Why We Do What We Do, *TED*, [Online] http://www.ted.com/talks/tony_robbins_asks_why_we_do_what_we_do#t-221391

5 Bandura, A (1994) Self-Efficacy, *Encyclopedia of Human Behavior*, New York, Academic Press. (Reprinted in H. Friedman [Ed.], *Encyclopedia of Mental Health*, San Diego, Academic Press, 1998) [Online] http://www.uky.edu/~eushe2/Bandura/BanEncy.html

6 Duckworth, A (2013) The key to success? Grit, *TED*, [Online] http://www.ted.com/talks/angela_lee_duckworth_the_key_to_success_grit

7 Madanes, C (2009) *Relationship Breakthrough: How to Create Outstanding Relationships in Every Area of Your Life*, Rodale Books

The 7 keys to project leadership

You are starting to form a picture of the power of project leadership and the ways in which it can help you add more value to your clients and fulfil the needs and desires that drive you. Now it is time to look at each of the 7 keys in depth and provide you with specific ideas and strategies that can help you to step up and lead. The 7 keys are as following:

1 Be authentic.

2 Lead with vision.

3 Improve and innovate.

4 Empower the team.

5 Get close to your stakeholders.

6 Establish a solid foundation.

7 Work with intent.

Although these keys cover the full spectrum of project leadership attributes, it doesn't mean that you have to exhibit each and every aspect in order to be perceived as a leader. The 7 keys aren't meant as a prescriptive checklist, but aim to provide you with inspiration and suggestions of what good project leadership might look like. Leadership is not about blindly following a specific set of rules or a mentor, or uncritically implementing everything in this book. It is about marrying up what makes sense in the external world with the concepts and approaches that make sense in your internal world. So read the 7 keys with an open mind and adopt the attitudes, behaviours and strategies that give meaning to you in light of where you are and what you would like to achieve.

At the end of each key you will find a box called *your insights and intentions*. In this box I encourage you to capture at least three insights from each key along with three actions you will take to implement that key. In Chapter 4 we will then review your insights and decide which aspects are most relevant and what your most immediate priorities and actions should be.

Key #1
Be authentic

FIGURE 3.1.1

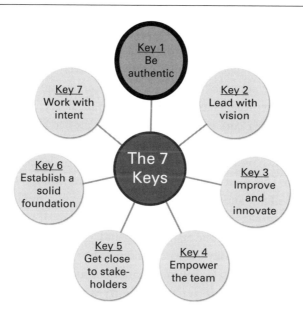

IN THIS KEY YOU WILL LEARN

- What it means to be an authentic project leader who has a strong sense of purpose and who leads according to personal values
- How you can become more centered and confident and learn to trust your instincts
- What your core values are and what the purpose of your leadership is

Authentic leaders live by their core values

The first of the seven keys to project leadership is to be authentic. This is the most fundamental of all the keys and represents a core aspect of leadership. If you attempt to implement a whole raft of strategies without being authentic, you may become very skilled at your job, but you will never become a truly inspiring and credible project leader. Leadership doesn't come from emulating others or from blindly following a specific set of rules. It is a deeply personal approach that is rooted in who you are as a person. Being authentic is about truly knowing yourself and what you believe in. It is about being the person you know in your heart that you have always been destined to be. When you know what you stand for, it is much easier to do the right thing in any given situation and to intuitively lead others. That is when you have the potential to be the best version of you.

Authentic project leaders are people with extraordinary integrity who are willing to live by their core values. When they are pushed to go beyond what they believe in, they will rarely compromise unless there is a meaningful reason for doing so. They have a strong sense of purpose and understand the motives that drive them. This is an insight they have developed through introspection, observation, feedback and years of experience. It is an insight that helps them stay grounded and be guided to make the right decisions. If you don't understand what the purpose of your management and leadership is, and what your big 'why' is, you will be easily influenced, not just by external events and other people's opinions, but also by your own emotions and impulses. That means that you will find it harder to act with integrity when the pressure is on and that you may make knee-jerk and poor decisions as a result.

The true test of authenticity is not what you say you will do, but how you actually behave. This is especially true when you are under pressure, as your true values will emerge when things aren't going your way. If you are not acting with integrity in those situations, by not living up to the values you professed, trust is broken and not easily regained. Being truly authentic means that your actions reflect your core values and that your purpose is aligned to those values. It means that there is harmony between what you think and feel on the one hand and what you say and do on the other.

When you are comfortable with who you are, and when you are able to use your inner guidance system to inform you about what is right and what is wrong, it will be easier to act with integrity and to make the best decisions, even if they are not popular. You will instinctively know when to step in and when not to, when to accept something and when to push back. You will have the confidence to stand up for yourself and your project and to protect

FIGURE 3.1.2   There must be congruence among what you think, feel, say and do

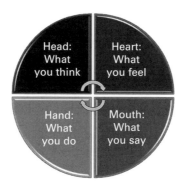

your team from unnecessary noise. But not least, you will have the desire to be true to your client's long-term vision (even when your client is not) and to deliver the project's outcomes and benefits in the most cost-effective and sustainable manner. When you have the courage to rely on your inner guidance system, you will be better able to serve your client and to build stronger interpersonal relationships because your actions will be congruent and consistent. People will respect you and want to follow you because you are honest, strong and reliable.

Authentic project leaders have a genuine desire to serve their client and to enable others to make a difference, more than they are interested in power, money or prestige for themselves. They have a clear view of what their client's true needs are, and they seek to fulfil them with utmost care and judgment. We could say that project leaders are *givers* who seek to empower people to contribute to the client's bigger vision. They naturally lead by example and recognize that being a leader is a real privilege and responsibility that must never be abused or taken advantage of. In that sense they are humble. They want to continue to learn and grow, as they know that becoming a leader is a journey that never ends. The opposite are *takers* who tend to take out as much as they can from their surroundings. They have a big need for *significance* and fulfil this need by serving themselves. These people often view situations, colleagues and subordinates as a means to gain greater power, money and recognition.[1]

But the goal of project leaders is not to serve themselves at the expense of others. Rather than being steered by self-enhancement values, project leaders are primarily driven by self-transcendent values linked to *growth, contribution* and *connection*. They gain satisfaction from contributing to a cause greater than themselves, from continuously learning, empowering others and knowing that they are doing the right thing. For that reason they don't play favourites or engage in dishonest politics, as that would undermine trust and collaboration and their core values. They have a genuine and honest approach to their work and attempt to be transparent and open about a situation. When things go well, they look out of the window and let others take credit. When things go wrong they look in the mirror and take responsibility.

In an interview with the APM,[2] Camila Batmanghelidjh, founder of Kids Company, says,

> If you're a project manager, provide for quality and truth, and success will come on the back of that. If you just go for success on its own it won't work. Generally there is an attitude of success being the end goal in everything, and sometimes people think up shortcuts just to have success whereas actually I think integrity is the most important thing. Sometimes you won't be successful, but integrity is a better driver of projects than the drive for success. If you have integrity, the outcome is success. What I would like project managers to be able to do is to face truth, stare it in the eye and then operate by it.

Always act with the best intention of the organization in mind – by Dave Sawyer

I've seen so many managers who are seeking to feather their own nests; bigger teams and bigger budgets, often to fuel big egos.
I have a small team that works well. I have a modest budget, but it's carefully managed to run the projects that I have. I work hard to try and benefit the organization, sharing new learning and helping to build the staff. I won't support anything that is 'selfish', and teams see that and understand what's going on. It's fairly simple advice really; act in the best interest of the firm!

– Dave Sawyer, Project Manager, UK Government

Listen to your intuition and gut instinct

The key to being authentic is knowing in your heart and in your head what you stand for, what you *will* and *will not* compromise on, and then being true to that. As a project or change manager, it is not unusual that from time to time you will feel pressured to respond to awkward and challenging requests. These pressures, and your need to please others, may cause you to detour from your authentic self or from what is in the project's or client's best interest. When you get too far off course, your internal compass will tell you that something is wrong, and if you take the message seriously, you will be able to make a correction. It requires strength of character, courage and determination to resist these constant pressures and to take corrective action when necessary.

When project leaders are under pressure, they stand out by openly admitting it. They don't pretend to be perfect or make out that they have all the answers even if people expect them to. They accept that complexity is so great that they cannot possibly know or control everything. And instead of feeling pressured to arriving at a conclusion on their own – which may be a poor one – they will draw on their team and support network. The true genius of project leaders is that they enable others to grow and contribute. In doing so they build trust and collaboration and they turn their own limitation into strength by considering different viewpoints and multiple perspectives. Asking others for help is not a sign of weakness or a lack of self-awareness. It is a sign of courage and a desire to obtain as much information as possible before making a decision. Having the ability and willingness to draw on good people is not only a great way to empower others, it is also one of the main ways in which project leaders stay healthy and avoid excessive levels of stress.

But project leaders do more than consult others when making decisions. They also listen to their intuition and gut instinct. At the end of the day, they are the ones to make the final decision – or select which options to recommend to the client or project sponsor. It is not uncommon that a decision needs to be made quickly and that time doesn't allow for each option to be investigated in depth. We operate in environments where change happens rapidly and where we have to make decisions on the fly. Nothing is fixed or certain, and the fear of taking a wrong turn can be frightening. The trick is to accept that uncertainty is everywhere and that from time to time we are going to make mistakes. We have to embrace uncertainty instead of resisting it, and the better we become at listening to our gut instinct, the easier it will be.

Project leaders often have a hunch that something isn't quite adding up or a feel for which of the options presented to them is the right one. Consider some of the most important decisions you have made in your life, such as buying a house, changing jobs or deciding to get married. Did you let the unknown paralyze you and did you rely solely on facts and logic in these cases? Probably not! Part of your decision-making would have involved your gut feeling or your heart. Project leaders don't solely make decisions based on logic or the information available to them. They do look at facts and consult others, but once they have obtained the data they will draw on their other senses and come to a conclusion. It may be that the conclusion is to follow the team's recommendation or to delegate decision-making to a particular individual. But even so they consulted their inner guidance system in the process.

The key is to admit that our gut instinct plays a role and to hone it over time. The more we tune in to it the more we can trust it and start to rely on it. It's about developing our awareness and then allowing our intuition to move from the gut to our mind. Sometimes, it's as simple as asking, *What is my gut telling me about this – what is my intuition?* Other times we have to specifically shut down our rational thinking and reflect in a quiet setting away from distractions. Unfortunately, reflecting and listening for insight has almost become a lost art in our increasingly fast-paced projects. But if we fail to cultivate the intuitive half of our decision-making abilities, we become less than our best as leaders and merely rely on the facts at hand.

FIGURE 3.1.3 Use your gut and inner guidance system in the decision-making process

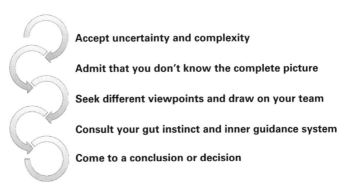

Accept uncertainty and complexity

Admit that you don't know the complete picture

Seek different viewpoints and draw on your team

Consult your gut instinct and inner guidance system

Come to a conclusion or decision

Good leaders have good instincts that they listen to – by Julia Strain

One of the things that distinguish a project leader from a project manager is the ability to interpret and challenge data. Managers can take detail and add things up, but leaders will step back from the detail, listen to their gut feeling and then marry up the two. There's a

huge difference. If you don't have the ability to stand back and use your instinct, you'll be a manager because you're relying on the detail. When you look at an estimate, for instance, you've got to stand back from the detail and ask yourself if it feels wrong or if it feels right. The same is true when you have to learn to trust people in your team. You have to take into account what they are saying and weigh it up with your gut instinct.

Good leaders have good instincts that they listen to. They follow what they believe in, which makes them much more likely to succeed. Choosing one option and bringing everyone along with you sounds so basic, but it works. One of the major differences between a manager and a leader is that a leader can formulate a clear strategy and can bring people into that strategy. That's very hard to do unless you've honed your instinct and unless you're prepared to take risks. It all adds up to an inner belief, risk-taking, confidence, working outside your comfort zone and not being afraid to make a mistake. Instinct is somewhere alongside that. It's a very powerful thing that drives a lot of our behaviour. Most of the time your instinct is absolutely right.

I'm a great believer that people need to hone and listen to their instinct more. Project managers at all levels can do that by observing things that work out well and not so well on a day-to-day basis, and tying that to their gut feeling. They can start off gently by asking themselves what they thought was wrong and what was right. How did they feel when they first did something? Nine times out of 10 people will find that they had a funny feeling, and that's what they need to capitalize on.

– Julia Strain, CIO, Standard Bank

Understand the values that are authentic to you

Becoming an authentic project leader can take months – or even years – of self-reflection, observation and development. But looking within yourself and gaining greater self-awareness is essential, as it will help you to lead yourself and in turn lead others.

Bill George, the bestselling author of *Authentic Leadership* and *True North*, writes that,

> In studying leaders who have failed, I realized that their failure resulted from their inability to lead themselves. As we discerned from our interviews, the hardest person you will ever have to lead is yourself. When you can lead yourself through the challenges and difficulties, you will find that leading others becomes relatively straightforward. Leading yourself starts with understanding your life story, your unique gifts, the challenges and crucibles you have faced, and the source of your passion to lead others and to contribute to the world. In interviewing 125 authentic leaders, we learned that their calling to lead emanated from their life stories. When you understand your life story and experience life's challenges, you can find your passions to lead and, in turn, the purpose of your leadership. This is what I consider is your calling to lead.[3]

EXERCISE   Uncovering your core values

Let's spend some time finding out what your internal guidance system and core values look like. You will already have a sense of it from Chapter 2, but in this exercise we will have a closer look at your values in regards to your profession. Please grab hold of pen and paper and write down your answers to the following questions.

- What is most important to you in your job as a project manager?

- What does it mean to you to be a good leader? What do great leaders do?

- Describe a time when you felt most fulfilled at work?

- What has to happen for you to be happy in your job and feel that you are contributing to a worthy cause?

- Which situations typically make you feel upset or angry?

- What would you most like to change in your current job or on your project?

From the preceding questions, what would you say your most important values are? In which situations do you feel that your values are being compromised, and what can you do about it? To what extent is there congruence between your personal purpose and that of your project?

Following your inner guidance system is not about being arrogant or headstrong, but about being true to who you are. It means that you have a strong sense of self without being egotistical and self-serving. It means that you are centred because you know what your purpose is and what your values are.

Being authentic also means that there is congruence between your personal values and beliefs and those of the project you are leading and/or the organization you work for. If there is a conflict, how is it possible to live by your core values? If, for instance, the project you are running is delivering a product that you find unethical, or if some of the subcontractors are using immoral or unsustainable methods, you will not be authentic if you fail to address your concerns. Not only will you be compromising your own values, but you will also find it hard to fully engage in the project and to serve your client.

When your values and beliefs are fully aligned to those of the organization – or the project you work on – there will be nothing that can hold you back or distract you. There will be a strong synergy between the purpose of the project and the organization on the one hand, and your personal purpose on the other. As a result you will feel an unlimited amount of energy and fulfilment from the work you do. The more synergy there is between your needs and your project's needs, the greater your chances of becoming the best version of you and ultimately being able to serve your client.

You will know within yourself if there is congruence between your personal purpose and that of your project, and if you are leading in accordance

FIGURE 3.1.4 Authentic leadership is about knowing your values and living by them

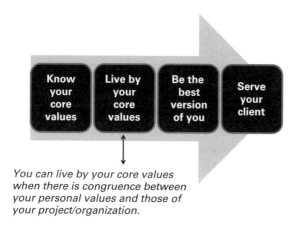

| Know your core values | Live by your core values | Be the best version of you | Serve your client |

You can live by your core values when there is congruence between your personal values and those of your project/organization.

with your values, or if you are not. If you are not, you will feel it, because you aren't getting the results you want and because you aren't fully engaged or able to serve your client. You may find that certain aspects of the project feel wrong – or upsetting – or that you feel discomfort and distress. This could be caused by what psychologists call 'cognitive dissonance' – a state of inconsistency between your attitudes (what you think and feel) and your behaviours (what you say and do). This inconsistency means that you are not centred and that you may doubt your inner guidance system. You may find that you are easily influenced by other people's opinions or by external events and requests. After all, it takes great courage, insight and stamina to steer a project through troubled waters and to know when to cut through and assert yourself, and when not to.

Some of the situations that you may find challenging and that may test your authenticity muscle are:

- Senior management is putting pressure on you to kick off the project and to commit to timelines before the project has been defined and before you know what the client's real needs are.

- Internal resource managers or department heads insist that certain people are deployed on your project for practical reasons, even it it's clear that they are not the best fit and that it will not serve the project in the long run.

- One of your team members has made a mistake and your executive sponsor demands that you remove them from the project.

- A severe error has been discovered during testing of your product and your client insists that you personally handle it even though you know that your team is perfectly capable of taking care of it.

- A team member who had committed to an important deadline hands in the work late and to a significantly lower standard than agreed. He doesn't take the issues seriously and his only comment is that the task was more complex than he had expected.

- From detailed analysis it becomes clear that the agreed solution will not serve the client's strategic vision and that an alternative approach will produce far better results in the long term. However, when you suggest that the project be revisited, you experience pushback from your managers. They seem to be focused only on the short-term benefits that the original solution will produce.

Next time you find yourself in one of these situations, what can you do and say to be true to your values? How can you calmly find a mutually acceptable resolution instead of succumbing to the pressure and pleasing others? Could you pause, take a step back and make the other parties aware of the adverse impact of their demands and actions? Could you coach them to make them see what you see, rather than either lecture them or blindly agree with them?

Your role is to show the way, to do the right thing and to focus the team on that which adds the most value to your client's end goal in the most effective manner. That's the kind of project leaders and role models we need. And that's the kind of leadership you have the potential to show when you act with integrity and authenticity.

Courage – by Benoit Jolin

Making the right decisions requires courage, even more so when the right thing to do is to course correct or halt an investment. Too often, pleasing key stakeholders supersedes rational decision-making. Data and the insights resulting from a test-and-learn approach are powerful allies and will help product leaders make (and sell internally) the right decisions.

– Benoit Jolin, Head of Global Supplier Experience, Expedia Inc

Be ready to stop the project – by Julia Strain

If your users don't make it clear what they want, or if decisions aren't being made by the right people, you should be prepared to stop the project! It's hard to stop something, but it forces people to think.

– Julia Strain, CIO, Standard Bank

Building self-esteem

When you are comfortable being authentic, it also means that you are comfortable standing out. It means that you have found your unique voice and that you are proud of it. Many of us feel more at ease blending in and following others than standing out and taking the lead. When we follow we don't have to take full responsibility and we are less likely to be criticized. But project leaders think and behave differently. They are happy to put their unique stamp on the project and to lead the way. They take full responsibility for their actions and accept that it is an approach that is not risk free. Fear of failure does not deter them from standing up for what they believe is right. To them the risk is far bigger in trying to be someone who they are not. Project leaders give it their all or nothing and implicitly set a good example. Emulating others in order to gain recognition – or seeking to fit in out of fear of being criticized – is not something they prefer to do.

You don't have to do it like they do; be authentic – by Eileen Strider

I was a department manager, with six or seven project managers reporting to me, and I didn't think it possible to progress to a director-level position. There was only one female director in the very large company (almost 100,000 employees) where I worked, and she was in HR. There were no female directors and never had been in IT where I worked (3,600 employees). Then I attended a class where the instructor asked us to close our eyes and picture having a career dream come true. I was having trouble picturing myself as a director. When the instructor asked me why I thought I was having trouble, I said, 'Because all the directors are male'. Then she said, 'What makes you think that if you are a director, you have to be like them?' A light bulb went on for me. I realized, 'Oh, I don't have to do it like they do it! I can do it like I would do it'.

To me, this is at the heart of being an authentic leader. Just be yourself. You are an authentic person; there is no one else just like you; you are unique. It can sometimes be scary to just be yourself; you have to find your courage. In fact, you already have it; all you need to do is practise it. Take a step back, observe what is going on and integrate what you learn with your own wisdom. Don't just mimic what you see and hear; make it your own. Look outward and observe the big picture, then look inward and use all your senses and your intuition to make meaning from it. That is how you build authenticity. Make an intention; do what is right and be courageous enough to say the truth. Lead yourself in ways that demonstrate your authenticity, and this will encourage others to be honest and authentic too. But as we all know it can be hard to be introspective on your own and read the label from inside the jar. So find a good mentor whom you can learn from and who can support you. Someone who exhibits the exact characteristics you would like to have, and if that means working with several mentors then that is fine too.

— Eileen Strider, co-founder and President of Strider & Cline Inc

It's OK to be you and it's OK to be honest – by Sam Fleming

It is very important that you learn to understand who you are and when you are at your best. Leadership excellence is all about knowing that it is OK to be you and that it is OK to be honest. Outstanding leadership is just you on a very good day! The major affliction, however, is that vast swathes of us suffer from a fear of failure, meaning that we either never try to apply ourselves to great leadership or only shoot for goals that are easily within reach. I see this frequently in my team, which frankly stuns me; these folks hold millions of pounds in budgets and yet are too nervous of failure to really attempt to try anything different from the standard pattern of project management.

— Sam Fleming, Head of Project Delivery, British Gas Plc

Accepting yourself the way you are, and being happy to stand out and be unique, is something that comes more easily if you hold yourself in high regards. There will always be people who are more talented, knowledgeable and successful than you, but that's OK. You are truly gifted in your own way. You have unique strengths – and weaknesses – and you strive to learn and better yourself. When you learn to accept yourself the way you are, it will be easier to show the world what your authentic self looks like. It will help you to be more honest about what you have to bring to the table, and it will be easier for you to challenge others when your boundaries are being breached.

A good way to build self-esteem is to practise appreciation and to notice what you do well. Write down your strengths and achievements in a notebook, and find new areas and capabilities to appreciate every day. See yourself as the confident and authentic leader you want to be and take credit for the tasks and activities you do well. Resist the temptation to focus only on what you feel is missing, and make an effort to see the positive in every situation.

Try it out now. Identify a situation where you recently doubted yourself or your abilities as a project manager. Maybe it was during a steering committee meeting or when dealing with a particularly challenging client or team member. Bring yourself back to that time and consider how you felt and what caused you to feel that way. Was it a rational and reasonable feeling, or did your lopsided perspective in any way influence it?

Now try to reframe the situation and take a different view. Look at the situation from the completely opposite angle. From that angle, in which ways did you behave really well? In which ways were you being true to yourself? Which skills, attitudes and behaviours did you bring to the situation, and in which ways did it help you to grow and develop? Can you see how important it is to go back to these 'sticky' situations and see them in a different light?

FIGURE 3.1.5   Strategies to build your self-esteem

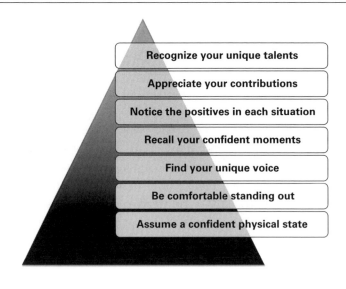

It can take time to build self-esteem, but with the right focus, support and willingness, you can change the way you feel about yourself more quickly than you think. You can accelerate the process by reading uplifting and motivational books, working with confident mentors and coaches and up-skilling yourself in areas where you feel you are lacking in competence. Empower yourself by being proactive and by continuously learning and developing.

Another way to strengthen your self-esteem is to remind yourself of the situations in which you are truly confident and to notice where you feel it in your body. Try it now. First, think of a point in time when you felt really confident. Close your eyes and imagine it. Where were you? What did you do and who were you with? Focus on the feeling you had in your body at that time. Where in your body did you feel a confident sensation? In your stomach, chest, arms or face? Be specific and recall the feeling in your body. Really go into it and try to amplify it until you know with certainty how your body reacts and feels when you are confident.

The easier it is for you to access this confident state in your body, the more you can take advantage of it in situations of doubt. Your mental state is closely linked to your physical state, so if you need to drum up support and increase your confidence so that you are better able to stand up for what you believe in, first bring yourself into a confident physical state. For most of us it means that we straighten our back, lift our chest and look up. Crouching your back and looking down is not a good position to be in when you want to be an authentic and strong project leader.

Learn how to be self-aware – by Hala Saleh

Leaders understand that their attitudes and even emotional state has an impact on the team and people around them. People naturally want someone to lead them, and they want that person to be confident and generally positive. Providing that type of energy for a team is critical. I don't mean to imply that a project manager should fake positivity or feign confidence when unsure about something. Rather, allow your confidence and sense of positivity to shine through when you experience them, and point out when things are going well.

– Hala Saleh, Director of Projects and Agile Coach

EXERCISE   Overcoming roadblocks to being authentic

Let us have a look at some of the roadblocks that might be preventing you from being truly authentic and acting according to your core values and beliefs.

- You work with some demanding managers for whom it is 'my way or no way'. You find it easier to just accept their way and play by their rules even if they contradict your own.

- Up until now you have never really thought about what your internal guidance system and values were. You just tend to get on with the job and deal with issues as they arise.

- You don't feel you have enough experience (either with project management or with the client organization or industry) to know what is right or what is wrong. As a result you are more inclined to look to others for guidance and decision-making.

- You are polite and respectful and find it hard to speak up and assert yourself when others aren't acting with integrity. As a result you end up suffering in silence when you feel your boundaries are being breached.

- You work in an industry or with a product that you find unethical. You have accepted that your personal purpose and need for growth and contribution cannot be satisfied by your current project.

- You work in a company culture where there is a lot of backstabbing and dishonesty. You have kind of accepted that way of working, as it seems to be the only way to progress in your career.

Which of the above scenarios do you recognize – if any – and in which ways do they impact you? Are you saying or doing things out of habit, or are you saying and doing them because you truly believe in them? How can you start to practise your 'authenticity muscle' and how can you start to follow your head, heart and gut in everything that you do? Do you have the courage to give it a go?

How to embed the new behaviour

In this key we talked about what it means to be authentic and how it is linked to honesty, integrity and self-esteem. Authenticity is about being who you are, listening to your instincts and standing up for what you believe is right. It is about creating consistency among what you think, feel, say and do – something that is easier when your personal purpose matches that of your project or organization.

How to embed the learning

- Regularly spend time examining your behaviours – particularly in stressful situations – and notice how you behave. Do you act with integrity by doing what you said you would? And do your promises and actions reflect your internal thoughts and feelings? If not, begin to understand the causes of the disharmony and how you can handle similar situations differently going forward.

- Spend time establishing what your core values and beliefs are and what the purpose of your leadership role is. Which aspects are most important to you on your project, and how can you emphasize them?

- Analyse to what extent you are using your current project to serve yourself in order to gain power, money or prestige, or whether you are driven by the desire to serve your client and empower your team members to contribute to something bigger than themselves.

- Actively work to increase your level of self-worth and appreciate your unique talents. Unearth the leader you were meant to be and practise standing out and showing the way.

Checklist: Do you master the learning?

- You appreciate what your core values and beliefs are and regularly spend time on self-reflection and personal development.

- There is congruence between what you feel, think, say and do, and when there is not, you revisit the situation and make a correction.

- You always seek to act with integrity and do what is right.

- You are aware of your strengths, your big 'why' and what the purpose of your leadership is. You actively look for opportunities to work on projects where there is a high degree of synergy between your personal purpose and that of your project.

- You know that you have a unique leadership style and that it serves your client and empowers those who work with you. You are happy to stand out, take the lead and make use of your genius. In fact you see it as your duty to bring the best of you to the team and the rest of the world.

Your insights and intentions

Write down at least three insights you have gained from this section along with three actions you will take to embed this key.

_____

_____

_____

_____

Notes

1 George, B [accessed April 2014] The Spirituality of Authentic Leadership [Online] http://www.billgeorge.org/page/the-spirituality-of-authentic-leadership

2 Camila Batmanghelidjh CBE, founder of Kids Company, APM conference 2014, New Frontiers, London. [Online] https://www.youtube.com/watch?v=y57ZC0xzLDc&list=PLQzq_ylfBVzJpc3u_Inr2owS1v1pS8izo&feature=share&index=2

3 George, B [accessed April 2014] Truly Authentic Leadership [Online] http://www.billgeorge.org/page/truly-authentic-leadership

Key #2
Lead with vision

FIGURE 3.2.1

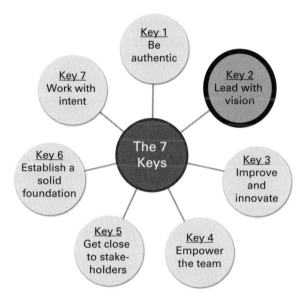

The importance of having a clear vision

The second key, leading with vision, represents another cornerstone in project leadership, as it is concerned with setting the direction and end goal for what the project is meant to achieve. The vision clarifies the clients' or sponsors' strategic objectives, focuses the team and provides a target to plan against. It gives you a view of where your client wants to go, but it won't give you all the stepping stones to getting there. The stepping stones will be derived by the team and will typically consist of tangible deliverables and outcomes. It is not unusual for the vision to be dependent on a collection of projects and initiatives, meaning that your project is part of a bigger picture or programme of work. For the vision to be as effective as possible, it should be clearly articulated, have an inspiring and energizing effect and be aligned to corporate strategy.

According to *Harvard Business Review* (HBR),[1] being forward-looking and enlisting others in a shared view of the future is one of the attributes that most distinguishes leaders from non-leaders. In an ongoing survey, HBR asked tens of thousands of people around the world what attributes they were looking for and most admire in a leader. The number one requirement – honesty – was also the top-ranking attribute of a good colleague. But the second-highest requirement, being *forward-looking*, applied only to

FIGURE 3.2.2 The importance of being forward-looking as an attribute in either colleague or leader

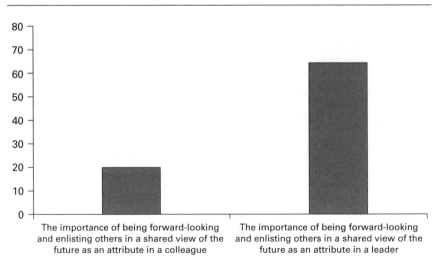

the leader role. Just 27 per cent of respondents said it was something they wanted in a colleague, whereas 72 per cent wanted it in a leader. Among respondents in more senior roles, the percentage was even greater, at 88 per cent. No other quality showed such a big difference between leader and colleague.

Being forward-looking and inspiring people to share a common vision is an essential attribute of project leadership. Project leaders are visionary and *begin with the end in mind*, as Stephen Covey put it in his best-selling book *The 7 Habits of Highly Effective People*. They partner with the client and play an active role in helping to define the project's vision, goals and benefits rather than just accepting it as a given by senior management or the client. They help shape it and challenge it until they understand it just as well as the client – or maybe even better. The main benefit of engaging at a vision level is to help ensure that there is congruence between the strategic objectives of the project and the actual deliverables. This means that you actively contribute to delivering what the users *need* rather than what they *want*, and that you are able to better engage the team members by sharing the vision with them.

This may be a new way of thinking for you if you are used to the traditional way of operating as a project manager. Traditionally, project managers are concerned with delivering an *output* or a *product* rather than the big vision. Customers normally specify what they want, and as project managers

FIGURE 3.2.3 Project Leadership is concerned with outputs and outcomes as well as business benefits and the vision

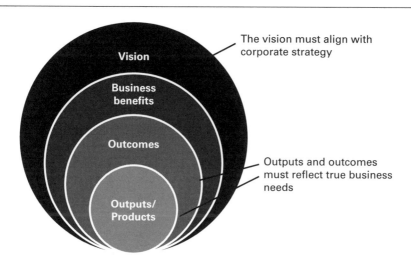

we help deliver it. We happily leave the big-picture thinking to the client or to the project sponsor – or to whoever else we feel is closer to the business and the decision-making process than we are. But project leaders think and act differently. They know that they have an opportunity to improve the project and increase its success rate and value by getting involved in the big picture and by fully engaging with the client's views and ideas.

Many project managers miss out on an exciting opportunity to have real impact and to help increase the project's value because they are excluded from the goal-setting part of the project. As a result they may end up with a disconnection between the project's tangible outputs and what the customer really needed. The project fails to deliver the expected benefits, either because the customer's needs weren't fully understood and therefore not reflected in the project's requirements, or because the initiative wasn't fully thought through and maybe not aligned with corporate strategy. According to PMI's research,[2] 60 per cent of projects are not aligned to strategic objectives although such an alignment has the greatest potential to add value to an organization. As a result it is not uncommon that projects are delivered more or less to specification, but that the end product ends up not being used or not adding as much value as it could have.

In the project management profession, it is mostly assumed that the clients or the executive sponsors know what they need and that they have analyzed their current challenges and opportunities in depth. But unfortunately, that's not always the case. Whereas the clients, or business owners, know their day-to-day operations better than the project team, they may not be skilled at specifying how their current and future needs can be met by a new product or service. They also may not be able to predict what the positive and negative impacts will be of a major change programme and what to do about it. Ultimately this may lead to a failed project. In some cases you will be fortunate enough to work with executives who know exactly what they need, how the project adds value in the short, medium and long term, and how it supports corporate strategy. But in other cases the set-up will be different entirely, and there may well be an opportunity for you to bridge the gap.

Partner with your client

Unfortunately it is not uncommon for clients, teams and delivery partners to start blaming each other when there is lack of clarity and alignment between the tangible outputs and the true business needs. Project teams blame the client for delivering a poor specification, and the client blames the supplier or delivery team for producing the wrong product. What is needed for successful delivery is joint responsibility and real partnerships. We need collaboration at all levels, even where rigid contracts are in place between supplier and customer. When we fully collaborate it means that the supplier (or project team) is a business partner to the client rather than a subcontractor. This is a mindset shift that implies that the project team shares the responsibilities for a successful strategic outcome and for the realization of the project's bigger vision. The aim is to create *one team*, encompassing client and supplier, and one shared goal.

In situations where project managers don't lead with vision, they become subcontractors working on a brief that has been passed down to them. They become followers who assume that someone else knows better than they do. They fail to share the responsibility for achieving the vision and cannot easily make decisions, or motivate the team towards the great new idea, as they are unlikely to have fully bought into it themselves. Sure, they will be able to plan within the confines of the brief that the client has provided and deliver the specified output, but that may not be enough to de-risk the project and ensure that the strategic objectives are achieved.

Many project managers feel inferior to their client and senior stakeholders, which reflects in their relationships and makes it difficult to lead. If you believe that your client's opinion is more valuable than yours, you are not creating a partnership based on equality. You are creating a relationship

FIGURE 3.2.4   Do you fully partner with your client? Do you have a mindset of equality, or do you see yourself and your team as being inferior, subcontractors?

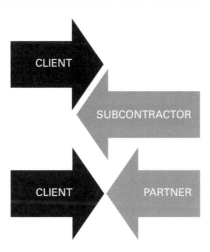

where you have subdued yourself. When you truly partner with your client, it means that there is complete transparency, trust and mutual respect between you, more so than equal measures of knowledge or seniority. Building strong relationships of trust is something we will examine in more depth when we come to key number five: *Get close to your stakeholders.*

Stepping up and applying yourself as a project leader requires not only that *you* personally partner with the client, but that you involve the delivery team in this level of engagement. Create the space for your team members to play an active role and to interface directly with clients and their organizations. When the team is directly engaged, everybody's knowledge and ability to add value is enhanced. People need to be given a chance to buy into the project's strategic objectives, which in turn will help them take ownership and feel motivated to contribute. Many teams intellectually understand what the project is trying to achieve, but are not emotionally engaged. They have only a high-level view of the project's objectives and don't appreciate how the end product impacts the users once it is operational or how it will ultimately benefit the business.

Partnering with your client is an engagement and a motivational exercise as much as one of knowledge sharing. It facilitates buy-in, accountability and a sense of community – and it enables you to lead and to add value in all that you do. How else can you effectively make decisions and motivate people to contribute? If you don't partner with your client, or project sponsor, you won't be able to come up with great, innovative ideas and you won't be able to judge which way to go. For that to happen you need an incredible amount of business acumen and you need to be brave enough to face off to your client in a like-minded manner.

FIGURE 3.2.5   The benefits of leading with vision

The best way to engage your client, and extract the goals, objectives and benefits, is to ascertain why the project is being carried out and what they want to achieve in the short, medium and long term. You need to establish what the strategic drivers are, what the business context is and how your particular project can help enable that. Below is a good set of questions that can help you get started:

- *What would you ultimately like to achieve?*
- *Which problems or constraints would you like to address with this project?*
- *In which ways will this project help you in the short, medium and long term?*
- *Who are the end beneficiaries and in which ways will they be impacted by the project's outcomes?*
- *How will the company or department operate differently as a result of this project?*
- *Why are these goals essential and how will they benefit the business financially?*
- *Which other projects need to happen in order for these goals to be fulfilled?*
- *Which other areas of the business will be impacted (positively or negatively)?*
- *What could affect the overall vision and change the objectives of the project?*
- *How can we measure the success and ultimate benefits of this project?*
- *What is the time frame for measuring that?*
- *Which other factors is this project dependent on?*

Asking these questions makes it clear what the project is aiming to achieve, why it is important and what your ultimate focus should be as a project leader. In addition you should ask yourself if you would be willing to invest your own money in the project. Answering that question will give you a good indication of whether the project is sound and if it makes good economic sense. If the benefits do not stack up, you should raise it to senior management and question the project's viability.

FIGURE 3.2.6 The answer to this question will indicate if the project makes good economic sense.

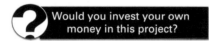

Unfortunately projects often get approved even if their foundation is weak. When you partner with your client and help analyze the business drivers, it gives you the confidence to judge the viability of the project and to tell the truth if something doesn't seem to make sense. Honesty and integrity are key project leadership values. Your job is to serve your clients and to look out for their interests. That means not just delivering the project's outputs, but ensuring that the long-term benefits are achieved as a result of those outputs.

EXERCISE Overcoming roadblocks that prevent you from leading with vision

Let's examine some of the roadblocks that might stand in your way. Some scenarios could be:

- You don't feel that you have sufficient business acumen to start engaging in discussions around the vision.

- Interfacing with your client and enquiring about the ultimate benefits is unfamiliar to you and quite firmly outside your comfort zone. You are not sure you have sufficient confidence and gravitas to face off to the client.

- Your project has clearly defined roles and responsibilities; it is the role of the client to provide the specifications and the role of the executive sponsor to provide the business rationale for the project. Your role is to deliver what they want, not to question it.

- You don't have direct access to the client, as a more senior manager does most of the communication. You deal only with one particular work stream and feel excluded from client interaction.

- Spending time understanding the bigger vision is not what you have been told to do by your boss, and it is not generally 'the done thing' where you work. Normally you leave that to senior management.

- You are nervous what the implications might be if you take joint responsibility for achieving the ultimate business benefits in case the initiative fails. You feel more comfortable, and safe, taking responsibility for delivering the tangible outputs only.

- You feel that you are too busy with day-to-day work to engage in the big-picture view.

Consider the particular reasons why you might not be leading 100 per cent with vision and which of the above roadblocks apply to you. Could it be that some of them are perceived roadblocks rather than real hard roadblocks? Could it be that you are using them as excuses because you deep down feel uncomfortable with the thought of stepping up and leading? Could it be that you are holding yourself back unnecessarily due to some limiting beliefs that you are not good enough, senior enough or clever enough to have these conversations?

Consider what you can do to overcome these roadblocks. Could you, for instance, get more exposed to your clients and learn more about their business? Could you start to partner with them in a new and different way? It is in everybody's interest that you step up and start to take part ownership for achieving the overall goals. You are not serving anyone by playing small. Be honest with yourself about the aspects that are holding you back. Acknowledgment is the first step. Then surely but safely put in place stepping stones that will help you to gradually lead with vision.

Test and question the business case – by Dave Sawyer

I don't really like to deliver anything where there isn't an obvious business case. If it isn't obvious, I'll ask if I can test it and check that the benefits really stack up. If I can't test it, and we're not running a pilot, I'll flag up to senior management that perhaps they need to reconsider the project. Generally those types of projects go to a project manager who doesn't ask the questions. I've spent years building up a good reputation as a safe pair of hands, and I'm not going to risk that by agreeing to deliver an absolute pig. We have to be selective and do the things that give the best bang for bucks.

– Dave Sawyer, Project Manager, UK Government

Focus on motivation, vision and project objectives (MVP) – by Thomas Juli

The big question project leaders need to ask is what they really want to achieve on behalf of the project and on behalf of the team. This is not just about project deliverables, but about project success as a process. It is about considering the overall picture with all its constituent parts. Project leaders understand the purpose/motivation, vision and objectives of the project, and they know that the heart and soul of every project is the team. They ensure that the team has a common understanding of the MVP – motivation, vision and project objectives – as it gives the team a strong common denominator. Motivation addresses the purpose of the project. Vision describes the ideal state after the identified problem has been resolved and gives the project a direction. Project objectives clarify and qualify the vision and describe the stepping stones toward that vision.

In my own experience, most project teams may know the project objectives. But they often lack the understanding of the overall meaning of them, how they were developed and, more important, why. But, it should not stop there. As a project leader, what you should do next is ask your individual team members about their personal MVPs. That is, what motivates them to be on the project? What do they envision for themselves personally, and what are their personal objectives and aspirations? Give your individual team members time for reflection, and then ask each person to share his or her MVP. This requires openness and trust, two ingredients of great leadership. As a leader reach out to your team and create an environment where it feels right to share this. If you find it difficult to answer the MVP questions, ask: What makes you happy and why? How do you want to feel on this project? How do you want to be treated? And how do you want to treat others in their pursuit of personal happiness on the project? 'After all, the only way to do great work is to love what you do, and to do what you love'.[3]

The personal MVPs complement the MVP of the project. And yet, it shouldn't stop there. The third dimension is the MVP of your team and community. Hence, ask your team what your MVP as a team should be. How does it fit in with the MVP of the project and how do you accommodate the individual MVPs within it?

I have found these MVP exercises the most valuable investment in a project. Leaders understand these three dimensions. They know that successful projects are not just about projects, but about people and a group of people forming a team or even a community. The overlap of these three levels of MVPs can spark a WOW project where there is common understanding of the motivation and direction of the project as well as the drivers, visions and objectives of each individual and the team as a whole. This is a very, very strong foundation for project success.

– Thomas Juli, author of *Leadership Principles for Project Success*

The importance of business acumen

Common for all project leaders is that they have an incredibly good understanding of the business drivers of their project. They understand the context in which their client is operating and they understand the industry. They also have a good view of the particular issues that their client is facing and of the ways in which the project's outcomes will help resolve them. They have acquired this knowledge in a multitude of ways – through project experience, theoretical learning and by observing or assisting clients with their day-to-day business. They have a passion for their industry and are keen to learn.

Some people believe that it is possible to be a good project manager without having much business acumen. But in that case your role will be confined to one of upholding project management processes and planning to a given specification. Project leaders aim to deliver *more* benefit to the client with the same or fewer resources – something that is not possible without an in-depth understanding of the business. This is not to say that project leaders must have the same skill set as the business analyst or that they should personally carry out the detailed requirements gathering. Far from it. Their primary role is to inspire and build a great team of skilled people and then get out of the way so that the team can do its best work. They are by no means micromanagers.

One of the best ways of acquiring business acumen is to facilitate workshops with clients, where they walk you through their business model, their challenges and what they are looking to gain from the project. In such situations, make sure you involve all key players of the team. Make an effort

FIGURE 3.2.7 Having business acumen means that you under-stand the business drivers, business context, industry standards, client needs, and goals and objectives.

to be as inclusive as possible, as it can be very demotivating for a team member to be excluded from key meetings. The last thing you want is to create a divided group of A players and B players. If you feel it is inappropriate to invite too many people to meet the client early on, make sure you at least set up debrief sessions where the information is disseminated and elaborated on. Your job is not to control information but to make sure that it flows freely to those who need it – including your remote teams.

What is your current level of business acumen and is it appropriate for the role you are in? Does it allow you to guide the team and to add maximum value to your client? And what about each member of your team? Do they all have a good enough understanding of the context in which they operate?

Don't ask, rather try to live their reality – by Benoit Jolin

Spend time with your clients understanding their world, their preoccupations, their pain points, their hopes and desires and what is important to them. Don't ask, rather live their reality. Spend a day in their shoes, shadowing them. Feel what they feel. They will like you for it, and it will make you immensely successful. You need to continuously focus on how you can increase your contributions to their success. When you become a subject matter expert and understand the customer, you gain so much more authority in the eyes of others. This also helps you to become more assertive and to say no. More than anything, your ability to influence will come from your ability to be perceived by others as a subject matter expert.

– Benoit Jolin, Head of Global Supplier Experience, Expedia Inc

Understand how the end result will help the business – by Julia Strain

Let everyone know the bigger picture and why they are doing something. It's important they understand what the end result is and how it will help the business. It's also a good idea to get someone from the business or key stakeholders to talk to team members every now and again so that they can relate their tasks to something that people are going to use. It makes a big difference when people know that the piece they are working on actually is going to have an impact in the real world.

– Julia Strain, CIO, Standard Bank

Understand the business – by Harlan Bridges

Great project managers bring business acumen to the project and focus on results over process. They think and act strategically and understand the business, the market, the competition and how projects fit in this mix. They know how the project brings value to the business and understand that project success is based on that value, not on cost, schedule and scope. We are slowly realizing that projects are not separate from the business but rather an integral part of the business and as such are successful only when they bring value to the business. Project managers must not abdicate the responsibility to deliver business value and must manage projects in such a manner that delivers the highest possible value to the business. Sadly some of the greatest resistance to this need comes from project managers.

– Harlan Bridges, PMP, BOT International

The strategic measures of success

Leading with vision requires you to consistently keep an eye out for the strategic and long-term benefits of the project – as well as the short-term benefits. In project management circles, a project's value is often measured according to the *iron triangle*, which states that projects must be delivered to the triple constraints of time, cost and quality. The triangle is useful for understanding the tradeoff among time, cost and quality from a planning perspective and for ensuring that the outputs are successfully delivered according to these measures.

But the triple constraints represent a narrow view of success, as they are concerned only with the tactical aspects of project management. The problem is that the concept of 'quality' may be too narrowly defined and captures only the quality of the project's tangible outputs, rather than the long-term benefits. In light of the many failing projects, is it possible that we need to give more consideration to the strategic value of projects and their potential to generate a real competitive advantage and economic value? Meridith Levinson writes that project managers need to be more focused on business value. They must see their primary role as delivering value to the company – not just completing projects on time and on budget.[4]

Dr. Knut Fredrik Samset – a professor at the Norwegian University of Science and Technology – says that a marker of success is the delivery of benefits in a *strategic* context. He argues that the triple constraints of time, cost and quality are tactical success criteria, whereas factors such as sustainability, relevance, impact and effect are strategic success criteria. In *Making Essential Choices with Scant Information: Front-end Decision Making in Major Projects*, Knut Samset writes,

> Judged in a broader perspective, a successful project is one that also significantly contributes to the fulfillment of its agreed objectives. Moreover, it should have only minor negative unintended effects, its objectives should be consistent with needs and priorities in society, and it should be viable in the sense that the intended long-term benefits resulting from the project are achieved. . . In essence, five requirements or success factors are fulfilled: efficiency, effectiveness, relevance, impact and sustainability. These are tough requirements that go far beyond the issues usually covered by many planners and decision-makers. What is termed efficiency represents only the immediate indications of a project's success in delivering its outputs. Clearly, there are many examples of projects that score highly on efficiency, but subsequently prove to be disastrous in terms of their effect and utility. There are also numerous projects which fail to pass the

efficiency test but still prove to be tremendously successful both in the short and the long-term.

The distinction when applying the success criteria above is the project's tactical and strategic performance. Success in tactical terms typically would be to meet short-term performance targets, such as producing agreed outputs within budget and on time. These are essentially project management issues. Strategic performance, however, includes the broader and longer-term considerations as to whether the project would have sustainable impact and remain relevant and effective over its lifespan. This is essentially a question of getting the business case right, by choosing the most viable project concept.[5]

As you engage with your client in understanding what will ultimately make the project a success, you have to consider the three tactical dimensions of time, cost and quality, as well as the strategic dimensions of effect on the project's objectives, relevance to its users and whether the project will have a sustainable impact. The iron triangle is great for helping you deliver the project's scope to the stated requirements and constraints, but the strategic triangle will help you ascertain the long-term viability of the project. The strategic triangle simply provides a set of further success criteria that need to be considered in the short, medium and long term, but does not otherwise indicate any interrelatedness between these factors.

FIGURE 3.2.8   To measure success, consider the project's tactical as well as strategic triangle

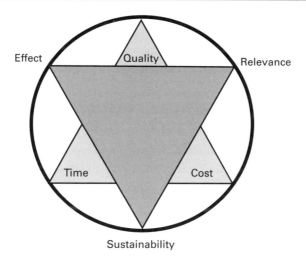

When considering the project's long-term viability, be clear on the time horizon you are measuring to, as the result may be very different if you measure the effect of the project after 10 years as opposed to 3 years. You also have to be aware that the project's objectives – and therefore success criteria – may change as the project progresses, perhaps due to a change in market conditions or corporate strategy. Your job is to work with the executive sponsor and client to adjust the project's measurement criteria so that they remain relevant in light of the context in which the project is being executed.

It is also worthwhile keeping in mind that the success of a project can be measured in both tangible and intangible ways. If, for instance, a product is being developed to specification, but the users for some reason don't like it, it will not be perceived as a success, as the users don't believe it is *relevant* and are likely to reject it.

Steve Pikett explains that in his experience, project managers are rarely equipped to deal with the emotional response from users who don't like a product or a service delivered to them. He says that it's insufficient to refer back to the tangible requirements if the users fundamentally don't like what they see. In order to deliver a successful outcome, we must have the courage and insight to ask the users how they *feel* about the product that is being developed. We have to listen for the meaning behind the words and be brave enough to ask them if they would be comfortable using it. Steve also explains that ascertaining the user's sentiment becomes easier the better we are able to prototype the solution and work closely with the end users. It's about making the product relevant and usable by focusing on the user experience.

Take a long-term view and deliver business benefits that add sustained value – by Rich Maltzman

Project leaders bring the long-term, enterprise view of the organization to the project team and help them make sustainably good decisions. This long-term thinking means that project leaders envision the project's deliverables beyond the handoff and well into the future, considering the use of the product in its steady state, i.e., when the product is fully operational. They take into consideration how the product performs and behaves over time with respect to market impact, competitive impact, investor impact, industry impact, as well as lasting ecological, societal and economic effects.

If, for example, your project involves the introduction of a new single-serve coffeemaker, are you merely planning for the handoff of the machine to the manufacturing process? Or, are you applying sustainability thinking by considering the fact that the coffeemakers will continuously use over tens of billions of non-recyclable coffee pods that are (A) filling up landfills and (B) contrary to your company's or client's stated sustainability goals? Project leaders consider and apply this long-term holistic mindset, including the use (consumption of power and material), waste (items such as the coffee pods) and reuse (recyclability) aspects of the project's product.

For project managers and their teams to make sustainably good decisions, they must first and foremost consider the steady state of the products, what they consume in that state and what the social, economic and ecological impacts are. They should be empowered to implement the company's stated corporate social responsibility (CSR) goals and apply this power and authority when initiating, planning, executing, monitoring and controlling, and closing the project.

> – Rich Maltzman, co-author of the Cleland Award-winning *Green Project Management* and *The Sustainability Wheel*

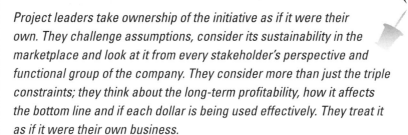

Project leaders have an entrepreneurial spirit – by Robert Kelly

Project leaders take ownership of the initiative as if it were their own. They challenge assumptions, consider its sustainability in the marketplace and look at it from every stakeholder's perspective and functional group of the company. They consider more than just the triple constraints; they think about the long-term profitability, how it affects the bottom line and if each dollar is being used effectively. They treat it as if it were their own business.

> – Robert Kelly, Managing Partner, Kelly Project Solutions

Always keep an eye on the benefits – by Dave Sawyer

Many projects just focus on delivering technology without considering the change holistically or the cultural or procedural implications of the change. These projects almost never achieve the claimed benefits or end up getting culled because there is no user requirement. I'm aware of a fairly high-value (nearly £100m) project that isn't being used properly because there wasn't a robust need for it and because the team didn't prepare the organization for its introduction.

I've been quite lucky avoiding this kind of thing because I tend to ask some really searching questions, and that often means that the main culprits steer well away from me when they're looking for a project manager. I'm not negative; we just have a really honest discussion, and perhaps their plan has to be thought about some more. I always recommend the use of benefits maps that show the alignment to the organizational strategic objectives. If you can't see the benefits in what you're being asked to do, it's probably best to think about whether the project is worth doing at all.

– Dave Sawyer, Project Manager, UK Government

The human aspect of change

Ensuring that everyone has a common view of what the project is trying to achieve, and that people feel inspired and ignited by it, is an art that only the best leaders master really well. They do this by involving the team, by showing them how they fit in, and by providing them with as much information as possible about the reasons behind the project. They share the exciting implications of the project's vision and embed it into everything that they do. They talk about it at every chance they get and use it daily to make decisions and solve problems.

But project leaders do much more than talk about the vision. They are mindful as to how the project and its outcomes affect the human condition and they tailor their approach, interactions and messages accordingly. They draw people in, address their concerns and anxieties and demonstrate what is in it for each person or group. Instead of exclusively dealing with tasks, activities and objectives, they delve into deeper layers and consider the psychological aspects. Project leaders know that most people resist change because they are uncertain about how it will affect them – whether consciously or unconsciously – so they take great care to remove resistance by addressing people's worries and by making them feel safe.

Resistance to change is an interesting phenomenon that is often quoted as the number one reason why projects and change programmes don't deliver the results they set out to. At its core, resistance to change is a label we apply when people seem unwilling to accept or help in implementing an organizational change. But oftentimes it isn't the change itself that people resist. They resist because they believe they will lose something of value (such as status, belonging or competence) or because they fear they will not be able to adapt to the new ways. It is a big part of human behaviour to hold on to the status quo because it's a safe port. We know what we have, but we don't know what we will get.

Emotions are important in understanding and addressing resistance to change. It is a very personal thing. Rebel Brown states that the easiest and fastest way to shift humans away from the way they've always done something and into a place where they think differently is to make the status quo unsafe. 'We have to make the status quo less appealing by pointing out the challenges, the risks, the downside potentials of remaining in that very status quo', she writes. Change does not happen unless the pain of stasis exceeds the pain of change. She also points out that this is not about scaring people or making them fearful. That would have a negative effect. Resistance to change cannot be overcome through authority or by forcing the unconvinced against their will.

Junior project managers may not be so aware of the emotional side of change and how important it is to listen to everyone who is being affected by it and ensuring that their needs are being met. Project leaders, on the other hand, adopt a holistic view and don't ignore the human aspect. They know that when people feel uncertain, they crave clear information and empathy. As a result project leaders make sure that there is a dialogue with everyone affected. On large projects they may even identify a team of change leaders throughout the organization who can help create this dialogue and instill a positive feeling towards the new products, procedures or services.

When Rod Willis researched why people resist change, he found that in the majority of cases, leaders and managers don't possess the necessary understanding of human psychology to effectively deal with the typical resistance-to-change symptoms.[6] He concluded that most managers operate at a *capability* level and fail to engage at a deeper level. This means that they consider what someone is capable of doing and how they do it as a function of their skills, rather than considering *why* people do what they do and what they believe about themselves.

The majority of the resistance-to-change symptoms (or causes) that Willis identified were a result of people's values and beliefs, sense of identity and personal purpose not being met. People don't leave their emotions, doubts, fear or lack of trust at home. They bring them to work where they may be perceived as resistance. Willis concludes that there is a direct correlation between a manager's ability to work at a deeper psychological level and bringing about successful change. It is when managers and leaders focus on building trust and removing doubt and fear that resistance disappears. It is not enough to simply communicate more. Overcoming resistance to change is about understanding people's psychology and getting to the root cause of the opposition. This is a process, which will take time. According to Professor Eddie Obeng, resistance to change comes about when we go too fast. He says that the natural remedy is to *go slower*.[7] He also suggests that we allow people to be part of the story and that we ask more questions. Questions are a great way to open up and allow co-ownership.

The ability to communicate the impact of your change initiative well, and to address people's underlying fears and uncertainties, could easily be the aspect that leads to the ultimate success of your project. If you understand how to do that well, not only will you get people's buy-in, you will also create a loyal and inspired team. Your focus should be to remove people's uncertainties – be it team members' or users' – by enhancing and highlighting the positive effects of the changes. You can do that by listening intently

FIGURE 3.2.9 Strategies to overcome resistance to change

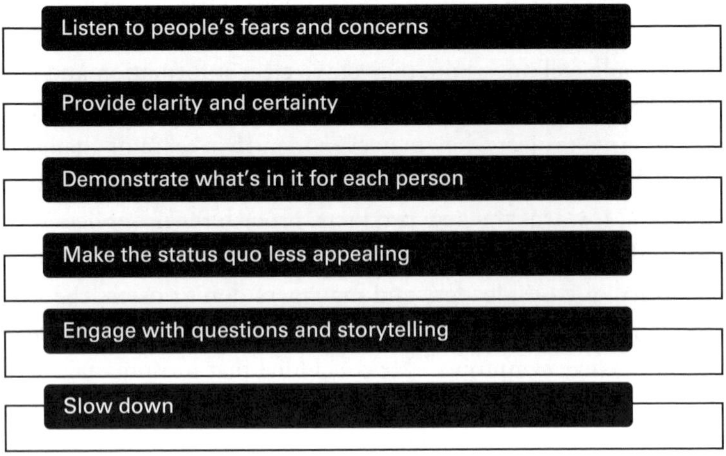

- Listen to people's fears and concerns
- Provide clarity and certainty
- Demonstrate what's in it for each person
- Make the status quo less appealing
- Engage with questions and storytelling
- Slow down

to people's hopes and needs and by understanding the things that matter to them. If you try to force people into a one-size-fits-all, you will cause upset even if you ultimately deliver what they need.

When embarking on this journey of deeply listening to and engaging people, consider the six human needs that we discussed in Chapter 2. How are the needs of the project's stakeholders, team members and end users affected in the short and long term as a result of the project?

- *Certainty* – Change initiatives are full of uncertainty and doubt, which makes people nervous. How can you add some security and stability into the picture? Which assurances can you give about the future that make the outlook more positive and credible?

- *Variety* – How can you appeal to people's need for excitement and stimuli when talking about the change? If people are worried that there is too much ambiguity about the outcome, how can you help reframe it so that risk is turned into opportunity? How can you show them that what they gain far outweighs the things they have to give up?

- *Significance* – Everybody wants to feel special. In which ways will the project and its outcomes help people gain new skills that will enhance their position and make them more employable and attractive in the future?

- *Connection* – How can you use the project's vision to unite people around a common goal? How can you make them feel that they are part of a community of like-minded people?

- *Growth* – We all have a need to develop and learn new skills – something that most projects provide ample opportunity for. How can you help people grow and develop and use that to create a positive feeling towards the project and the future?

- *Contribution* – Finally, in which ways can you show people that their efforts matter and that by supporting the project and its goals they contribute to a worthy cause greater than themselves?

How to embed the new behaviour

This key was all about how you can partner with your client and take joint responsibility for delivering the project's ultimate goals and objectives. We talked about the importance of considering the project's strategic as well as the tactical success factors and how you can overcome resistance to change by slowing down, providing clarity and listening to people's fears and concerns.

How to embed the learning

- Consider to what extent you lead with vision and what you can do to embrace it further. Do you fully partner with your client and share the responsibility for achieving the ultimate business goals? Are you conscious about uniting the team around a common vision and do you listen to people's concerns and seek to make the future more certain and enticing?

- Spend as much quality time as possible with your client or business users, understanding how they operate and what is important to them. Map out their vision, goals and objectives and involve your team in the process.

- Read up about your industry, organize knowledge-sharing sessions and walkthroughs and encourage your team to get to know the client.

- Work with the executive sponsor to create a comprehensive business case where all costs and benefits are quantified and where objectives are measurable. Demonstrate a clear link between project outputs, outcomes and the business goals.

- Address all team members, stakeholders and user groups and show them what they will gain from the project and its outcomes.

- Identify people who feel unsure about the change, listen to their concerns, hopes and aspirations and consider how you can meet their basic needs – in particular their need for certainty.

- Learn to tell an inspiring and believable story about the project that people can relate to, a story that motivates people and that ignites them around a common vision.

- Engage with your client and ensure you have a common view of your project's tactical success criteria (time, cost and quality) as well as the strategic ones (effect, relevance, impact and sustainability).

- Download a business case template from www.powerofproject leadership.com and check out some videos that will test your ability to keep an eye on the bigger picture.

Checklist: Do you master the learning?

- There is a high degree of trust and transparency between you and your client. You work as one united team and share the responsibility for achieving the project's long-term benefits.

- Your project's success criteria are a mix of tactical and strategic factors that are tracked by you as well as by your client.

- You feel at one with your project's strategic goals and your team members have an excellent understanding of the business context. They are able to make joined-up decisions and interface directly with the client.

- You are mindful of how the various stakeholders, team members and user groups are affected by the project and its outcomes and you have successfully communicated the benefits to them and addressed their concerns. People are generally positive and excited about the future.

Your insights and intentions

Write down at least three insights you have gained from this section along with three actions you will take to embed this key into your daily work.

_____

_____

_____

_____

Notes

1 Kouzes, J M, and Posner, B Z (2009) To Lead, Create a Shared Vision, *Harvard Business Review* [Online] http://hbr.org/2009/01/to-lead-create-a-shared-vision/ar/1

2 PMI (2014) *PMI's Pulse of The Profession, The High Cost of Low Performance 2014,* Project Management Institute (PMI)

3 Scharmer, C O, & Kaufer, K (2013) *Leading from the Emerging Future: From Ego-System to Eco-System Economies* (p 287), San Francisco, Berret-Koehler Publishers

4 Levinson, Meridith (2009) Top 10 Skills You Need to Succeed as a Project Manager @*itbusinessca* [Online] http://www.itbusiness.ca/news/top-10-skills-you-need-to-succeed-as-a-project-manager/14232

5 Williams, T, Samset, K, Sunnevaag, K, (2009) *Making Essential Choices with Scant Information: Front-end Decision Making in Major Projects,* Palgrave Macmillan, ISBN 978-0230205864, [Online] Chapter: Projects, their quality at entry – and challenges in the front-end phase http://www.concept.ntnu.no/attachments/058_Samset%20-%20quality%20at%20entry.pdf

6 Willis, Roderick Clarke (2014) What Drives Resistance to Change? A Leader's Perspective, *Academia.edu,* [Online] http://goo.gl/7msEvQ

7 Professor Eddie Obeng at APM conference, 2014, New Frontiers, Closing speech, London

Key #3
Improve and innovate

FIGURE 3.3.1

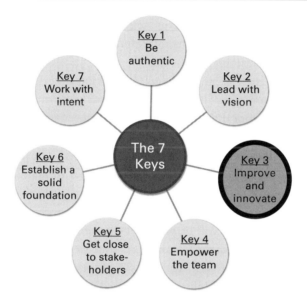

The status quo is not an option

As project managers we know all too well how demanding it can be to run a project and how easily we get absorbed in the detail. Just keeping our head above the ground and ensuring that the project stays on track can be difficult at times. Knowing when to dig into the detail and when to come back out and take a high-level view is an art more than a science. But taking a high-level view, and putting in place mechanisms that allow us to do so, is essential to project leadership. Project leadership is not about micromanaging the detail or about executing projects in the same way as they have always been done. Rather it is about setting a new standard based on the philosophy that we want to do the right thing and deliver our projects in the most effective and sustainable manner.

Project leaders are exceptionally good at taking a step back and observing the project from afar. They take a helicopter view of the project. They study the project from different angles and perspectives and assess which parts are working and which are not. And even if something is working relatively well, they consider how it could be improved. The process requires courage, energy and clear sight, as it is much easier to maintain the status quo than to question it and improve upon it. But the path of least resistance is of no interest to project leaders. They know that if we continue to do what we have always done, we will be no better off than before.

Project leaders are willing to take risks and step outside their comfort zone to see their ideas through. They go out of their way to help the project perform to the best of its ability, and they are not afraid to put their neck on the line for the things they believe in. Even when their views and proposals are being challenged, they are not discouraged. The status quo is not an option, and opposition does not frighten them or deter them.

What drives them to persist is their ongoing commitment to provide the best value for money and the knowledge that standing still is the equivalent to moving backwards. They understand better than anyone that it's not enough to simply turn up and do a good job. They work to a new standard and seek to be *outstanding* rather than *good*. The way to be outstanding and to generate competitive advantage is to consistently look for new and better ways of doing business, saving money, optimizing human potential and providing an outstanding sustainable service to customers. It's essential to question each part of the project, its inputs and outputs, and look for opportunities to better utilize resources, people, technology, processes, knowledge and ideas. That is the best way to serve the client – and besides, there is great satisfaction in doing something well and in jointly identifying the best way forward.

FIGURE 3.3.2 Challenge the status quo by finding more effective ways to serve your client

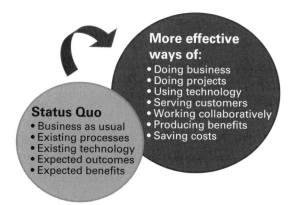

Challenge the assumptions – by Robert Kelly

I once took on a project with a company that was a product manufacturer and was tasked to develop the first 'non-tied' or 'stand-alone' service. Essentially, we wanted to develop a service offering that our customers could purchase without having to buy the product. As we launched the product, every regional executive said that we couldn't do it. We could only sell the service with the product. Here I was new to the company and senior executives were telling me we couldn't do it. I was ready to set my scope and run with their recommendation when I decided to reach out to some folks in the finance space to understand why this was. After several meetings and pulling in folks from finance, tax, legal and a few others, we were able to identify over three dozen countries where we could sell this 'stand-alone' service. It's so important for project managers to dig into the assumptions, and not get caught up in the mentality of 'this is how we always did it'. Had I simply run with the initial direction, I would have launched a programme in less than half the number of countries and made the firm uncompetitive in this space. What's more, my first project would have been a loser.

— Robert Kelly, Managing Partner, Kelly Project Solutions

> I realized that becoming an expert in my field came down to how much I really wanted it – by Hala Saleh

In 2011, after spending a little over a year at a job where being a good employee meant following the rules and not questioning authority, I attended a session at our local PMI chapter. The speaker was someone who worked in the exact opposite environment to mine; he was full of life, vibrancy and passion and, most important, he had the confidence to challenge the status quo. At that moment I realized that I had more to offer than I was sharing at the time, and I realized that becoming an expert in my field came down to how much effort I put towards that goal, and how much I really wanted it. Since that day I have shifted my project focus to people, thereby becoming full of passion and enthusiasm for what I do. I have also ceased to accept the status quo wherever it doesn't feel right to me.

— Hala Saleh, Director of Projects and Agile Coach

What is holding us back?

If challenging the status quo is such an important aspect to success, how come so many project managers are not doing it? What is holding them back and what is holding *you* back, if anything? Do you make an effort to rise above the day-to-day activities and assess how things could be done better? Are you willing to take the lead and stand up for what you believe is right? Do you involve your team in the process by challenging them to help find the answers? And do you have sufficient knowledge and interest in your job to do so?

Most project managers would probably say that they have their hands full. They are too busy keeping track of what is going on to be able to also spend time improving and innovating. In addition they may feel that they don't have sufficient knowledge of the project or the client's business to be able to suggest meaningful improvements – or they simply don't perceive that there is enough benefit in doing so. After all, everybody wants to leave the office at a decent hour, and if the price is to stay late in order to work on something that no one has asked for, then the motivation may quickly tail off.

But beneath these factors we find other reasons that help explain our lack of innovation, which relate to how we think and behave. As we saw in Chapter 2, everybody has a need for significance and a feeling of being unique and different, but at the same token we don't want to stand out *too much*, as we also have a need for connection and for being accepted as part of a group. When we lead the way, by proposing new and sometimes unconventional ways of doing things, it means that we break away from the pack. We take a standpoint and a risk by stepping out and saying, '*Hey, this is what my team and I believe in. It's different, but let's try it*'.

There is a real risk that people who are too critical towards existing ways of working will be seen as disloyal and skeptics towards the department or the company. To stand out as leaders doesn't mean that we are following the easiest or the safest path. It means that we are doing the right thing. And there are ways in which we can do that in an elegant and non-obstructive manner, through collaboration and by winning the support of people. But the fear remains that if we get it badly wrong, and if our ideas fail, it may cost us our job.

Great leaders understand that. They are willing to put their reputation at risk by endorsing ideas and initiatives even if they might not work out. Best-selling author and marketing expert Seth Godin puts it this way: 'Fitting in is a short-term strategy that gets you nowhere; standing out is a long-term strategy that takes guts and produces results. If you care enough about your work to be willing to be criticized for it, then you have done a good day's work'.[1] Having said that, the goal of project leaders is not to stand out for the sake of being different, but to stand out as an advocate for new ideas that will genuinely produce more for less and add value to the client.

FIGURE 3.3.3 Consider the benefits of innovation compared to staying in the status quo

In most cases it is easier for people to look for *marginal gains* – that is small and gradual adjustments to processes, tools and technology – as opposed to making radical changes. Identifying marginal gains is something that doesn't require too much risk-taking. It is one of the quickest and safest ways to optimize a project and definitely has its place. It is an approach where we improve tools, fine-tune workflows and increase motivation and engagement of the team. It's about mapping out all of a project's moving parts and looking for any improvements that can be made. But as Tim Harford, author of *Adapt*, points out, we get only so far with marginal gains. The big quantum leaps and breakthroughs don't come from optimization or modernization. They come from innovation, experimentation and risk-taking. Taking risks is part of the equation, and that invariably means that we have to be prepared to fail and to be wrong! And therein lies the problem. Many organizations have a very low tolerance towards risk, not least because of the drive to bring down cost and produce quick results. As a consequence we are finding ourselves in a bit of a dilemma; we want more for less, but in order to get more we have to innovate. We have to be prepared to risk something, unless we stick with the marginal gains.

Sir Ken Robinson, an author, speaker and international adviser on education, argues that most organizations are designed to execute rather than innovate and that they stigmatize mistakes. He also explains that most adults are frightened of being wrong and that if we are not prepared to be wrong we will never come up with anything original.[2] Furthermore, Seth Godin argues that creative and innovative thinking is hampered because we have been taught to conform and to follow for most of our lives. In his *education reform manifesto*, Godin argues that our school system was invented to produce 'compliant factory workers' to support the growth of businesses

FIGURE 3.3.4   Marginal gains versus innovation

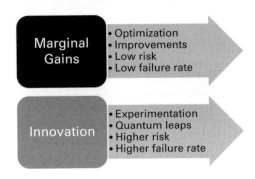

during the industrial revolution. School teaches us to comply and to fit in, not to stand out and lead.[3]

In the *Harvard Business Review* article 'Playing It Safe Is Riskier than You Think', Bill Taylor writes that there are all sorts of reasons why so many big organizations can be slow to make innovative changes. Most of them relate to the simple fact that they *don't have to*. There is no pressing need, and the risk of trying something bold or striking out in a new direction may seem too high. These organizations are far less adept at realizing the risks of staying the course and of not making any changes. They need to become aware of the worst that can happen if they do more of the same. Taylor says, 'In a very real sense, the first job of leadership is to identify and overcome the costs of complacency. To persuade colleagues at every level that there are genuine risks for the failure to take risks – that the only thing they have to fear, is the fear of change itself'.[4]

As project leaders we have to do what we can to influence and remind the organizations we work for that it's OK to experiment and to fail – and that in fact it is necessary at times. How else can we find that ingenious new solution to our client's problem? Trial and error is one of the most effective problem-solving techniques we have and the only sustained way to innovation. Many managers and leaders, however, are expected to deliver projects in line with agreed budgets and timelines, and that makes them choose the safe option that guarantees quick wins and fast results. But instead of automatically discarding the high-risk options, out of fear that they will fail or be rejected, we have to encourage people to at least identify and debate them – and maybe trial them through a prototype, pilot or proof of concept. We have to look at all scenarios objectively and assess if the potential

FIGURE 3.3.5 The inhibitors of innovation

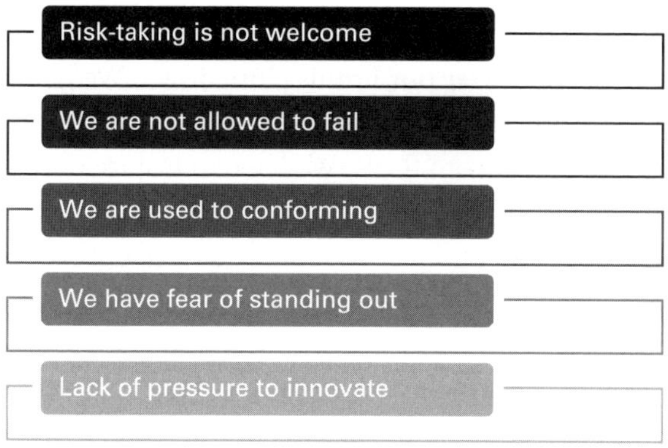

FIGURE 3.3.6 What is your risk IQ?

What	Do you allow yourself and your team to experiment?
is	Do you encourage risk-taking?
your	Are you prepared to be wrong?
risk	Do you remind others that it's OK to experiment and fail?
IQ?	How cautious are you?
	Do you consider how to best manage risk?

benefits *could* outweigh the risks. When we look at the worst-case scenario, and determine how the team would deal with it, we often find that it is much more manageable than we initially imagined. If we really want to, and are ready to stand out and take the lead, we can create a compelling business case that demonstrates the potential long-term benefits of taking a higher-risk approach and trialing a new concept.

What would you say that your own risk IQ is? Do you allow yourself and your team to experiment and make mistakes for the sake of being creative, or do you feel more comfortable sticking to the parameters that have been given to you by other managers? Are you a cautious type of person, or are you prepared to be wrong in order to come up with something original? What would be the best way for you to manage an innovative and risky element of your project? Could you, for instance, plan for a separate feasibility project with clearly defined measurement criteria?

The key is to *fail productively*, as Tim Harford put it. We have to learn from our failures and accept that mistakes can be good as long as they genuinely help us advance and get closer to our end goal. The question is how quickly we learn from them, adjust and adapt. When something fails, we often get angry at ourselves and instead of using the failure productively and refining the course, we let our brains close down. We go into meltdown and make even more mistakes and worse decisions. The trick is to make our failures smart by learning from them. We have to inspire our teams to move forward in spite of uncertainty and create an advantage out of what could have been a demotivating and threatening failure. To prevent a meltdown, identify the ways in which the failure *benefited* you and the team. What did you gain in terms of new knowledge, insight, experiences and improvements? Then look at what you can do to generate a better outcome next time. Making the same mistake over again is dumb and has to be avoided.

Reduce risk during early stages of the project – by Benoit Jolin

Despite a good appreciation of the customer's problems, many of the initial product assumptions will be wrong. This is not a bad thing as long as care is taken to validate these assumptions early on – something that requires that management allows and encourages rapid failure. An effective way to do this is to clearly define key metrics that would indicate if an assumption is valid and to test each assumption before any material investment of resources and cost is made. Data should inform product investment decisions and help refine the solution. At times, it will be necessary to course-correct or halt an investment, but too often, pleasing key stakeholders supersedes rational decision-making. In such situations project leaders must find their courage and do the right thing. Data and the insights from test-and-learn approaches (such as fast-failure models, high-fidelity demos or prototypes) are powerful allies that will drive the right decisions. Continuous testing is a great way to eliminate HiPPO (highest-paid-person opinion) decision-making, reduce risk and make the product stronger over time.

– Benoit Jolin, Head of Global Supplier Experience, Expedia Inc

Project leaders continuously learn and improve – by Dave Sawyer

Project leaders are not just thinking about the old 'time, cost, quality' thing, but also about how to continuously improve and how to help their teams better. I'm constantly reading, seeking new information to fill in the gaps, and I really care about doing things in the best way possible. It's about continuously listening, reading and learning in general. I've met a few project managers who seem to think that just doing things is enough, but 'competence' = 'learning' x 'experience'. You have to always be learning! Keep up to date with the best practice, and anything else you can get your hands on. Try out ideas on a small 'pilot' scale and see if it works. If not, why wasn't it successful? Ask yourself and others if it was the right thing to do,

or if you could have done things better. Keep thinking, reviewing and asking questions. And accept that you're going to get criticized; that's inevitable.

Whenever we are doing new things, I tell my team that we are breaking new ground and that we probably are not going to get things right the first time. We plan, and then we change the plan as we go along; circumstances change and we learn new things about how we work and about the project environment. I expect us to make mistakes, and we need that room to explore and experiment. As time goes on, we tighten things up and by the end of the project we are running like a well-oiled machine – but you have to go through that initial learning curve to get to the end point.

— Dave Sawyer, Project Manager, UK Government

Innovation requires you to break the rules – by Colleen Garton

In reality, not everyone will become a leader. Being a leader takes humility, genuineness and the willingness to let go of control. Some people will never be comfortable letting go of control. When you stop controlling outcomes, it means that others can fail and their failures will reflect on you. Leadership is not just about basking in the glory of success; it is also about justifying actions that lead to setbacks or failures. If you believe in what your team is doing, you will be able to justify actions and results successfully. If you have to know the exact outcome of every single thing, you may become a fairly good manager (to people who need a lot of direction) but you will not be a leader. Depending on what industry you are in, management skills may be more important than leadership skills. In some industries, having strict rules and demanding that they are followed at all times is a necessity. A software innovator would not thrive in such a rules-driven environment. Innovation requires breaking all the rules and approaching design from different and sometimes bizarre perspectives.

— Colleen Garton, author of *Fundamentals of Technology Project Management* and *Managing Without Walls*

Overcoming roadblocks

Exercise: Overcoming roadblocks that prevent you from optimizing and innovating

Let's examine some of the roadblocks that might be preventing you from stepping up and applying yourself as a thought leader and innovator. Some scenarios could be:

- You don't feel that you have sufficient knowledge about the status quo (business acumen, project management processes, technology, your team members, etc.) in order to challenge it.

- Your project is going through a tough patch at the moment with lots of issues and you simply don't have the capacity to extract yourself from the detail and think about innovation.

- You know it is important to take a big-picture view of the project, but you somehow never get around to doing it.

- Your team is inexperienced and needs a lot of direction. You don't feel the members are mature enough to assist with value-added idea generation.

- You have lots of innovative ideas and an appetite for making changes, but the organization you work for is conservative and risk-averse and you have difficulties securing buy-in to bring about the quantum leaps you dream of.

Consider the particular reasons that are preventing you from continuously improving and innovating. Look at the particular roadblocks that are in your way. Be honest, and decide what you want to do about it. How much of it stems from lack of ability or knowledge and how much is related to simply not perceiving it as a high enough priority? What can you do about it, and more important, what *will* you do about it?

Remember that the status quo is not an option. Challenging it may not be the easiest thing to do, but it is the only way to create progress. The world is moving very fast, and your project needs to move with it. New methods, tools and technology become available every day. It is your job – in collaboration with your team – to assess how to best make use of them.

One of the key mindset shifts you can make is to *not* let the roadblocks you just identified put you off. There will always be reasons not to do something, but the trick is to ask *'how can we?'* How can we better serve our clients? How can we move forward and prove that there is value in this great idea? How can we become better at innovating and accepting the risks associated with it? How can we become more creative and learn from other industries? When we start to look at *how* we can do something, our minds open up and become more resourceful.

But it takes more than a mindset shift to start challenging the status quo. You and your team also need a good level of business acumen and an understanding of what the current state of play is. In order to improve something, we first have to see things the way they are. We need to observe, listen and learn about the current state of affairs – including our clients' needs and desires. Which business processes does the client use on a daily basis and what are its products and services? Which technology and company procedures are available and in use by the project team? These aspects represent the status quo. The status quo is concerned with how we normally go about things and how we usually execute projects. It is also how the client normally does business. When we keep our mind open and our ear to the ground, we understand the playing field and start to appreciate where the problems and opportunities for improvements might be.

Once we clearly see things the way they are, we need to form an equally clear picture of how we would like to change them. That means seeing things *better* than they are. We must have the ability to be inspired and imagine what the future would look like if we made use of more simplified processes, new technology, innovative ideas, a more inspired team, and more affordable tools and materials, had better relationships with our customers, and were able to improve the way our clients do business. What would the future look like if you were able to meet the needs your clients are not even aware they have? Look at the end game, that of adding value in a faster, simpler and more affordable way.

Diversity of thought powers innovation

During the process of continuously improving and innovating, project leaders make use of their excellent interpersonal skills to engage people and make them see what is in it for them. Through their insightful questions they get people to step into the challenge and endorse a new way of working – or even thinking. They challenge, question and listen, and they draw on the team as much as possible. They are keen to learn from others and are under no illusion that they personally have all the answers. They know that creative ideas that add value often originate from different ways of seeing things and, therefore, act as a facilitator and enabler more so than an oracle who holds all the answers.

In her book, *Multipliers,* Liz Wiseman distinguishes between a *Multiplier* and a *Diminisher*. She defines *Multipliers* as leaders who use their intelligence to amplify the smarts and capabilities of the people around them. Her description is relevant to project leadership. She writes,

> Multipliers liberate people to think, to speak, and to act with reason. They create an environment where the best ideas surface and where people do their best work. . . The question 'why' is at the core of their thinking. They ponder possibilities. They want to learn from people around them. At the heart of any challenge is intellectual curiosity. *I wonder if we could do the impossible?*. . . How do multipliers get people to step into a challenge? They shift the burden of the thinking to others. Initially, when they establish a concrete challenge, the burden of the thinking sits with them as the leader. But by asking the hard questions and inviting others to fill in the blanks, they are shifting the burden of thinking onto their people. It is in this shift that the Multiplier creates intelligence and energy around him or herself.[6]

The opposite of a *Multiplier* is a *Diminisher* and a good reminder of the attitudes and behaviours that we are trying to steer clear of. Wiseman writes:

> Diminishers tell and test. Like the stereotypical Know-It-All, they tell people what they know, tell people how to do their jobs, and test other people's knowledge to see if they are doing it right. Diminishers consider themselves thought leaders and readily share their knowledge; however, they rarely share it in a way that invites contribution. They tend to sell their ideas rather than

FIGURE 3.3.7 Project leaders are multipliers, not diminishers

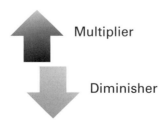

Multiplier

Diminisher

learning what others know. . . They ask questions to make a point rather than to access greater insight or to generate collective learning. . . Rather than shifting responsibility to other people, Diminishers stay in charge and tell others – in detail – how to do their jobs. . . They are debaters, not Debate Makers.

Innovation – by Julia Strain

As a project leader your role is not necessarily to come up with new ways of doing things but to give people the means and the environment in which they can do it. It's an enabling function. If someone from your team has a great idea, get the person to assess how it links to cost savings, impacts delivery and improves what you are doing. It's not enough to just come up with a random idea; the individual must be able to apply it to the project's drivers in a practical way.

– Julia Strain, CIO, Standard Bank

One of the best ways to innovate is to bring people together with different backgrounds and to stimulate their curiosity. Diversity of thought powers innovation, so mix people up and invite outsiders into the team – maybe even from different industries – who have a different background and who aren't close to the subject matter. They bring a new perspective and often ask questions that expose a completely different set of options due to their alternative background.

You can also fuel new ideas by rotating people so that they get exposed to new ways of doing things. We are really able to improve, question and challenge the current state only when we have seen different ways of working. As Pablo Picasso said, 'Good artists copy; great artists steal!' So encourage job rotation and mobility and get people to talk across projects. Give them the space and opportunity to share their know-how and to learn *in* the experience rather than *from* it. As Liz Pearce, CEO of LiquidPlanner, puts it, 'Enabling transparency across the project team and understanding what other teams are working on can mean the elimination of costly redundancies, the identification and exploitation of powerful new ideas and the facilitation of powerful cross-team collaboration'.[5]

Learning from different teams, industries and projects also applies to your role as a project manager. The more projects, environments and clients you have been exposed to, the more knowledge you will have about what

FIGURE 3.3.8 Strategies that help stimulate innovation

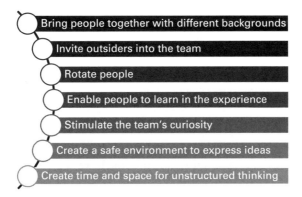

Bring people together with different backgrounds

Invite outsiders into the team

Rotate people

Enable people to learn in the experience

Stimulate the team's curiosity

Create a safe environment to express ideas

Create time and space for unstructured thinking

is likely to work and what is not. If you have worked on large projects that take years to complete, you will have seen fewer cycles that you can learn from. To make up for this you can facilitate knowledge sharing across teams, physically spend time on other people's projects, and involve external facilitators and mentors to help you think in new and unfamiliar ways. The use of observers from the outside can also help you understand the market-place better and stay connected to external stakeholders and user groups.

Many managers are very controlling of their teams and believe it is a waste of time to explore areas slightly off the beaten track. But leaders see this differently. They understand the value of creativity, learning and innova-tion and have seen the motivational effects it can have on a team in addition to the ideas it generates. They deliberately stimulate the team's curiosity and encourage it to find inspiration from other groups, industries and depart-ments. Their goal is to create a safe environment for team members to express their ideas and to remove the factors that may otherwise cause peo-ple to doubt and hold back. As Rebel Brown writes in *The Influential Leader*,

> Our conscious mind can only tap into its innovative capabilities when our unconscious mind tells it that there is no threat in our environment. As influential leaders we must quiet the unconscious survival mind to empower innovative results. That means removing stresses, pressures and negative potentials that threaten our teams. If we want true innovation, we need to be innovative leaders who create a positive environment for our team. We need to deliver what they need to be productive and creative.[7]

In order to aid idea generation, it's important to create the space and time for unstructured thinking and to give people the autonomy to think freely. According to Daniel Pink, there are many examples of innovative products and solutions to existing problems that have come about by telling engineers that for the next 24 hours they can work on anything they want and wherever they want. During those 24 hours there are no schedules and no mandatory meetings. The engineers get complete autonomy. The only rule is that they show their result at the end of the 24 hours. The outcome is astounding. Productivity, engagement and satisfaction go up and a raft of new ideas and solutions are generated. To Daniel Pink the results aren't that surprising, as several studies show that autonomy, mastery and purpose are the building blocks of a new way of doing things.[8] We will look at the self-determination model in more detail in the next key, *Empower the team*.

The power of questions

One of the best ways to take a big-picture view of the project and identify new and better ways of operating is to take a step back on a regular basis and ask questions – of yourself and others. When you ask questions that challenge conventional thinking, you open up and invite discovery. You become a leader who explores better ways of doing things, who acknowledges that you don't personally have all the answers and who encourages others to share their views and ideas. Taking a helicopter view of the project and asking questions can help you ascertain how the team can work smarter, understand why people act the way they do, learn how to better use people's strengths, and determine what the big opportunities and risks are. Taking a big-picture view allows you to notice connections and opportunities you haven't noticed before.

Asking questions as a matter of course is an essential component of leadership and of making progress. Voltaire said that we should 'judge a man by his questions rather than by his answers', and Albert Einstein was obsessed with questions, or more precisely, with getting to the *right* question. Another smart mind, Peter Drucker, stated, 'The more serious mistakes are not being made as a result of wrong answers. The truly dangerous thing is asking the wrong question'. That's an interesting observation. How often, for instance, have you seen organizations and projects waste time and money in the pursuit of ideas based on having asked the wrong question? When so many projects end in failure, is it fair to conclude that we have to some extent been asking the wrong questions?

Tim Brown (chief executive and president of IDEO) also has a view on the importance of asking questions. He says, 'It's very easy in business to get sucked into being reactive to the problems and questions that are right in front of you. It doesn't matter how creative you are as a leader, it doesn't matter how good the answers you come up with. If you're focusing on the wrong questions, you're not really providing the leadership you should'.[9]

The first step in asking better questions is to pause and set time aside to observe and query what you are currently doing. Unfortunately we don't often build time for contemplation or exploration into our day. We are expected to *think* in our spare time and to do actual work during working hours. We feel that we should be focusing on the detail and telling people how to do things, but oftentimes the best we can do is to get out of the way. So claw back some of that thinking time and start to observe and question what is going on.

Get into your helicopter and fly as high up as you need to. Get away from your desk, as that is where you think in familiar patterns and are likely to have a mindset of executing activities, following procedures and giving direction. It is much better to go somewhere where your thoughts can flow freely, for instance in an open space, a nice meeting room or a walk around the building. When you take a helicopter view, you get a much better sense of what is important, where the roadblocks are and what you can do to overcome them. You will discover opportunities, links and routes that you didn't know existed, and you will find that the right questions come to you. Your job is to observe and ask, and then to listen to what comes back.

In the beginning these trips may seem out of place, and you may feel that you are not doing any real work or accomplishing anything specific. But as you get better at stepping back from the detail, you will start to enjoy the ride and begin to appreciate its value. How can you start to practise that right now? Could you begin by scheduling helicopter time with yourself once a week for just 20 or 30 minutes? What time of week would work best for you? When are you normally less busy and when will it be easier for you to step away from your desk?

When you *do* step away from your desk, bring a set of insightful questions to kick off the process. Initially you will ask these questions of yourself, but later you will want to also ask them of your team. Don't be in a rush to find the answers and don't force anything. Just observe, ask and listen. Remember that it's not for you alone to come up with the answers.

- What are we trying to achieve?
- What do our customers and executives keep complaining about? What can we do about it?
- Which bad decisions have we made that need to be reverted?

- What is our feeling about the project? What does our gut tell us?
- Have we scrutinized the rationale for the project and any alternative solutions?
- What are we not seeing that is new or different?
- What have we not yet invested in that could make a big difference to our performance?
- How can we stay updated with changes in the market and in our industry?
- What is working really well for other teams and industries that we can replicate?
- How do we better access the team's knowledge and creativity?
- How do we improve our ability to learn from experience?
- How can we improve our working relationship and our ability to listen to our customers?
- What can get in our way of achieving the end-project goal?
- How can we focus more on product quality and minimize mistakes?
- What would we do differently if we bet our own money on this?
- What if we could make things simpler and more affordable?
- What if we could fulfil some of our customers' needs that they are not yet aware of?
- What if we were the best team in this organization or in our industry?

At the end of your helicopter time, choose three of your best insights, ideas or questions and canvass them with the members of your team. Putting these exploratory questions to them will stimulate their thinking and allow you to access their genius. You demonstrate that you value their input and that you trust their judgment. Having to find their own answers and solutions will have an empowering and motivating effect and over time create a critical mass of new thinkers.

Liz Wiseman writes that good leaders 'ask the really hard questions that challenge people not only to think but to rethink. They ask questions so immense that people can't answer them based on their current knowledge or where they currently stand'. She further writes 'because the opportunity has been planted but not fully grown, others are taken through a process of discovery. This process of exploration and discovery sparks intellectual curiosity and begins to generate energy for the challenge. And because the answers are clearly not formed, people know "there is still something for me to do" and they can step in to be involved'.[10]

On the topic of great questions, it is not enough to ask open questions that begin with who, what, when, where and how, as they aren't necessarily the best at opening our minds to move beyond the status quo and into innovation and creative thinking. We also need to ask 'what if' questions, as they tend to free our minds to focus on possibilities. Examples could be, 'What if we could solve the problem better than anyone else? What if we put ourselves in the user's shoes? What if we could not fail?'

As you begin to ask these great questions, encourage your team to see the project and its products from the customer's point view. At first, you will have to show the way and share some of your own thoughts. But later, when the team becomes more familiar with generating and implementing ideas, you can start to take a step back and give space for others to lead and take responsibility.

Be careful not to come across as negative or constrained as you evaluate new ideas. When we challenge others to think critically, it's easy to slip into a mode where we are too analytical and make people feel that their ideas aren't good enough. There is a fine line between someone perceiving an inquiry as helpful or experiencing it as criticism. What's important is that you create a safe and inspiring environment and that people feel excited and motivated by the opportunity to make a difference. Your role is not to overrule anyone, but to listen, inspire and encourage people to share and think their best thoughts. You can practise holding back by deliberately limiting

FIGURE 3.3.9 Guidelines on how to empower the team with questions

your contribution in meetings to only five comments, for instance. That will help you to filter your thoughts for only the most essential and to look for the right moment to insert your ideas.

Don't give up if people are initially hesitating and not contributing. Be persistent in your pursuit of answers and reward those who embrace a new and different way of thinking. Avoid a situation where you tell people, 'You found the problem; now it's your job to fix it', as that's a certain way to get people to stop finding problems and asking questions. Most people aren't seeking to add to their workload, and the question they've identified may be too big for them to answer on their own. A better approach is to ask problem-finders how much they want to be involved in working on that issue or idea – with the understanding that they will be given time and support as needed, and that, even if a resolution is never found, they have earned credit just by asking it.

How to embed the new behaviour

In this key we discussed the importance of challenging the status quo and encouraging your team to think unconventionally. You can do that by introducing diverse points of view, asking (what-if) questions, creating the space for unstructured thinking and making it safe for people to express their ideas. We also looked at the inhibitors of innovation and how many people have been brought up in a culture of compliance where risk-taking isn't welcome. They hold themselves back due to a fear of failure.

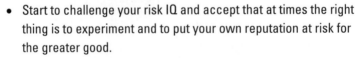

How to embed the learning

- Start to challenge your risk IQ and accept that at times the right thing is to experiment and to put your own reputation at risk for the greater good.

- Balance out negative aspects with the positives. Consider the implications of not taking risks and be conscious of how dangerous it is not to innovate.

- Invite guests from other projects and industries to spend time with your team so that you can get inspired and learn from them.

- Set aside 20–45 minutes each week to take a helicopter view with the sole purpose of observing the project from afar. Look at what is working and what is not, and ask 'What am I/we not seeing that is new or different? What am I/we not seeing that could add tremendous value to the client?'

- Shift the burden of thinking onto others. Set up creative review sessions where you train yourself to ask questions and invite the members of your team to fill in the blanks. Ask 'How can we?' and 'What if?'

- Create the space and time for unstructured thinking and make it safe for people to express their opinions and suggest ideas.

- Check out the inspiring TED talks with Seth Godin and Sir Ken Robinson. You can find the link at www.powerofprojectleadership.com.

Checklist: Do you master the learning?

- You regularly step back from the detail and take a big-picture view of the project.

- You have an eye for spotting and exploiting opportunities and you are not afraid of putting a case forward to senior decision-makers in order to get a new meaningful method or idea approved.

- You see yourself as a catalyst for change and a debate-maker rather than an oracle who holds all the answers.

- You encourage job rotation, mobility and knowledge sharing with other groups, industries and departments.

- Through your inquisitive and probing questions, you have created a mass of critical thinkers on your team. New ideas regularly surface and there is a culture of continuous learning, improving and innovating.

Your insights and intentions

Write down at least three insights you have gained from this section along with three actions you will take to embed this key into your daily work.

_____

_____

_____

Notes

1 Godin, S (2013) Stop Stealing Dreams, TEDxYouth@BFS [Online] http://www .youtube.com/watch?v=sXpbONjV1Jc

2 Robinson, K (2006) How schools kill creativity, *TED* [Online] http://www.ted .com/talks/ken_robinson_says_schools_kill_creativity

3 Godin, S (2012) Stop Stealing Dreams (What is school for?) [Online] http:// www.sethgodin.com/sg/docs/stopstealingdreamsscreen.pdf

4 Taylor, B (2013) Playing It Safe Is Riskier Than You Think, *Harvard Business Review* [Online] http://blogs.hbr.org/2013/09/playing-it-safe-is-riskier-than-you-think/?utm_source=Socialflow&utm_medium=Tweet&utm_campaign=Socialflow

5 Interview with Liz Pearce, CEO of LiquidPlanner, February 2014

6 Wiseman, L (2010) *Multipliers: How the Best Leaders Make Everyone Smarter*, Harper Business

7 Brown, R (2013) *The Influential Leader: Using The Technology of Our Minds to Create Excellence in Yourself and Your Teams*

8 Pink, D (2009) The puzzle of motivation, *TED* [Online] http://www.youtube .com/watch?v=rrkrvAUbU9Y&list=TLubtQgNESVgeg4S-PDiwGT6RwEf-r2BBC

9 Wiseman, L (2010) *Multipliers: How the Best Leaders Make Everyone Smarter*, Harper Business

10 Wiseman, L (2010) *Multipliers: How the Best Leaders Make Everyone Smarter*, Harper Business

Key #4
Empower the team

FIGURE 3.4.1

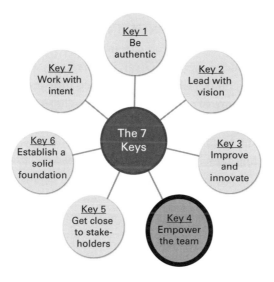

IN THIS KEY YOU WILL LEARN

- What the characteristics are of high-performing teams and what you can do to create a fully engaged and motivated team

- What the three key communication dynamics are that affect team performance

- Why you need a high degree of supporting yin as well as challenging yang to effectively lead others

- How you can manage poor performers and adapt your leadership style to cater for each individual player

- The differences between hygiene factors and true motivators and why we need more than money to become truly fulfilled at work

Great leaders create space for others to grow and excel

Project leaders know better than anyone that they alone don't hold all the answers or possess all the knowledge to deliver a project. Environments are too complex for one person to know it all, and project leaders certainly don't pretend that they do. Leadership is not about finding a hero who can make all the decisions and tell people what to do. It's about facilitating collaboration at all levels, instilling the right culture and enabling the team to do what it does best.

Peter Drucker said, 'The first secret of effectiveness is to understand the people you work with so that you can make use of their strengths'. And Global Project Leaders[1] writes: 'Great leaders facilitate growth in their teams, which means on occasion you have to do little more than encourage individuals to play more of a leading role in the right situation'. Project leaders understand that in order to serve their client they have to do everything they can to help the team collaborate, excel and win.

Instead of feeling they have to know all the answers, project leaders are excellent at identifying people who *do* know the details and at enabling them to do their best work. They inspire, mentor and provide the team with a clear focus and otherwise get out of the way. They drum up support and energy for the project's goals, but are far from autocratic generals who direct the troops and singlehandedly make decisions. People don't want to be tightly managed or told what to do. They want to feel appreciated, have the autonomy to decide *how* to do their work and be led by someone they respect. This is even truer of younger generations, who are used to a collaborative approach and who want to understand why something has to be done. As a result, project leaders *lead by objectives* and *outcomes*, meaning that they agree what needs to be done rather than defining *how* to do it. They empower the team to find the 'how' – something that takes courage, as the team may have its own unconventional ways of working.

Project leaders are mindful of not micromanaging people unless it is absolutely necessary. This doesn't mean that they leave the team to its own devices. On the contrary; they consistently observe and monitor and offer guidance and support where needed, but they don't *do* the team members' work for them. They don't jump in and take over when something goes wrong – just like in football where the coach also doesn't run onto the pitch and start kicking the ball, as it simply isn't the person's role. They stick with what they do best – supporting and challenging from the sideline, asking, listening and

FIGURE 3.4.2   Strategies to empower the team

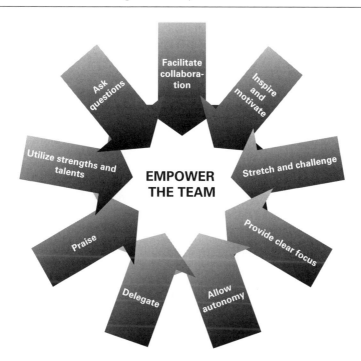

removing obstacles. They assume the role of an enabler, guide and coach who makes it possible for the team to produce its best work. Initially project leaders may take more of a hands-on role, but as the team matures they gradually step back and allow the team to think and work independently. Not only is this more rewarding and empowering, it also frees up the project leader to attend to the bigger picture and to the road that lies ahead.

Project leaders spend a lot of time and energy creating a high-performing team where all members thrive and deliver their best work. They have a can-do attitude and find a way to inspire, grow and motivate any team irrespective of location and circumstance. They are unlikely to let cultural or geographic barriers stand in their way and will only rarely give up on a group that is inexperienced or disillusioned. They know that with the right approach, and by deeply understanding and connecting with each individual, they are able to dramatically increase its performance. They do this by investing in the team and ensuring that each person feels appreciated, engaged and stretched. When all team members get to use their unique talents and contribute to a compelling vision – in a way that gives them meaning and purpose – they feel more inspired and engaged. In turn they generate a higher performance, which again adds to their professional development and overall job satisfaction.

How do project leaders find out what motivates and drives each person? They observe, ask and listen. They might, for instance, ask: *What do you like the most and the least about your role? What would you like to have happen for yourself on this project? How can I fuel your energy? In which situations do you feel the most inspired and motivated?*

But project leadership is not just about engaging people. It's about engaging people at the *right level*. It's the quality and depth of the interaction that matters and whether we can relate to people emotionally and understand their values and beliefs. One of the most powerful exercises you can do to better relate to people and build a high-performing team is to imagine that all your team members were volunteers. Try it now. Imagine that everyone turned up to work not because they got a salary for it, but because they got to contribute in a way that they found deeply fulfilling and meaningful. What would that look like? What would you need to do in order to create such a team of 'volunteers'? You might find the question unusual in a work context, but outside of work people frequently volunteer their time. Just consider the Olympics, an event where thousands of people volunteer their time for weeks at a time – not because they get a salary for it, but because they find fulfillment in other ways. When you are able to answer the question of what could make people turn up to work without getting a salary for it, you are well on your way to becoming a leader of people rather than a manager of tasks and processes.

FIGURE 3.4.3 Understanding why people would volunteer gives you great insight into their true motivators

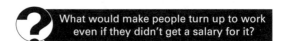

What would make people turn up to work
even if they didn't get a salary for it?

Co-creating is the most engaging way of relating
to others – by Penny Pullan

Leading a team is way more than telling. Telling someone what to do is the least engaging way to relate to others, closely followed by selling. Much more engaging are consulting and (best) co-creating.

– Penny Pullan, co-author and editor of several
project management books

Support others to be the best they can be – by Colleen Garton

Unfortunately, most project management training includes very little people skills development. You can't replace soft skills with spreadsheets, but many project managers try to do so because they are not sure how else to manage problems. This is also the root cause of micromanagement and people not being given the time to experiment and develop new skills. If you always assign tasks to the people who already know how to do them, how will your less experienced team members ever gain the experience they need to excel? People management means trusting people to do things their way, even if it takes longer than if you did it yourself. A leader's job isn't to be better than everyone else; it is to support others to be the best they can be.

To learn how to be a good leader you have to learn how to be a people person. You can't learn it from developing a spreadsheet or reading a book. You have to believe in people. You have to be brave and let go of control so that you can truly become a people-centric manager/leader and those you are leading can develop their full potential in their own way. You have to start asking questions and really listening to the answers. Not just hearing what you want to hear. Not dismissing the things you don't think are realistic or acceptable. Not arguing or contradicting what others tell you. Listening and understanding. Not everyone is the same as you, and your way may not be the best way. The way to lead is to learn every day from those you are leading. Accept that their way is different but not necessarily inferior to yours. Be a role model. Act the way you want your team to act. Treat others with respect – all the time, and don't bad-mouth other departments, clients or management. Imagine yourself in their shoes before you judge them. Being able to experience the world the same way as others is what enables you to understand and connect with them. If you can't do this, how can you lead them? Be positive and empower people so they can follow you in their own way. Let them use their own road maps. Why should they have to follow yours? As long as they end up in the right place at the right time, it doesn't matter if they took a different route.

– Colleen Garton, author of Fundamentals of Technology Project Management and Managing Without Walls

Project leadership is a team effort – by Michael Fleron

I have seen many project managers carry out planning, analysis and risk identification on their own and then subsequently communicate the result to the team by mail – and if they ask for feedback they never use it. That's a big mistake. Project leadership is a team effort, not the result of a single person's achievement. I experienced this firsthand one morning when I was told by the Board that the project suddenly had to shave 20 per cent of its cost. I didn't know how that would be possible, so instead of making the decision myself, I got the team together and presented them with this burning question. Three days later we had found the savings – collaboratively. It was a great moment for us, which really added to the team spirit. The lesson is that we have to let the team do the work and be engaged in it. Otherwise its engagement and motivation vanishes and the project slowly dies one day at a time.

– Michael Fleron, adviser and PRINCE2 Trainer

The importance of energy and engagement to team performance

Before we look at how project leaders go about creating a high-performing team, let's briefly examine the characteristics of such a team. In a study led by Sandy Pentland, a group of researchers at MIT's Human Dynamics Laboratory set out to investigate why some teams consistently deliver a high performance while other, seemingly identical teams struggle. In their study of 2,500 individual team members, from a broad variety of projects and industries, they found that the most important predictor of a team's success was its communication patterns. Those patterns were as significant as all other factors (intelligence, personality and talent) combined.[2]

According to their research, individual reasoning and talent contribute far less to a team's success than one might expect. They concluded that the best way to build a great team is not to select individuals for their intelligence or accomplishments but to learn how they communicate and to shape and guide the team so that it follows successful communication patterns. According to Pentland's study, the successful teams shared the following defining characteristics:

- Everyone on the team talked and listened in roughly equal measure, keeping contributions short and sweet.
- Members faced one another, and their conversations and gestures were energetic.
- Members connected directly with one another – not just with the team lead.
- Members carried on back-channel or side conversations within the team.
- Members periodically went exploring outside the team, and brought information back.

In addition to these characteristics, Pentland and his team identified three key communication dynamics that affect team performance: *energy, engagement* and *exploration*.

1 The first dynamic, **energy,** is measured by the number and the nature of exchanges among team members. The most valuable form of communication is face-to-face. The next most valuable is phone or videoconference, but with a caveat: those technologies become less effective as more people participate in the call or conference. The least valuable forms of communication are e-mail and texting.

2 The second important dimension of communication, **engagement,** reflects the distribution of energy among team members. If all members of a team have relatively equal and reasonably as many exchanges with all other members, engagement is extremely strong. Teams that have clusters of members who engage in high-energy communication while other members do not participate don't perform as well.

FIGURE 3.4.4 The three communication dynamics that affect team performance

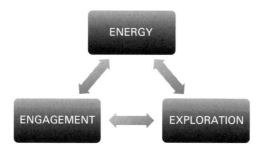

3 The third critical dimension, *exploration*, involves communication that members engage in outside their team. Exploration essentially is the energy between a team and the other teams it interacts with. Higher-performing teams seek more outside connections. Exploration is most important for creative teams responsible for innovation, as they need fresh perspectives.

The data showed that exploration and engagement don't easily coexist, as they require the energy of team members to be put to two different uses. Energy is a finite resource. The more energy people devote to their own team (engagement), the less they have available to use outside their team (exploration), and vice versa. But they must do both. Successful teams, especially creative ones, alternate between exploration for discovery and engagement for integration of the ideas gathered from outside sources. The study proved that the most effective work was done by teams that were high in energy and engagement, but it also showed that as soon as either energy or engagement dropped, so did the performance. For the best performance, team leaders need to keep energy and engagement in balance as they work to strengthen them.

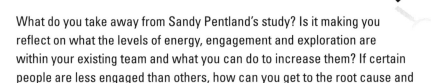

EXERCISE   Is your team fully engaged?

What do you take away from Sandy Pentland's study? Is it making you reflect on what the levels of energy, engagement and exploration are within your existing team and what you can do to increase them? If certain people are less engaged than others, how can you get to the root cause and address it? Consider the following:

- Are people trying to contribute and being ignored or cut off – either by you or other team members?

- Do they hold themselves back due to lack of skill or confidence?

- Do they communicate only with one or a few other team members, maybe because the group consists of cliques?

- Is their communication style unclear?

- Is the team leader too dominant, or are you doing most of the talking at meetings and not giving others enough chance to participate?

To get to the root cause, keep asking 'why': Why is someone holding back? Why are they being interrupted? Why are they not collaborating? Finally look at what you can do to help improve the situation and raise the energy and engagement levels.

Act like the best leaders do – by Dave Sawyer

As a project manager you are either helping or you are in the way. If you are getting in the way of the team's productivity, or they are raising issues that you are not dealing with, then you are chaff and not really contributing to the overall picture. I think of myself as the oil that keeps the machine going, and sometimes that means doing things that I don't want to do to make life easier for the team. I clear the politics and barriers, sort out ordering or delivery problems and generally try to make things work well. People tend to notice that kind of behaviour and react well to it. One of my pet hates is managers who treat their staff like slaves. Staff hate managers like that, and will go to the nth degree to make their life more difficult. Instead, be the best you can be, be clear about what your game is and communicate that. As Reginald Harling said, 'Get ahead; then give others a helping hand to catch up'.

— Dave Sawyer, Project Manager, UK Government

The yin and yang of project leadership™

Project leaders are excellent at connecting people and at engaging everybody in short, high-energy conversations. They tend to be democratic with their time, communicate with everyone equally and make sure that all team members get a chance to contribute. They listen at least as much as they talk, and are fully present with whoever they are in conversation with. Although project leaders aren't necessarily extroverted, they feel comfortable engaging with others in energized discussions. They enjoy building rapport and are genuinely interested in seeing others thrive. They listen with a view to understanding what each person's desires are, and they actively seek to uncover people's unique strengths and talents. By making use of these strengths, not only do they maximize each person's value to the project, they also create a deeply satisfying and rewarding position for the individual team member.

But project leadership is much more than utilizing people's strengths, listening and ensuring that everybody participates. It is also about holding people accountable and expecting that they do their best work. Project leaders provide their team with all the support they can, but in return they look for a great outcome. They ask challenging questions, set high standards and expect the best quality. They coach and spend time with people who need to learn, but at the same token do not hesitate to address poor performance. They need all members of the team to contribute to the common goal, as otherwise it can jeopardize success.

The ability to fully support and enable the team to grow *and* at the same time challenge and stretch it to deliver an outstanding outcome is an art that only the best leaders do well. Project leaders give themselves fully; they are 100 per cent invested in creating an outstanding and high-performing team. That is why they support and challenge in large measures. Dave G Jensen put it this way: 'Leaders need to understand that they should access their wonderful "empowering" style of serving others, and at the same time, they must also stretch to access their "commanding" style. Supervisors need to learn how to counsel underperformers, conduct excellent performance

FIGURE 3.4.5 Yin and Yang of Project Leadership™

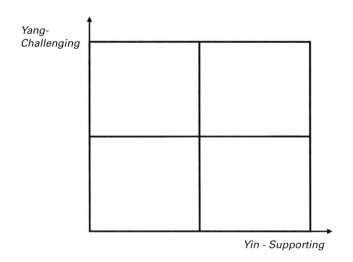

reviews and create individual development plans by applying both empowering and commanding leadership styles'.[3]

Many managers are not 100 per cent invested when it comes to leading a team. Their primary concern is getting work done and telling people what to do. They may be demanding and expecting tasks to be done on time, but they might not understand their own role in helping the team live up to these demands. They expect people to simply turn up and do a good job. But people are complex beings, and leading a team is not that simple. By looking up from our desk, tuning in and connecting with the individual, we can start to appreciate that complexity and how to best work with it.

How good are you at tuning in to people? Do you understand what each person's needs, desires and strengths are? Do you often ask people what they worry about, what is holding them back, what they like the most or the least about their job and how you can help them move forward? And do you consider team-building and motivation to be a core part of your role?

Let us turn to the diagram in Figure 3.4.5 and examine in more depth how project leaders go about supporting and challenging their team members. On the horizontal axis you find 'Yin' – the supportive element of leadership – and on the vertical axis you find 'Yang' – the challenging aspect of leadership.

Yin symbolizes feminine elements, such as listening, supporting, coaching and maintaining stability. These are characteristics that are hugely important when establishing a high-performing team, especially in the early days when people don't yet trust their own abilities or roles within the team. Project leaders use the supportive yin element to build the team's confidence and develop skills that are lacking. They encourage collaboration and provide a safe environment for team members to work together

FIGURE 3.4.6 Yin leaders support; yang leaders challenge

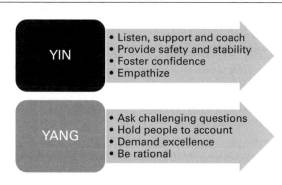

and come up with their own solutions. Supportive yin leaders have a deep respect for people and want to understand what drives and motivates each person. They often spend one-on-one time with people, assisting them to grow and develop. They are good at praising people for a job well done and will often ask what type of help the individual needs. Yin leadership is enabling and is concerned with making it possible for others to flourish, lead and contribute.

But what happens if leaders only use yin, if they don't possess the demanding yang element? Then they run the risk of being too soft and nice, supporting people without looking for a return. Project leaders aren't in the game to be nice. They are in the game to serve their client and to develop people in the process. But developing people cannot be at the expense of what the client needs. Adding value comes first; developing people comes second.

Yang symbolizes the masculine element, which is challenging, demanding and factual. This side of leadership sets a high standard and expects the team to deliver to it. Yang leaders have a strong sense of direction. They are action-oriented and results-driven. They ask challenging questions, hold people to account and may come across as forceful. They are assertive and push the team to deliver to the best of its ability and expect nothing but excellence. It is the yang element that pushes the team to continuously improve and innovate, and the yin element that steps back and enables the team to do so.

FIGURE 3.4.7   Project leaders use a lot of Yin and Yang

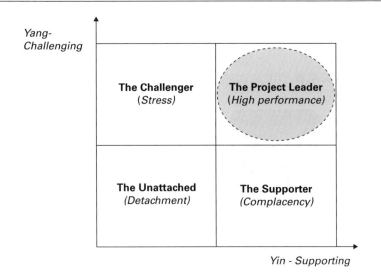

You could say that yin is a predominantly heart-based approach, whereas yang is a predominantly rational or head-based approach.

Leaders who have a lot of yang and very little yin tend to create stress around them. They demand a lot but don't give the team the security, confidence and space it needs in order to perform. They can be short-tempered and tend to take over if they aren't satisfied with the results. If they come across poor performers, they will be more inclined to move them out of the way than spend time building up their skills and confidence levels.

As illustrated in the figure 3.4.7, project leadership encompasses a high degree of yin as well as yang. People need both in order to perform and thrive. Project leaders support and enable others to lead on the one hand, whilst on the other they challenge and drive results. Combining these two opposite approaches in a holistic way is an art and a balancing act. When these two elements are combined, we find tough project leaders who care about people; they care about their client and they care about their team. They involve people in the decisions that affect them and they ask questions that empower and stimulate creative and innovative thinking. These project leaders are committed to excellence, and they know that they will get there only by focusing 100 per cent on the team's performance and well-being.

Poor managers neither support nor challenge. They are unsure and afraid of taking a stand. They fear they will come across as being either too soft or too forceful and end up being neither. The result is indecisiveness, inconsistency and a lack of clear direction. The team becomes frustrated, disengaged and underutilized. In the preceding matrix, we have labeled this 'Unattached' in the bottom left-hand quadrant.

One of the ways in which project leaders manage performance – including poor performance – is to create transparency around what they expect from each person. They set SMART (specific, measurable, achievable, realistic, time-bound) objectives in cooperation with each team member so that there is no doubt what an excellent piece of work looks like. They favour personal development plans, goal setting and one-on-one performance reviews because they are great tools to manage expectations and performance in a fair and transparent manner. One-on-one meetings can be used to focus on what has been achieved (yang) as much as what kind of support the team member needs (yin) in order to excel and meet the objectives.

Many yin-oriented leaders are uncomfortable addressing poor performance, because it requires them to inform someone that they are not doing their job well enough. They feel they are giving someone bad news. But we have to take a different viewpoint. We are not doing anyone any favours by hiding or ignoring someone's poor performance. Most people want to be given the chance to do well and improve. Not pointing out how they can do that shows lack of insight and concern for the individual. The way to manage performance elegantly is to agree with the individual up front on specific goals and measurement criteria, and then meet up regularly to discuss and update them. In that way performance becomes a mutually agreed target and not a subjective expectation.

When managers have a preference for either yin or yang, they can develop a lopsided or dysfunctional style. Either the yin or the yang element has grown to dominate and stunt the other. As a consequence the team feels either too pressured or too complacent, neither of which leads to high performance. Teams need the dynamic tension of both aspects, and leaders need to reconcile the two. Leadership is not about 'either/or' but 'and'. We must be enabling *and* forceful, forgiving *and* demanding, flexible *and* tough, supportive *and* challenging. Robert E Kaplan and Robert B Kaiser put it this way:

> According to the concept of yin and yang, the harmonious vibration between opposites constitutes the very stuff of existence. Versatile leadership arises from the continuous vibration between pairs of opposing impulses: to be forceful and at the same time enabling; to be visionary and at the same time to get things done. Being a versatile leader is more than having a wide repertoire of skills. It is having a wide repertoire of 'complementary' skills that can be adapted in infinite combinations, each specific to the task at hand. The idea is to modulate or adjust your approach, including cranking up to the maximum setting if necessary. In fact, it is completely consistent with the idea of versatility to take a strength to the extreme if that is what the situation calls for, just so long as that is not your default approach to every challenge. The more versatile the leader, the more effective he or she is.[4]

As Kaplan and Kaiser explain, we may in some cases have to make more use of one aspect than the other. The trick is to observe the team and understand the dynamics in order to best judge what is needed at any particular time. Leadership is about adapting our approach to any given situation. When a team is newly formed, for instance, or when it has experienced a setback of some kind, it is prudent to take a more supportive yin approach. When the team is established, however, and the goals are clear and people feel comfortable with their particular roles, it may be beneficial to become more yang oriented.

Are you aware of how much yin and yang you use to lead and manage people? Why not ask the members of your team how they perceive you? You may find that their perception of how challenging and supportive you are is very different from what you imagined.

EXERCISE   Creating a high-performing team

Take a moment to examine your own approach to leading a team, and where you would position yourself in the above yin and yang matrix. Consider the following;

1 How much attention do you give individuals within your team, understanding what they each need in order to contribute and perform better?

2 How good are you at balancing the two approaches of yin and yang? Do you tend to be more demanding than giving or vice versa?

3 How comfortable are you asking tough questions and challenging people to deliver their best performance?

4 What can you do to infuse as much yin as yang into your work and continuously keep the team's communication and engagement levels high?

People take much more ownership when setting their own deadline – by Morten Sorensen

I wasn't long out of university when I was asked to take my first project management role. It was after a couple of months in that role working with a highly skilled team of senior professionals that I realized how much more effective project leadership is when you let each team member take responsibility for his or her own assessments and commit to due dates and deliverables. People take much more pride and ownership when setting their own ambitious deadlines and then work harder and smarter to meet them.

– Morten Sorensen, Area VP, Global Client Services
at Verizon Enterprise Solutions

Don't be afraid to make the hard decisions – by Julia Strain

You can't bury yourself in the detail and in the tasks. If you don't understand the team dynamics, you'll end up with a task-driven project that can never be as successful as having a team work together. And don't be afraid to make that hard decision if someone is not pulling their weight. Do something about it, as otherwise it festers in the team. The way to do it is to test people and to give them one or two chances. You make it fairly open with the individual. Then you give them a choice.

– Julia Strain, CIO, Standard Bank

Treat people as strong and capable – by Paul Chapman

People will tend to meet your expectations, so treat everyone like the best person they can be. You will doubt in the abilities of some of your team at times, but if you show this, it will dispirit them and their performance will suffer. Instead, treat them as strong, capable people, and they will be inspired to be worthy of the respect and support you are giving them. This may seem counterintuitive, but it is how true leaders get the best from their people.

– Paul Chapman, Programme Manager, Financial Services

The Tuckman model

Bruce Tuckman's *Forming, Storming, Norming and Performing* model of the different development stages a team goes through is a further illustration of how managers and leaders need to adapt their approach to suit the circumstances and the team's maturity. Tuckman's original model describes four stages of team development: Forming, Storming, Norming and Performing. In the *forming* stage, when the team is just coming together and roles and responsibilities are unclear, project leaders bring structure, set objectives, provide direction and lay down the ground rules. In this early stage, project leaders will likely be more directing than at any other point during the project.

Relatively soon after the team has formed, it moves into a *storming* phase, where positions, roles and objectives are challenged. Some members feel overwhelmed by how much there is to do, or they are uncomfortable with the approach or the objectives. During this stage project leaders make use of their listening, mediating and conflict-resolution skills. They make people feel safe, address their concerns and build relationships among people. The focus is on building trust and planning collaboratively so that the team can concentrate on the actual objectives instead of becoming distracted by emotional issues.

Gradually, as the structure of the team is established, and roles and responsibilities are accepted, the team progresses into the *norming* stage. Team members come to respect one another and start to bond. Decisions are made in agreement, and some start to show ownership and take responsibility. The project leader's role in this phase is to support and guide the team and to encourage collaboration. They are mindful of each person's talents and needs and gradually take a step back as individuals start to engage and take responsibility.

The last of Tuckman's original four main stages is the *performing* stage. Here the team is strategically aware and knows clearly why it is doing what it is doing. It works towards a common goal, has a high degree of autonomy and is able to stand on its own feet with little interference. In this phase project leaders delegate entire roles and work streams and observe the team from the sideline. They continue to inspire, support and challenge it to think in creative and innovative ways. Project leaders aim to get their team to the performing stage as soon as possible.

The four stages of team development are illustrated in figure 3.4.8. Can you see how you will need to use different amounts of supporting yin and challenging yang during each stage? As the team matures and becomes more self-managing, you are able to take a less active role and move into the background. But even so you still need to stay abreast of progress and help your team to continually improve. Your inspiration, support and insightful questions will always be needed, albeit at varying degrees.

In addition to adapting your style to the maturity of the team, you also need to adjust it to each individual within the team. As a team develops and becomes more independent and self-managing, so does an individual. You will find that some people on your team have relatively low levels of confidence and skill. In that situation you will have to spend more time with them, nurturing and supporting them, and building up their confidence and competence. That requires a lot of yin support.

As people gain experience and as their drive and motivation increases, you can start to demand more from them and increase your yang level.

FIGURE 3.4.8 Tuckman's four stages of team development

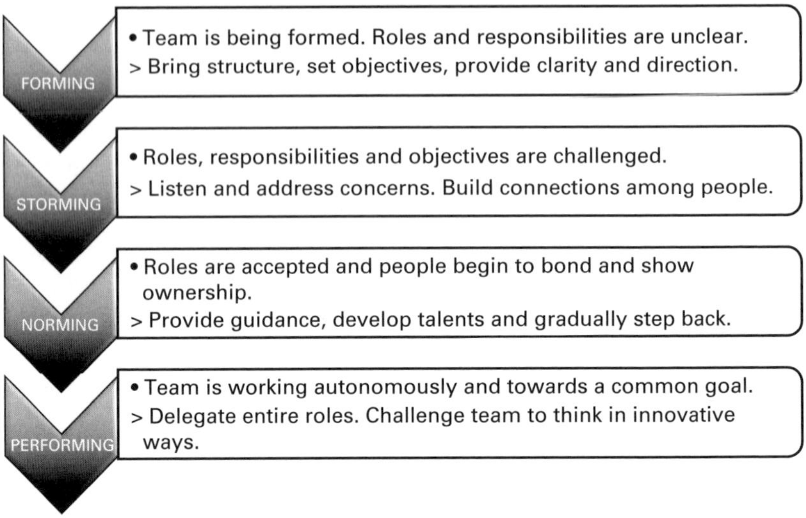

FORMING
- Team is being formed. Roles and responsibilities are unclear.
- > Bring structure, set objectives, provide clarity and direction.

STORMING
- Roles, responsibilities and objectives are challenged.
- > Listen and address concerns. Build connections among people.

NORMING
- Roles are accepted and people begin to bond and show ownership.
- > Provide guidance, develop talents and gradually step back.

PERFORMING
- Team is working autonomously and towards a common goal.
- > Delegate entire roles. Challenge team to think in innovative ways.

But be careful not to be too challenging and demanding with someone who lacks confidence and clarity. Just because someone is skilled doesn't mean that he or she is mentally ready to be challenged by you. Remember that the amount of support you provide must be tailored to the individual's situation. By keeping an open mind, enquiring and observing, you will be able to judge how much support, guidance and challenge each individual needs.

EXERCISE Adapting your leadership style

Take a moment to consider how good you are at adapting your leadership style to the different development stages of your team and to the needs of the individual.

1 How mindful are you with respect to the particular development stage your team is in?

2 To what extent do you provide direction and lead with vision during the forming stage?

3 Do you actively resolve conflict and make people feel secure during the storming phase?

4   Do you coach, enable and encourage collaboration during norming?

5   How good are you at giving the team space to perform and take responsibility as it matures and moves into the performing stage?

6   Do you tend to use a supportive yin approach when team members lack confidence?

7   Do you increase your level of challenging yang when you sense that people can handle it and are comfortable with their role?

The six human needs

You will remember that we examined the six human needs in Chapter 2 and also referred to them when we discussed how to overcome resistance to change in key number two. The six human needs are also relevant with regards to how you lead your team. Understanding each of your team members' needs, and how they change throughout the project's development stages, will help you to better fulfil them. Let's briefly revisit the six needs.

Certainty – The need for security, safety, stability and predictability. People need to understand what their role is, what the project is trying to achieve and how they can best help contribute to that.

Variety – The need for change, excitement and new stimuli. People like to feel alive and engaged in something new and exciting.

Significance – The need to feel important, unique and special. People want their work and life to have meaning, importance and significance. They want to know that their involvement matters and is being appreciated.

Connection – The need to feel connected and affiliated with like-minded people and to be part of a larger community. People have a desire to be accepted by the team and to be affiliated with it.

Growth – The need to learn, grow and expand personally and professionally. People want to be given the chance to learn about the project, its tools, techniques and context so that they feel they are evolving.

Contribution – The desire to make a difference and to serve and support something bigger than ourselves in a meaningful way. People like to know that their work is adding value to a worthy cause.

Each of your team members will have different degrees to which they value and prioritize these six human needs. Some will value variety over certainty and some will put a higher emphasis on connection and affiliation as opposed to significance – and vice versa. The question is, to what extent are you aware of people's individual needs and how are you trying to meet them?

It is worth noting that significance is often the largest reason for conflict on a team. If people don't feel heard or recognized, they might create a situation that makes them stand out and be noticed. They may draw undue attention to themselves in a manner that is disruptive and counterproductive. You can avoid that by listening to people, recognizing their contributions and publicly praising them. But your praise needs to be 100 per cent authentic and genuine in order for it to add meaning. Disruptive behaviour may also happen if people feel bored and don't feel that there is enough variety in their job. They may then create small dramas to get stimulated.

Your team members' needs show up differently during the different stages of the project. During the storming stage, for instance, conflict arises because people don't have certainty about the end goals and how they fit into the overall picture. They want to know what is in it for them. When you next kick off a new project, consider carefully which needs you can help satisfy during the initial discussions and kick-off meeting. This is an ideal opportunity to bring up topics that will help satisfy each of the six human needs. You can, for instance, talk about the project's overall vision, purpose, plans, roles and responsibilities and development opportunities. Also touch upon the social aspect; get the team members to introduce each other in a personal way and create a feeling of camaraderie.

We need more than money to be truly fulfilled

Many old-school managers are still of the belief that only a few common incentives motivate people, such as money and status. But research shows the opposite. People are not as heavily influenced by money as some think. One such study was carried out by Development Dimensions International and published in the *UK Times* newspaper. Development Dimensions International interviewed more than 1,000 staff from companies employing more than 500 workers and found many to be bored, lacking commitment and looking for a new job. Pay actually came fifth in the reasons people gave for leaving their jobs. The main reasons were lack of stimulus (variety) and limited opportunities for advancement (growth).[5]

In addition to empirical evidence, several theories point in the direction that people are motivated by different factors rather than just the desire for money or advancement. Frederick Herzberg was a clinical psychologist and the first to show that satisfaction and dissatisfaction at work are caused by two different factors: *hygiene factors* and *true motivators*. He believed that hygiene factors explain why we become de-motivated or dissatisfied by something, whereas the true motivators explain why we become motivated or satisfied by something.

According to Herzberg, hygiene factors – which cause dissatisfaction if they are not met – relate to aspects that define the job *context* such as salary, job security, work conditions, status and the relationship with supervisors and colleagues. The true motivators, on the other hand, relate to aspects that are directly involved in *doing* the job, such as professional development, responsibility, creativity, achievement, advancement, recognition and the work itself. These aspects represent a far deeper level of meaning and fulfillment. Herzberg's research proved that people are not truly motivated by the hygiene factors, but only by the true motivators. We strive to achieve the hygiene factors only because we are unhappy without them, but once satisfied the effect soon wears off. Many people are still under the impression that money is a primary motivator. But rather than motivate us, money has the power to de-motivate us if it is below par. There is a big difference. Although money is important, we need more than that to be truly fulfilled at work.

The Self-Determination Theory (SDT) developed by psychologists Edward Deci and Richard Ryan further supports this view. The Self-Determination Theory focuses primarily on internal sources of motivation, such as a need to gain knowledge or independence, which is known as intrinsic motivation.

According to SDT, people are intrinsically motivated, and become self-determined, when they experience a high degree of competence, connection and autonomy. *Competence* reflects the need to gain mastery of tasks and learn different skills. *Connection* (or relatedness) is about feeling a sense of belonging and attachment to other people, and *autonomy* is about being in control of our own behaviours and goals. When these needs are thwarted, people's performance and well-being suffer as a result.

According to Deci, giving people extrinsic rewards (such as money, prizes and acclaim) for already intrinsically motivated behaviour can undermine performance. The reason is that the behaviour starts to become controlled by an external reward, meaning that people begin to feel less ownership and control of their actions. Deci also suggests that offering unexpected positive encouragement and feedback on a person's performance can increase the level of intrinsic motivation. Why? Because feedback helps people to feel more competent, which is one of the key needs for personal growth.[6]

FIGURE 3.4.9 The three intrinsic motivators according to SDT

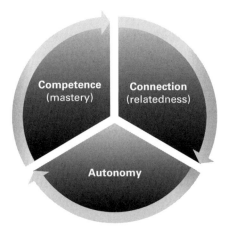

EXERCISE How good are you at catering to people's emotional needs?

Take a moment to consider how good you are at identifying and helping fulfil each of your team members' personal needs. Note that this is not about bending over backwards and giving in to everyone's desires and creating a group of prima donnas. It is about understanding people's deeply rooted emotional drivers and removing the noise and concerns that otherwise will prevent them from fully performing within the team.

1 How good are you at making people feel secure, at addressing their worries and removing uncertainty and distractions?

2 In which ways do you ensure that there is enough variety, challenge and excitement for people?

3   In which situations do you make people feel important and praise them for a job well done?

4   How often do you engage people in one-on-one conversation, and do you enquire about what they like the most and the least about their job?

5   In which ways do you help create a great team spirit that people can be part of?

6   What do you do to help people grow and acquire new skills, and to what extent do you make use of people's many talents and strengths?

7   In which ways do you support people in working autonomously?

8   How do you help people see that by working on the project they are making a difference and doing a meaningful job?

Overcoming obstacles

EXERCISE   Overcoming roadblocks to building a high-performing team

Let's examine some of the roadblocks that might be preventing you from truly connecting with people and empowering your team. Which of the following scenarios do you recognize?

- You work in a matrix organization where people on your project don't report to you. As you are not their line manager, you feel that you have limited scope to motivate them.

- You work with a team that is inexperienced and de-motivated. One person in particular is difficult to manage and is a poor performer. You have escalated this to the person's line manager.

- You would like to grow and develop your team, but you don't have a training budget.

- Your team is performing really well in isolation, but your organization has lots of red tape and rigid procedures that are negatively impacting team morale.

- You work with a global team that is based in many different locations. Communication can be difficult because of language and cultural barriers and because you don't see each other face-to-face. You believe that such a diverse team can never be high performing.
- You have taken a hands-off approach to the team and let the members make their own decisions. You are reluctant to get involved although the team isn't functioning optimally.

After having read this chapter on empowering the team, can you see how you can begin to overcome these roadblocks? Can you see that by prioritizing people more, spending one-on-one time with them and tuning in to their strengths, needs and desires, you will be able to find a way? And can you see that even if people don't report to you directly – or if they are poor performers – you can raise their level of contribution by actively engaging them, strengthening their competence and autonomy and setting measurable objectives? Even if people work in a different country and you can't see them in person, it is possible to create a strong bond through telephone conversations and video conferencing if you show a genuine interest for the individual and take the time to really listen. Global teams are here to stay, and the onus is on you to make them work.

Working with remote teams – by Paul Chapman

If you work with a remote team, try to visit the members in person. This is not always easy, but nothing beats face-to-face interaction. Also identify a local leader whom you can rely on to help you with issues, and build a strong relationship with the person. Occasionally I like to run a meeting with a remote team that is in a significantly different time zone at a time that is convenient for the rest of the team and inconvenient for me. (Note that I make sure very carefully to inconvenience only myself and not other members of my team.) For example, if working with a team in Singapore, I might occasionally hold a 6 am meeting with them rather than asking them to stay back to 7 pm. You don't have to do this very often to send out a powerful message that they matter to you and you acknowledge the sacrifices they make to work in a global team.

– Paul Chapman, Programme Manager, Financial Services

Virtual team building for project success – by Peter Taylor

What's different about running project teams remotely?
In a virtual situation, a lot of the power issues that otherwise arise during the 'storming' phase can be hidden, so as the leader you almost have to force the matter. If at all possible, make the investment in a 'hothouse' face-to-face meeting. By this I mean an intensive, almost 24/7 five-day team experience. Make the business case that this is an investment that will pay off. And by 24/7 I mean not just work but social activities as well – dinners with the team members, activities that bring people together and that are fun and visits to local sights and events. At dinners why not let the team organize the evening plans, what food to get and where to go? Let them work together and learn in simple ways. Based on the individual's personal ambitions and likes, you can bond the group by agreeing to goals for each team member that the group can follow, maybe to lose a little weight, or train for a sporting event, or visit somewhere special, or write an article for a magazine – it doesn't matter what it is, just that the team have some insight into each other's lives. If this is financially impossible, then you may just have to accept that the 'storming' phase will be longer than usual.

Once the team is up and running, what do you do to maintain the virtual team spirit when you can't just head off to the pub for a beer or two? One technique I have used is the 'It's Friday' e-mail exchange. On a Friday, it is encouraged that all those funnies, Dilbert cartoons, YouTube videos and so on are shared amongst the team. Be careful though—err on the side of caution of what is funny to whom; culture, sex and beliefs can vary a huge amount in a team. Another technique is to explore what you don't know about the team members. Each week on the team calls, get one or two to share hobbies or something unusual that they do outside of work hours. Making new connections with common hobbies help bond a team.

Thirdly, rotate the team calls. Don't take the lead each time yourself. Hand it over to a team member to take some time to share what that person has personally been doing in the past week. There is nothing worse than a conference call that is just a one-way piece of communication and you wonder if anyone is actually listening. By allowing the team members to regularly lead the call, their interest and interaction should increase significantly. Finally social media can be a great way to maintain a close network of support amongst the team – not least as they progress onwards after the project finishes. Who knows, you may all meet up sometime in the future on another new project.

– Peter Taylor, author of *The Lazy Project Manager*

How to embed the new behaviour

In this key we looked at how you can increase motivation and collaboration on your team by tapping into people's strengths and desires and by understanding what makes each person tick. Building a high-performing team is about building rapport, listening, enabling, providing autonomy and acting as an inspirational mentor and guide. It's about providing the right amounts of supporting yin as well as challenging yang in light of the individual's needs and the team's development phase.

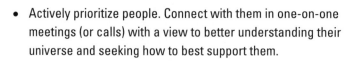

How to embed the learning

- Actively prioritize people. Connect with them in one-on-one meetings (or calls) with a view to better understanding their universe and seeking how to best support them.

- Map out each person's desires, needs and strengths, and determine how you will meet them and utilize them.

- Don't get frustrated if your team appears less motivated than you would like. Find out the reasons and do something about it. If someone is de-motivated or classified as a poor performer, there will be a reason for it.

- Imagine your team members were volunteers. What would it take to make all of them turn up to work and do their job even if they didn't get a salary for it?

- Assess the situations in which you need to either challenge or support people more and how you can begin to do that.

- Become aware of your team's communication patterns. Who is actively engaged and who is not? Look at the root cause and seek to improve energy, engagement and exploration.

- Adapt your leadership style to each person's level of competence and confidence and according to the development stage of your team.

- Write down all the roadblocks you feel are in your way and identify the best ways to overcome them.

Checklist: Do you master the learning?

- You regularly prioritize people over tasks and you often have one-on-one meetings that help you connect with the individual and discuss what you need from each other.

- You support people as much as you can but you also demand that they produce the best they are capable of.

- You understand and utilize each person's strengths as far as possible, and you are aware of the things that drive and motivate each individual.

- Your team's communication and engagement levels are high and everyone collaborates across geographical boundaries.

- Your team is high-performing and no longer needs your hands-on guidance. You continue to inspire and stimulate it to grow and develop and deliver great value to the clients.

Your insights and intentions

Write down at least three insights you have gained from this section along with three actions you will take to embed this key into your daily work.

_____

_____

_____

_____

Notes

1 http://www.projectleaders.com – see the psychometric report

2 Pentland, A (2012) The New Science of Building Great Teams [Online] http://hbr.org/2012/04/the-new-science-of-building-great-teams/ar/2

3 Jensen, D (2013) How Leaders Should Think about Leadership Models [Online] http://www.pmhut.com/how-leaders-should-think-about-leadership-models

4 Kaplan, R, and Kaiser, R (2013) The Yin and Yang of Leadership, American Management Association [Online] http://www.amanet.org/training/articles/The-Yin-Yang-of-Leadership.aspx

5 BusinessBalls.com [accessed February 2014] Frederick Herzberg's Motivation and Hygiene Factors [Online] http://www.businessballs.com/herzberg.htm

6 Cherry, Kendra [accessed February 2014] What Is Self-Determination Theory? *About.com Psychology* [Online] http://psychology.about.com/od/motivation/f/self-determination-theory.htm

Key #5
Get close to your stakeholders

FIGURE 3.5.1

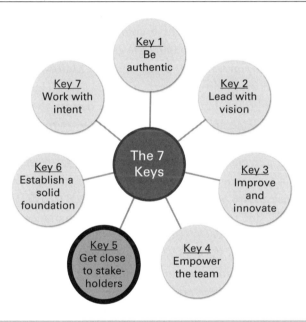

IN THIS KEY YOU WILL LEARN

- Why trust is fundamental to project success and what you can do strengthen it

- How you can win the support of your opponents and deal with difficult stakeholders

- How to strengthen your relationships with the project's most senior decision-makers and tailor your communication to their different types and styles

- What Transactional Analysis and the DISC model can teach us about relationship building

The importance of strong interpersonal relationships

Have you ever been involved in a project where there were too many misunderstandings and disagreements about scope and priorities and where it was a struggle to gain buy-in and traction for important decisions? Some stakeholders were not engaged, information wasn't flowing to those who needed it and internal politics were getting in the way of effective collaboration. At times people didn't show up for important meetings, and when they did, they spent more time questioning old decisions than providing support for the project.

Poor interpersonal relationships and communication are serious issues that contribute to project failure. PMI's *Pulse Report* states that high-performing organizations rate effective communications to all stakeholders, more than any other factor, as having the greatest impact on successful project delivery.[1] And Tim Banfield, Director at the Major Projects Authority,[2] says, 'It is people who deliver projects, not processes. The processes matter and they are important, but at the end of the day it's the people who will make it happen'. Time and time again projects go wrong because of poor relationships. Research[3] shows that strong working relationships deliver better projects and that they are absolutely essential to successful project delivery. In fact it's near impossible to deliver a major project successfully if the relationships are poor. The question you need to ask is whether your project is at risk due to poor relationships and communication among different parties. If the answer is yes, then what are you doing about it?

It is easy to fall into the trap of blaming someone else for a poor interpersonal relationship and for not understanding our messages. We may, for instance, believe that the project sponsor or client is too demanding or doesn't pay sufficient attention to the documents we send, that there is too much office politics and general tension, or that people have difficult personalities. We have probably all fallen victim of that way of thinking. But the truth is that we, as project managers and leaders, share the responsibility for creating a harmonious and dynamic stakeholder group – and that it is entirely within our sphere to do so. In his book, Wayne Strider describes this in a very honest way:

FIGURE 3.5.2 Time and time again projects go wrong because of poor relationships

I believe there is no such thing as a difficult person. There are, however, lots of people with whom I have difficulty. That does not necessarily mean that they are difficult people. 'NOT!' you may say. Ten years ago I might have agreed with you. But I have learned some things about myself since then that have changed my mind. One thing I have learned is that the difficulty is often more about me than about them.[4]

A constructive and engaged project sponsor and stakeholder group can have a tremendously positive impact on a project. People who are fully bought in to a change initiative will help shape, support and promote it and are much more likely to label it as a success. With the backing of powerful allies, it will be significantly easier to steer the project in the right direction, make decisions, resolve issues and avoid conflict. PMI's *Pulse Report* supports this view, as its research confirms that having an actively engaged sponsor is a top driver for project success. Unfortunately PMI's research also shows that fewer than two in three projects have sponsors who are actively engaged.[5]

The good news is that as project leaders we have the power to influence how the project sponsor shows up. By deliberately working towards it we can – through honesty, empathy and clear communication – encourage the sponsor's active involvement. Most sponsors haven't been trained in how to steer a project, so we need to help them and we need to openly explain what their role is and what we need from them. Through our questions and conversations we can influence them to think strategically, to promote a culture of learning, to endorse innovation and risk-taking and to make timely and sustainable decisions – preferably in consultation with the team.

Gregory Balestrero, a strategic adviser for International Institute of Learning (IIL), explains that major initiatives and complex projects must always be driven out of strategy. As such, there should be 'line of sight' direction through the organization, from the very top of the executive leadership to each member of the project team. He believes that all executives, team leaders and team members must share a clear understanding of the decision that led to this initiative and any subsequent decisions made to ensure the success of the project. In simple terms, this means that executives, especially project sponsors, must have a strong and positive relationship with the project team. As project development matures, and the surrounding environments begin to have an impact on the progress of the project, project sponsors and project team leaders must share the same enthusiasm and the same commitment to the success of the project. This is something that can happen either by increasing the project manager's remit or by strengthening buy-in from and access to the project's senior decision-makers.

Balestrero's point is very valid. We have to focus our efforts and relationships on the real decision-makers and on those who can help us move the project forward. What would the impact be on your project if there were complete transparency around the decisions made at the top? And how much time and effort could be saved if these decisions were always sensible and timely? Also imagine what the impact would be if your team was actively consulted before some of these decisions were made. If our relationships with senior executives are poor, they will negatively affect decision-making, execution time and the success of the project – and vice versa.

Project leaders are excellent at using their emotional intelligence to build strong interpersonal relationships and to gain buy-in from the project's most significant decision-makers. They have the courage to ask for help and guidance when required and to address conflict when it occurs. If the client or stakeholder goes off course and loses strategic focus – or makes a poor decision – project leaders refrain from bluntly pointing it out. Instead they will coach the stakeholders so that they come to realize it on their own.

As they do so they consider the stakeholder's individual motives as well as the project's big-picture vision. This insight into the client's universe and the underlying business drivers is one of the most fundamental cornerstones of project leadership and an important aspect of effective relationship building. In that sense, there is an interdependency between key number five, *Get close to your stakeholders*, and key number two, *Lead with vision*. You cannot effectively uncover your clients' vision and take joint ownership for delivering value to their business if you have a poor interpersonal relationship. But the opposite is also true. It is hard to build close relationships with your stakeholders or clients if you don't understand the context within which they operate.

The importance of trust

One of the most important prerequisites to building great professional relationships is *trust*. Without trust it's impossible for a project to function effectively, as people are unlikely to open up, collaborate and follow someone whom they feel they can't rely on. Trust can be described as the unquestioned belief that the other person has your best interests at heart – a belief that is built and earned over time by listening, sharing, asking questions and 'walking the talk'. It's a powerful force, which promotes loyalty, increases credibility and defines how people relate to one another. Trust is essential

for working together. Many team members and stakeholders have specialized jobs and responsibilities and the only way to collaborate effectively is
to understand each other, which is the core of trust.

Peter Drucker, the renowned management consultant, explained the
evolving role of trust in this way:

> Organizations are no longer built on force but on trust. The existence of trust
> between people does not necessarily mean that they like each other. It means
> they understand one another. Taking responsibility for relationships is therefore
> an absolute necessity. It is a duty.[6]

Terry Williams, the Dean of Hull University Business School, says that trust
is one of the biggest factors in projects. If you don't trust your client, or the
client doesn't trust the contractor, the whole thing starts to go wrong. But
unfortunately not much analysis is generally given at the beginning of the
project to what would happen if the trust relationship breaks down and
how we would manage it. How much analysis and attention have you personally given to that aspect?

For project management professionals, a high-trust environment is particularly important, as the very nature of our job is to lead people through
a period of high uncertainty and change. In addition we often interface with
people who are more senior than us and who don't report to us. As we
can't rely on hierarchical reporting lines to move things forward, we have
to make use of our interpersonal skills and our ability to influence people
in more subtle ways. If we want people to trust us and follow us, we have
to make them feel safe, keep our promises and communicate with absolute
clarity.

FIGURE 3.5.3 The benefits and dis-benefits of (lacking) trust

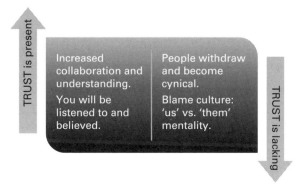

Project leaders generate trust by being fair and open and by emphasizing teamwork. On many projects there is an 'us vs. them' mentality that creates factions and a blame culture. There is only *one* team, and project leaders consistently play at that level. Because they are able to create a safe and transparent environment, they see increased levels of collaboration and willingness from stakeholders to support them. They have earned the benefit of the doubt and are more likely to be listened to, understood and believed – not least when a problem needs to be resolved. It is really easy to be nice to one another when everything is going well, but it is how people pull together and deal with problems that is the best indicator of effective collaboration.

When trust is lacking, people tend to pull back and withdraw rather than cooperate. They start to doubt and become cynical. Lack of trust is something that comes about when people fail to communicate important information or deliberately withhold information or when they are not truthful, reliable or consistent. Actions speak louder than words, so if something is not appropriately done or communicated it will create barriers even if the intentions were genuine.

The good news is that there is a method for building trust – and that trust can be regained even in situations where it is lacking. It does, however, require time, energy and conscious effort to do so. Let's examine the four main components of project leadership trust: *Competence, Honesty, Connection* and *Communication*.

FIGURE 3.5.4   The four components of building trust on a project

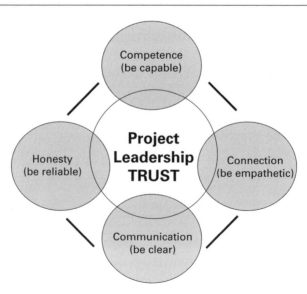

Competence – In order for your clients and stakeholders to trust you, it's imperative that they see you as an excellent and reliable manager who knows how to get the job done. They will admire you for being an effective person who keeps tabs on risks, issues, decisions and actions – and for being someone who is able to execute plans and generate the results you have promised. It almost goes without saying, but sometimes we overlook this reason for why people don't trust us. The quickest way to lose respect is to be careless, unstructured and unreliable. To your stakeholders it will look as if you are not in control or as if you don't care. Conversely, the quickest way to gain trust is to keep your promises and to consistently deliver a quality output.

Honesty – The second major component of trust is honesty. Many project managers are capable of excellent work but let people down unexpectedly when they come under pressure. They promise too much, and trust is broken when they later have to admit that they couldn't deliver the work they promised. Don't fall into that trap. If you are in a situation where you feel pressured to saying yes without wanting to, take time out and come back with an answer later. Or give small allowances by saying, 'We can't do A but we can do B'. Be strong and have an open conversation with people so that they don't expect something that is unrealistic. Project leadership is about doing the right thing, and that sometimes means telling the unpleasant truth and saying things the way they are. In the long run your stakeholders will respect you for being realistic and for having their best interests at heart. Being overly optimistic and promising too much helps no one.

Connection – The ability to deeply connect with people, relate to them and show them that you care is a third factor in building trust. We discussed this at length in key number four, *Empower your team*, and will continue to explore it in this key. In order to connect with people, you have to see them as individuals and spend time understanding their situation. Show them that you care and that you are able to put yourself in their shoes. Those aspects are the basics of empathy – being able to view situations and responses from the other person's perspective. It is not enough to have a superficial relationship. Real mastery and trust building comes from understanding people's psychology, their values, beliefs and identity. A good way to get started is to become an empathetic listener and to give people your full attention. But it's also important to share something about yourself and to show openness and willingness to cooperate.

Communication – The fourth major component in building trust is the ability to communicate clearly and effectively. Communication cannot make a person trust you if you are basically untrustworthy, but it can help create a culture in which trust can thrive. At ICCPM's Fourth Annual Research and Innovation Seminar, Jeff Wilcox, VP Engineering at Lockheed Martin, said that he had never seen a project fail that did not fail as a result of poor communication. PMI's *Pulse Report*[7] underlines this by revealing that it is indeed a major factor in half of all projects that fail. Project leaders address this risk by making use of *deliberate* communication. They purposefully influence the perception and behaviour of the project's stakeholders and don't leave anything to chance. They communicate openly, honestly and frequently and ensure that their messages are as accurate and clear as possible.

Learn to say 'Maybe' – by Michael Fleron

Far too many PMs say yes too quickly and too often. The best answer is to say, 'Maybe, it depends on. . .' and then come back later with an analysis of all the assumptions, constraints and preconditions. 'Maybe' is the best word to learn to say, since it narrows the gap between yes and no. It increases the possibility of a more accurate and reliable outcome.

– Michael Fleron, adviser and PRINCE2 Trainer

It is easier to say no if you know the facts – by Morten Sorensen

It is a lot easier to be comfortable saying no in a project if you have all the necessary analysis, facts and leadership endorsement behind you. Trust is earned through a track record of strong performance. Once you have that you can afford to stand firmer in debates and hold your position where needed.

– Morten Sorensen, Area VP, Global Client Services at Verizon Enterprise Solutions

Soft skills can be learnt – by Dave Sawyer

There is a big barrier out there because many people think that you can't learn soft skills and that you've either got it or you haven't. It's a total myth. People change throughout their life. One of the best soft skills that can be leant is active listening. If you don't listen properly, why would others listen to you? Doing a lot of requirements interviews helped me learn that, but I'm always striving to get better. As an ex-technician, I tend to give answers and it was really difficult to put the 'answer mode' on hold so that I could fully understand the problem.

— Dave Sawyer, Project Manager, UK Government

The best way to grow into a leader is to listen – by Sam Fleming

We often plan what we want to say (and how we want to be perceived) in our heads, rather than actually listening to the person talking. This promptly truncates your propensity to learn, as well as shuts down that emotional intelligence aspect of observing the 'awareness of others'. In addition, actively analyze leaders that inspire you ... and don't be afraid to experiment using similar techniques with your own team.

— Sam Fleming, Head of Project Delivery, British Gas Plc

Project managers fail to use their position to influence key decisions – by Hala Saleh

Project managers are in a unique position where they have access to intimate details about the day-to-day status of the project, and they also have access to key stakeholders and decision-makers. This puts them in a position where they should be able to help the stakeholders make key decisions about the project by communicating early and

often. In too many cases, however, I've seen project managers fail to take advantage of their ability to influence decisions by miscommunicating the project's status, or by not making the leap from purely transmitting information to making recommendations based on what they know. I witnessed this at a major financial services company where the project managers consistently changed any 'red' statuses of a very high-profile project to be 'less controversial' in order to avoid confrontation with executives. The project's issues kept compounding to the point where executives had to be informed that the project could not be delivered on time. As a result the executives took control from that point forwards, and the project managers became sidelined and served only as coordinators. Not only did the company lose money as a result, the project managers' reputations were severely tarnished and it took months to recover the trust of upper management.

– Hala Saleh, Director of Projects and Agile Coach

Communicate with clarity

The unfortunate truth is that many of us make basic mistakes when it comes to trust building. We are not sufficiently mindful of the person in front of us. We speak more than we listen and we are generally too concerned with our own situation and with what we want to say and do. We don't always see the situation from the other person's perspective and we are not good enough at tailoring our messages. We often provide either too much or too little detail, and in general we communicate too much in writing instead of face-to-face. Written communication is great for short messages without complexity, but should not be used because it's more convenient or because it saves us having a difficult conversation. Many misunderstandings and disagreements are born because we don't take the time to speak openly with people, understand their motives, identify common ground and prepare them for what is coming.

To move into project leadership we have to hone our emotional intelligence, tune in to people and tailor our messages specifically to our audience. We also have to communicate in a simple and clear manner without the use of jargon. Many stakeholders feel alienated when we use project management speak, such as 'benefit analysis', 'milestone report', 'risk assessment' and 'deliverables'. Instead, we have to use plain English and say things the way they are. When we communicate clearly and use the words that give meaning to our clients, we build trust as we demonstrate that we understand their world and what the project is trying to do for them.

'Inspiring leaders have an obsession with simplicity', writes Baldev Seekri in *How Perceptions Shape Realities*.[8] 'They speak softly, use simple words instead of business jargon, and the words come smoothly from them. With this style they make others feel that he/she is at their level. This is a powerful catalyst for undivided attention and willing participation of others'. If you are in doubt about how simple and clear your communication style is, try to express your message in 100 seconds. That will usually make the essence come out. And bear in mind that if you can't express your thoughts clearly, the recipient will have little chance of making sense of them.

Before you enter into a dialogue with someone, make it a habit to ask yourself what you want to convey and what you want to gain from the communication. How do you want people to *feel* when they hear or read your message, and what do you want them to do as a result? It is surprising how many of us don't take the time to ask those simple questions before we get in touch with someone. Knowing what you want to achieve means that you can compose your message in a much clearer and direct manner. Try it now. Think of your next steering committee meeting or one-to-one with an important stakeholder. How would you like the person to feel after the meeting? And, what do you want the individual to do as a result?

Effective communication means that the message you convey is being understood in the way you intended it. This is *your* responsibility, not the receiver's! In order for that to happen you have to adapt the content and communication method to the individual or group you are communicating with. Some clients may want you to alert them on the phone if a major issue occurs. Others are contented with a weekly status report. You have to tailor your message to people's individual filters and learning styles instead of defaulting to your own preferred style. Many of us default to written communication, but in general, face-to-face interaction is a *must* in situations where:

- the stakes are high (for instance, regarding an issue or a significant risk);
- you sense disagreement or conflict;
- you want to build trust and make sure you're on the same page;
- you want to ask for advice or feedback;

- you want to win your client's support for an important matter; or
- you want to understand your client's point of view and how to best communicate with the client.

How good are you at ascertaining each stakeholder's communication preferences and at engaging people in face-to-face conversations? Is it possible that you have let convenience and efficiency supersede impact and effectiveness?

It is also worth mentioning that most people think in pictures, and that a combination of pictures and words represents a far more effective way of communicating than words alone. Pictures can transmit a lot of information in an appealing, intuitive and memorable way. So include simple graphs, diagrams, illustrations and flow charts in most of your communication, weekly reports and meetings. But keep it simple. If you convey too much detail or complexity you may lose people.

EXERCISE Building strong relationships of trust with your stakeholders

Consider the five most important stakeholders on your project – those with the most power and influence. How would you rate the relationship you have with each of them on a scale from 1 to 10? Would you say that you sing from the same hymn sheet and that they support the project in the way that you need them to? Or do you sometimes struggle to get their buy-in and attention?

How many of these stakeholder relationships would improve if you were to put in more effort and communicate with them in a more regular, empathetic and clear manner? Can you see that improving these relationships would lead to increased support and better/quicker decision-making on your project?

To enhance the level of trust between you and your stakeholders, consider to what extent you can make each of the following aspects work for you. As you read through them, think of someone specific with whom you feel that there is room for improvement.

- **Take the first step** – Thinking of a situation where you feel trust is lacking, or not yet present, between you and a particular person, how open are you towards taking the first step and actively starting to demonstrate trust in the other? I mean, how ready are you to really show that you believe in the other person's abilities and value his or her contributions? If you want to transform a poor relationship, you have to be proactive and take the first step. If subconsciously you don't rate the other person, it will reflect in the relationship and undermine trust. You have to put your negative emotions aside, be forthcoming and show that you care.

- **Share reliable information** – Assess to what extent you are contributing to a high-trust environment by sharing accurate and timely information, for instance about the project's vision, plans, decisions, roles and responsibilities, risks, costs and progress. Is the information accurate and reliable and do you keep the right people informed? Do your stakeholders sometimes complain that they are not being kept informed or that the information you provide is incorrect or untimely? Have you considered what you communicate to whom and how often, or do you communicate in an ad hoc manner? Do you see communication as a key part of your role, or do you tend to down prioritize it and carry out a rushed job?

- **Be straight** – Is your communication open and honest also when it comes to mistakes and bad news, or do you tend to hide it? It's important never to withhold information, even when it's unpleasant news. Instead, ask how you can be transparent whilst also demonstrating that you are on top of the situation – for instance, by providing clear options, mitigating actions and contingency plans. The same is true when it comes to mistakes. The last time you made a mistake that affected your client, did you openly admit it and correct it – maybe with an apology – or did you hide it? Admitting a mistake, and being open about issues and delays, is a sign of strength as long as you demonstrate competence and sincerity in your communication. In which situations could you benefit from being more open and honest and straight about project issues and mistakes?

- **Listen** – How good are you at connecting with your stakeholders on a one-to-one basis and really listening to what they say? When you approach other people, do you first seek to listen and understand, or do you primarily try to make your own views come across? When I trained as a coach we were told that we have two ears and one mouth for a reason. That picture stuck with me. When we invest time in really listening and understanding the other person, the dynamics of the conversations change. People become more open, receptive and interested. As Ulrika Berg, project manager at BAE systems, puts it: 'Stand back and listen. It is all about communication. The rest is just technology'.[9]

  A good way to practise active listening is to ask open questions and listen just for the sake of listening. Put your tongue on 'pause', meaning that it neither touches the lower or upper part of your mouth. Positioning your tongue in this neutral way means that you are deliberately not speaking but listening. Try it when you are next in conversation with someone. Give the person your full attention and hold back your judgment.

- **Walk the talk** – Generally speaking, how good are you at walking your talk and setting a good example for others to follow? If you demand that people turn up to meetings on time, complete their actions and go above and beyond, are you also personally demonstrating those qualities? As a project leader you have to be a walking example of the vision and the values you communicate. If you say one thing and do another, people will quickly question your trustworthiness. Do you have double standards by expecting other people to do certain things whilst not doing them yourself? Or maybe you have a tendency to promise more than you can live up to. Committing to aggressive deadlines without delivering on them is one of the biggest causes of broken trust.

- **Be Confident** – Your stakeholders are much more likely to trust you, support you and let you get on with the job if you come across as confident. The more confident you are, the easier it will be for your stakeholders to relax, as it will make them feel confident too. But your confidence will need to be founded on real performance, good interpersonal skills and a firm understanding of your client and of project management practices. If you don't have sufficient knowledge and experience, your reliability and trustworthiness will quickly be questioned. Do your stakeholders see you as a knowledgeable project manager and a safe pair of hands? What are the areas in which you might need to improve? One of the quickest ways to boost your confidence is to take action and do something to strengthen the topics in which your knowledge is lacking.

- **Ask for feedback** – Have you built a habit of asking your stakeholders for feedback and verifying that you are providing them with the information and the outcomes they need and in the manner they want? Asking for feedback is one of the most powerful tools on your road to ongoing growth and development and is an excellent way to strengthen personal relationships. People sometimes shy away from asking for feedback because they are afraid what they will be told, but we are much better off knowing about it than not knowing. When was the last time you asked your clients how they feel about the project, and if they are receiving sufficient information about it? Can you see how asking these questions can immediately strengthen trust?

- **Be consistent** – On a scale from 1 to 10, how consistent are you in your way of managing the project and interfacing with the stakeholders? If you are very

attentive and great at following up and communicating clearly one day –
but not the other – you will undermine your good efforts. Your stakeholders
will be able to trust you only if they feel they can rely on you – something they
will be able to do if you are consistent in your approach. Building trust is not
something you attend to once in a while. It has to be present in everything
you do day in and day out – and not just when you feel like it or at the very
beginning of a project.

Stakeholder analysis

Stakeholder analysis is a great tool that can help clarify whom you are communicating with and how you can better tailor your messages and make
them more deliberate. At its core it will help you identify who the people are
who can help deliver the project. Although stakeholder analysis is a tool, its
power is not based on the process but on the human interactions, insights
and engagement that it brings. By systematically analyzing each player, you
leave nothing to chance and ensure that no one is overlooked. The process itself is concerned with identifying and analyzing people who will be
affected by the project and who have an interest in its conclusion. Some of
these people, groups or organizations will have a lot of power and influence
over the project and will be able to either block it or advance it depending
on how supportive they are.

FIGURE 3.5.5 Use the stakeholder matrix to identify your
Opponents and Allies.

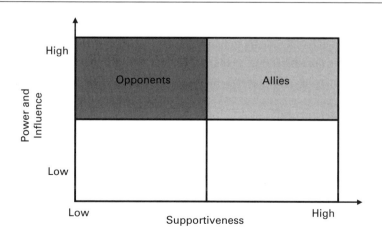

People who have a lot of power and influence and who are very support-ive are your closest allies. They genuinely want the project to succeed and are happy to assist whenever there is a need. This is the group to communi-cate new ideas to first, as they can help improve them and promote them to others. This is also the group to go to when we have major risks or issues that the project team cannot handle or resolve on its own. It's important to continue to nurture these relationships so that they continue to work in your favour.

On the other hand, people who have a lot of power and influence but who are less supportive – or who actively oppose your work – are your opponents. They have the power to negatively influence others and could derail the project if you don't win them over. When communicating with this group, it's important to be as flawless and pragmatic as possible. The key is to listen to their concerns and make a genuine effort to understand their points of view and the cause of their reservations. There will be a reason for their lack of support, and when you get to the root cause and address it, the dynamics of the project can dramatically change for the better.

EXERCISE   Engage your stakeholders

The purpose of this exercise is to help you uncover the needs, motives and characteristics of the most powerful and influential stakeholders on your project – and to gain their trust and buy-in. Put your investigative hat on and set up a one-to-one meeting with those who are best positioned to help you deliver the project's outcomes and benefits – whether directly or indirectly.

As you meet with each stakeholder, discuss what you want out of your relationship together, and try to find the answer to as many of the following questions as possible. Some of them cannot be asked directly, so you will have to glean the information from more informal conversations and indirect questions.

Project outcomes

- What is their interest (or stake) in the outcome of the project?

- What do they believe the short and long term benefits are of the project?

- What does success look like in their eyes, and how should it be measured?

- If they have been involved in similar projects before, what lessons did they learn?

- How can you best leverage their knowledge?

Reading between the lines

- What is their level of support and buy-in for the project?

- Why might they want to see the project succeed (or fail)?

- Who influences their opinion of you and the project?

- What could influence them to become more supportive of you and the project?

Current situation

- Is anything worrying them about the current project? If so, what is it?

- Are there any risks they feel you are not mitigating or issues you are not addressing?

- What are the consequences of any such issues?

- Do they have a view of what the underlying problem is?

- Which other risks can they think of?

Communication needs

- Are they happy with your current status reports and project communications?

- What type of information and updates are they most interested in?

- How would they like to receive it (face-to-face, e-mail, telephone, in a weekly report)?

- How frequently would they like to receive it?

Expectations

- What does your stakeholder expect from you, in general and right now?

- In what types of situations would the stakeholder like you to escalate to him or her – and how?

- What do you expect from your stakeholder, in general and right now?

- How will you be working together?

- Does your stakeholder understand and accept his or her responsibilities on the project?

As you engage with each stakeholder, really listen to his or her answers without interrupting. Forget your own agenda – ask questions and listen from the heart. Observe the stakeholders' body language and their tone and tune in to the meaning behind the words. What are they really saying? Put yourself in their shoes; empathize and enquire about their world, their views and worries. That is how great relationships are built.

Never copy your stakeholder analysis and communication plan – by Michael Fleron

One of my students was a very popular project manager and had just delivered a very successful project. The next project was just around the corner. To speed things up, he copied the risk-management strategy, stakeholder analysis and communications plan from one project to the other, as the two projects seemed very similar. However, the new project was in another country and in a completely different environment. The result was a deficit in millions and a project that was delivered late. The project manager was in a rush and didn't consult the team. I did the same once, but closed the project before it became a disaster.

– Michael Fleron, adviser and PRINCE2 Trainer

Show your clients that you care – by Paul Chapman

A bad client relationship usually stems from lack of trust from your client. Show your clients that you understand and care about their business by demonstrating that you are interested in it. The most straightforward way to do this is to ask them questions about their business and priorities, and don't constrain yourself just to questions that directly relate to what you are doing for them. Once they see that you are interested in their business – and are 'speaking their language' – you have a solid basis for a trust relationship.

– Paul Chapman, Programme Manager, Financial Services

Walking into the lion's cage

Whenever I coach or train a group of project managers, one of the biggest concerns they raise is how to deal with *opponents*, i.e., senior stakeholders and clients who have a lot of power and influence over the project but who are not supportive. Or at least they don't come across as being supportive. These people are unpleasant to deal with because they make us feel insecure and in doubt about the direction of the project. Most project managers interface with them only when they have to, but will otherwise avoid them. Why ask for unnecessary trouble? *But,* we should be doing the exact opposite. We should be *walking into the lion's cage,* so to speak, and addressing the stakeholders instead of avoiding the situation. How good are you at doing that? Do you sometimes avoid having a difficult conversation? And do you sometimes shy away from getting to the root of a conflict at work more so than you would in your private life?

When looking at your opponents, first consider how they are acting towards you. Are they indifferent, absent and maybe noncommittal? Could it be that the root cause of the problem is related to time management, rather than a substantial problem, where your project is simply further down on their priority list? If that's the case, how can you work on increasing their stake and interest in the project by making them see the benefits and what's in it for them? How can you help them focus on the value they provide and also help them rationalize and optimize the time they spend on your project?

If, on the other hand, their opposition isn't about time management but due to a deeper-rooted skepticism, you have to take a closer look at the emotions and reasons that drive their behaviour. What are the underlying needs that they feel are not being met? Could it be that they feel their voice and contributions aren't being appreciated and that the project isn't giving them what they were hoping for? What can you do to actively engage these people and uncover the reasons for their skepticism? Maybe it is time for you to 'walk into the lion's cage' to find out.

One of the best ways to address a skeptical stakeholder – or opponent – is to ask for advice and feedback. This is a very disarming move, which instantly opens up the relationship because you show that you care and that you are humble enough to ask for the person's opinion. Just imagine how your opponents might react if you said, '*I would like to ask for your feedback about the project. I value your opinion about how we can work more effectively and deliver a better product or service to you. Are there any aspects (e.g., requirements, risks or issues) that you feel we have overlooked? Which other tips and suggestions do you have for how we can improve?*'

These questions have the potential to work wonders for you – but only if you sincerely mean it and take the time to really listen to the answer and to the meaning behind the words. Leave your negative emotions by the door, put your tongue on neutral and just listen. If you take mistrust into a meeting that aims to build trust, you will undermine the process. We are often not aware of the emotions we bring to a situation ourselves – and neither is the other person – but subconsciously it always comes across. If you fundamentally don't trust or respect the individual you are interfacing with, the person will detect it, and it will undermine your relationship in more ways than you think.

Take a moment to reflect on what your true feelings are towards some of the people with whom you have a tense relationship. Do you look up to them or down on them? Do you fear them, or do you think they are laughable? In which ways would you say that this perception shows up in your relationship? Do you unintentionally exclude them from e-mails and meetings, or do you tend to speak badly about them to other people? I invite you to have a long and hard look at the emotions and attitudes you hold, as they affect your interactions with people even if you would like them not to. Building relationships is a two-way thing, and realizing that you can indeed help change the situation – if you choose to – is a powerful first step.

Lead through conversations – also the tough ones! – by Andy Taylor

From my observations, there is a particular breed of project leaders who really grab my attention. They are what I would call a 'people person', and what I like most about them is their natural inclination to lead their project through conversations – also the tough ones! When their team members don't deliver on a promise, they call it out. When stakeholders resist, they welcome it and ask for the truth. When their sponsors go invisible, they seek them out and ask for what they want. They are rarely on their keyboards or devices, but perch on the ends of desks, walk corridors at the end of the day or listen in a local bar later still.

The few project managers whom I really put high on a pedestal are those for whom tough conversation is so integrated in who they are that it seems easy, even enjoyable. They don't see difficult stakeholders as antagonists to be rugby tackled, but as equal people who walk in different shoes, and who have no less right to choose their own behaviour than we have. I suspect they see projects as a social system, possibly because it might be too obvious to consider that it might be a mechanical one. Whether they think this or not, they thrive on the fundamental ingredients – relationships, connectedness and trust. This is created through conversations, lots of them.

These project leaders have plenty of self-confidence, but it seems composed rather than brash. They take risks, but without seeming reckless. In fact there is little ego involved; the issues seem not to be about 'them', but just about what needs to be discussed. In our intellectual management culture we have a name for it – 'authenticity', but in truth I am not sure what the best word for it is. One client said to me, 'It's obvious, dummy – it's leadership'. We laughed, knowing there was truth in that. In any event I fully intend to enjoy watching it some more, and who knows, maybe emulating it a little each day.

– Andy Taylor, People Deliver Projects

Overcoming roadblocks

EXERCISE Overcoming roadblocks to building strong stakeholder relationships

Let's examine some of the roadblocks that might be standing in your way and preventing you from getting closer to your clients and stakeholders.

- Your stakeholders are too busy and are not located in the same office as you. That makes it hard to connect and get to know them better.

- You don't feel you have enough time to build better relationships. You barely have time to talk to your clients about essential project-related work and pressing issues.

- You have made a couple of mistakes and poor decisions in the past. Now you hesitate because you know that your knowledge isn't up to scratch in your stakeholder's eyes.

- You feel that senior managers don't take their project roles seriously and that they talk down to you. It undermines your confidence and makes it difficult for you to trust them.

- You are aware that you sometimes overpromise and that it affects your stakeholder's view of you. Overpromising happens because you commit to deliveries and deadlines based on poor estimates provided by your team. As a result your clients have lost trust in the team – including you.

- Some of your stakeholders are partners who work to contracts that are rigid and specific about how you are supposed to interface with one another. The contract is getting in the way of effectively collaborating and trusting each other.

Which of the above roadblocks do you recognize, if any? How can you begin to overcome them – even if your stakeholders are hard to track down or if you have to move outside of your comfort zone and have a tough conversation?

Transactional analysis theory

Eric Berne's 'Parent-Adult-Child' model is a building block of transactional analysis that can help us shed light on the communication patterns between people and how we can build better relationships. Berne devised the concept of ego states to help explain how we are made up and how we relate to others. The starting point of Berne's model is that every time two people encounter each other, they will communicate from one of three ego states. These ego states are called *Parent, Adult* and *Child* – labels that **don't** necessarily correspond to how they are defined in common English. Each of these ego states relate to how different parts of our personality think, feel and behave. The better we understand our own state, the easier it becomes to choose our responses and communication style. If we are not aware of our state, we could be responding inappropriately, damage relationships or aggravate a conflict.

Parent

The Parent ego state represents a set of feelings, thinking patterns and behaviours that we have copied from authority figures in the first five to six years of our life. As we grow up, we take in ideas, beliefs and behaviours from our parents, caretakers and teachers. Anything we have heard or experienced is

FIGURE 3.5.6 The three ego states of transactional analysis

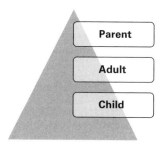

FIGURE 3.5.7 Characteristics of the *Parent* ego state

Parent ego state	*Taught* concept of life
	Feelings and behaviours copied from authority figures
	Critical parent:
	Lecturing, judging or criticizing – focusing on problems
	Nurturing parent:
	Consoling, advising and taking care of someone

stored in the form of a code for living, and as a result we say things in the exact same way as our parents and grandparents, even though we don't want to. Our Parent ego state is made up of a large number of hidden and overt recorded playbacks and can be referred to as our *Taught* concept of life.

The Parent state can be divided into the *Critical* Parent and the *Nurturing* Parent. When we operate from the Critical Parent, we are typically lecturing, judging or criticizing and focusing on identifying problems. A statement from the Critical Parent could be '*What? It takes five days to generate the report?*' and it could be accompanied by a pointed finger, folded arms or furrowed brows. Autocratic managers who make extensive use of authority and give little freedom to their teams operate primarily from this ego state.

When we operate from the Nurturing Parent state we are typically consoling, advising and taking care of someone. An example of a statement could be, '*Let me take care of that for you.*' In this state we may make plans for our team but fail to seriously take on board their input. The information flow is primarily downward from manager to team.

FIGURE 3.5.8   Characteristics of the *Child* ego state

Child ego state	*Felt* concept of life Our seeing, hearing, feeling and emotional part; playfulness, spontaneity and anger
	Adapted child: Submissive, complying to the adults' expectations
	Natural Child: Playful, impulsive, creative and fun

Child

The Child ego state represents the emotional part of our beings, which encompasses playfulness and spontaneity, but also anger, despair and depression. It holds the seeing, hearing, feeling and emotional body of data within each of us and can be referred to as the *Felt* concept of life. When anger or despair dominates reason, the Child ego state is in control.

The Child state can be divided into the *Adapted* Child and the *Natural* Child. When we operate from the Adapted Child, we are typically submissive and adapt to the Adults' expectations. In that state we might say, '*Sorry. I'll try to improve.*' When we come from the Natural Child, however, we will be more playful, impulsive, creative and fun, and we might say something like, '*Nobody follows that rule anyway*' or '*Let's take off work today*'. Physical signs that we operate from a Child state could be tears, temper tantrums, downcast eyes, laughter or giggling.

Adult

The third state is the Adult ego state, which can be referred to as the *Thought* concept of life. This is the independent part of us, which is able to think and determine action for ourselves and make rational decisions based on facts. The Adult in us begins to form at around 10 months old. It represents our primarily intellectual ego that helps us deal with situations in ways that are not negatively influenced by our past. It means that we take the best from the past and use it appropriately in the present based on positive aspects of both our Parent and Child ego states.

When we operate from our Adult state we are objective, rational and less emotional. It means that we see people as they are rather than what we project onto them. Instead of making assumptions, we ask for information and

FIGURE 3.5.9 Characteristics of the *Adult* ego state

Adult ego state	*Thought* concept of life
	Our independent part that makes rational decisions based on facts
	Objective and rational; see people as they are rather than what we project onto them
	Ask for information and solve problems based on logic and facts

we solve problems based on logic and facts. In the Adult state we might say something like, '*What are the alternatives?*' or '*What consequences will this action have?*' The physical clues are less explicit than in the other states, and mostly relate to signs that someone is listening intently. In the Adult state we engage others and give them the freedom to participate in problem-solving and in suggesting solutions. The emphasis is on the smooth functioning of the team with free flow of information. It's an environment that is conducive to self-development and for team members to utilize their potential.

To build the most constructive and enduring interpersonal relationships – with stakeholders and team members alike – it is recommended that we operate from our Adult ego state. We should neither speak down to someone nor up to someone but treat people as equals and communicate to them based on analysis and facts rather than preconceived ideas.

According to Transactional Analysis, not only is it most effective to operate from our Adult state, but communication between two people must also be *complementary*, meaning that individuals should respond from the same state as they are being communicated to. For instance, if someone speaks to you from an Adult state and you respond from either Parent or Child, it can cause problems in the relationship. Imagine someone saying, '*What time is it?*' (Adult-to-Adult message) and you respond, '*The clock is on the wall for you to see*' (Parent-to-Child message). It's easy to see how this lecturing comment can have a negative effect.

In a project environment we sometimes communicate from either a Parent or Child state without being aware of it – especially with people with whom we have a difficult emotional relationship or in situations that we approach with preconceived attitudes. If, for instance, you encounter a senior stakeholder who is impatient and finger-pointing and who uses critical words, he or she would be talking down to you in a Parent-Child pattern. If you then answer in a defensive and lecturing manner yourself, you will be escalating the conflict by also speaking in a Parent-Child pattern. To smooth the situation, you would be better off apologizing with a complementary Child-Parent pattern and then subsequently switching back into an Adult-Adult pattern by asking, '*What problems does this cause for you?*' and '*How can we reach a mutual agreement?*'

Transactional Analysis can help us recognize our communication patterns and do something about them. In which project situations would you say that you communicate from a Parent or Child state? Could it be, for instance, that you communicate from an Adult state when you are reprimanding someone, or that you assume a Child state when you are overly apologetic or rebellious? And what about the other members of your team? From which state do they most often communicate? What can you do to encourage Adult-to-Adult communication throughout the team?

Understanding personality types

Having an understanding of the basic personality types of people can further help you to build better relationships. To that end we will look at DISC, which is a leading personal assessment tool conceived by Dr. William Marston. It provides a simple way of explaining human behaviour and helps us adapt our style to get along with others. When used correctly, it has the potential to reduce conflict, improve productivity and build trust. The four different personality types of DISC are *Dominance, Influence, Steadiness* and *Conscientiousness*.

The model itself is centered on two basic observations about people's behaviour. The first observation is that some people are more outgoing and assertive, while others are more reserved and slow-paced. Those who are outgoing are mostly energized by events external to themselves, whereas the more reserved people are energized by their own internal drivers and may engage more slowly and be more cautious. The second observation is that some people are more task-oriented, while others are more people-oriented – something that we have already discussed in previous chapters. Task-oriented people are concerned with getting something done, whereas those who are people-oriented are more tuned in to the people around them and their feelings.

Looking at the illustration, you will see that the combination of these two observations creates four different tendencies with the labels *Dominance, Influence, Steadiness* and *Conscientiousness*. Everyone exhibits all four tendencies to some extent, but for most people one or two of the tendencies fit them well, whereas one or two other tendencies seem foreign. It is the balance of these four tendencies that shapes the way we see life and those around us.

FIGURE 3.5.10 The four personality types of DISC

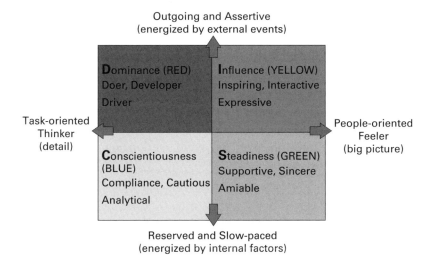

Style D

Dominance represents an outgoing, task-oriented individual who is focused on getting things done, accomplishing tasks, getting to the bottom line as quickly as possible and making it happen! They are also referred to as *Drivers*, and are associated with the colour red. They are goal-oriented, direct, competitive and sometimes impatient. They work and talk quickly and take charge in business situations. The most important thing to them is that they meet their goals and achieve results. They dislike it when people waste their time and prefer others to be straightforward and clear. Drivers have no problem giving out orders, and are less emotionally involved when dealing with someone who is not performing. Many managers, CEOs and executives have Driver personalities, as they are in a job where responsibility, decision-making and leadership are required. The key insight in developing a relationship with Drivers is *respect* and *results*. Be direct and to the point and give them the bottom line. Focus your discussion, avoid generalizations and repetitions and focus on solutions rather than problems.

Style I

Influence represents an outgoing, people-oriented individual who loves to interact, socialize and have fun. They are inspiring and charismatic people who want admiration, attention and friendship from those around them. We also refer to them as *Expressive* and associate them with the colour yellow. They have a great desire for novelty and stimulation and will often initiate positive changes within the company. They have highly developed people skills and build excellent rapport with their customers. Expressives are typically salespeople, PR representatives and customer service agents who sell their services through their winning way with people. They need a fast-paced and stimulating work environment and excel at recognizing and seizing opportunities. During a crisis, for instance, they will spontaneously take action, knowing exactly what to do. The key insight in developing a relationship with Expressives is *admiration* and *recognition*. By all means, share your experiences, but make sure to give them time to ask questions and to talk. Focus on the positives and avoid overloading them with detail.

Style S

Steadiness represents a reserved, people-oriented individual who enjoys relationships and who helps and supports others in working together as a team. They are also referred to as *Amiable* and are associated with the colour green. In most situations they will be reserved but kind, and will happily comply with what they're told. They are mostly concerned with harmony and want everyone to be happy. Within a company, Amiables can function somewhat as peacekeepers, seeking to resolve conflict. Although they are people-oriented, they tend to deal with people-related matters behind the scenes; they prefer to give the spotlight to someone else. Amiables excel at cooperation and dislike telling others what to do. You will usually find them working as receptionists, HR managers or therapists or in a teaching capacity. When communicating with S-style individuals, be personal and friendly and express your consideration for them. Take time to provide clarification, be polite and avoid being confrontational or rude.

Style C

Conscientiousness represents a reserved, task-oriented individual who is driven by value, consistency and quality information. These types of people focus on being correct and accurate and are associated with the colour blue. They are referred to as *Analytical*, as they thrive when working alone on a task that requires accuracy and analytical skills. They tend to be organized in their work and have a tendency towards perfectionism. They are skilled at fixing equipment, keeping track of data, solving puzzles or finding an efficient solution to a problem. Sometimes they come across as unfriendly, but that's because they are focused on understanding the facts of a situation and applying them towards an outcome. They work best when they are alone in a quiet area, solving a problem or making sure the details are right.

Most engineers, IT experts, accountants and researchers are Analyticals. When communicating with a C-style individual, focus on facts and details. Be patient and diplomatic and minimize small talk and emotional language.

It is not unusual for technical project managers to have a C-style behaviour and for the project sponsor to have a D-style or I-style behaviour. Can you see how those styles might clash if the communication approach is not adjusted? Analyticals, for instance, will prefer to spend time on their own, drafting a detailed e-mail in response to a request, whereas an Expressive stakeholder would prefer a quick summarized account in person or over the phone.

There may also be clashes when a Driver is communicating with an Amiable. The D-style personality will tend to be fast, direct and unemotional, whereas the S-style will be reserved and thoughtful. If neither adjust their communication style, the Driver will feel impatient and the Amiable will feel overruled and disregarded.

Which of the four DISC personality types would you say are most descriptive of you? And what types are your main stakeholders? In which ways can you adapt your communication style when interfacing with each of them?

How to embed the new behaviour

This key described how you can strengthen your relationships with clients, partners and customers in order to gain their buy-in and build a strong group of allies. We looked at the components that build trust (demonstrate competence, create connection, be honest and communicate clearly) and we discussed how you can win over opponents by walking into the lion's cage and asking for advice. We also looked at Transactional Analysis and DISC and how they can help you improve communication and cater to people's personality types and preferences.

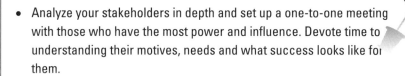

How to embed the learning

- Analyze your stakeholders in depth and set up a one-to-one meeting with those who have the most power and influence. Devote time to understanding their motives, needs and what success looks for them.

- Ascertain what the communication preferences are of each major stakeholder (or group) and seek to meet them.

- Develop your active listening skills by asking open questions, putting your tongue on pause and listening just for the sake of listening. Remember that you have two ears and one mouth for a reason.

- Make it a habit to ask your stakeholders for feedback on a regular basis and to verify that you are providing them with the information and the outcomes they need.

- Limit e-mail communication and see people face-to-face when you need to discuss a significant risk or issue. Also, see them in person if you sense disagreement, if you want to build trust or if you want to win your stakeholder's support for an important matter.

- Address opponents and skeptical stakeholders by asking for feedback and advice. Remove your negative emotions and ask them about their concerns and how they feel you can improve.

- Before you meet with someone, be clear on what you want to convey and what you want to gain from the communication. Use your knowledge of the DISC model to help ascertain their personality style, and tailor your approach and your message accordingly.

- Take one of the many DISC profile tests online. Find the links from www.powerofprojectleadership.com.

Checklist: Do you master the learning?

- You have analyzed your stakeholders and you know who the most powerful and influential decision-makers are.

- You have a good relationship with your client and the project's stakeholders and you regularly meet in person. You trust each other and you speak openly about risks and issues and how you can mutually move the project forward. When a mistake is made you discuss it in a constructive manner without getting into a blame game.

- The project sponsor is supportive and fully bought into the project. Decisions are made in a timely fashion and in consultation with the team. They are sustainable and take the project's tactical as well as strategic objectives into account.

Your insights and intentions

Write down at least three insights you have gained from this section along with three actions you will take to embed this key into your daily work.

_____

_____

_____

_____

Notes

1 PMI (2014) *PMI's Pulse of the Profession In-depth Report, Navigating Complexity*, Project Management Institute (PMI) [Online] http://www.pmi.org/~/media/PDF/Business-Solutions/Navigating_Complexity.ashx

2 Tim Banfield spoke at the Fourth Annual Research and Innovation Seminar in London in October 2013. At the time he was the Director of the National Audit Office.

3 Research by Roy Staunghton, MD, at SHAPE International Ltd. Was referenced by David Whitmore at the Fourth Annual Research and Innovation Seminar in London. 'Fruitful and enduring relationships hold the key to sustained growth, increased value in the supply chain, enhanced productivity and profit, and the creation of long-term competitive advantages that cannot easily be copied'. Roy Staunghton

4 Strider, W (2002) *Powerful Project Leadership*, Management Concepts

5 PMI (2014) *PMI's Pulse of The Profession: The High Cost of Low Performance 2014*, Project Management Institute (PMI)

6 Drucker, P F (1999) Managing Oneself. *Harvard Business Review, On Point* [Online] http://www.pitt.edu/~peterb/3005-001/managingoneself.pdf

7 PMI (2013) *PMI's Pulse of the Profession In-depth Report, The High Cost of Low Performance: The Essential Role of Communications*, Project Management Institute (PMI) [Online] http://www.pmi.org/Knowledge-Center/Pulse/~/media/PDF/Business-Solutions/The-High-Cost-Low-Performance-The-Essential-Role-of-Communications.ashx

8 Seekri, B (2012) How Perceptions Shape Realities, *ChangeThis*, Issue 97-05 [Online] http://changethis.com/manifesto/97.05.ShapingRealities/pdf/97.05.ShapingRealities.pdf

9 Ulrika Berg, project manager at BAE systems, spoke at the Fourth Annual Research and Innovation Seminar in London in October 2013.

Key #6
Establish a solid foundation

FIGURE 3.6.1

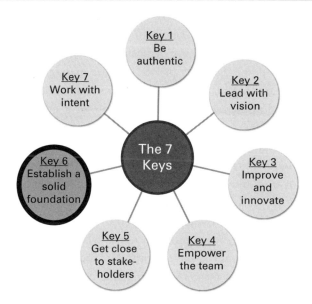

IN THIS KEY YOU WILL LEARN

- What the biggest process-related mistakes are and how you can avoid making them
- Why project management practices are fundamental to project success and how you can implement them on your project
- What the keys to good project estimation and risk management are and which questions you should ask when you start up a project

People deliver projects, but processes support them in doing so

The five keys to project leadership that we have discussed up until now are *Be authentic, Lead with vision, Improve and innovate, Empower the team* and *Get close to your stakeholders*. Our attention to fundamental project management processes and techniques has been limited. This is partly because project leadership is so much more than the application of processes and partly because you may already be familiar with them. Having said that, a book on project leadership would be incomplete without a chapter on essential practices, as it is near impossible to be a project leader without mastering the fundamentals of the profession. It is unfortunate that many project managers make basic mistakes and fail to put in place a solid foundation on which the project can progress. This is one of the aspects preventing them from stepping up, and why we have dedicated key number 6 to this topic.

Project leaders don't discount proven project management techniques. They are well aware that for the most part projects must be rooted in a logical and structured approach to delivery, as without it everything else falls apart. If we don't have a solid method for defining and controlling the project's scope, requirements, benefits, costs, quality, communication and risks, the project is unlikely to succeed even if the project manager is authentic, visionary, innovative and good at leading and motivating people. This comes back to The Project Leadership Matrix™, which we examined in chapter 1. Project leaders pay attention to people and strategy as well as tasks and processes. They strike the right balance and know when to prioritize one over the other. What's important is their continuous focus on the client and on delivering value-add. That means leveraging and developing people's potential, understanding the client's business drivers, building strong relationships of trust *and* supporting the delivery with the most appropriate set of tools, techniques and processes. It is true that people deliver projects, but processes support them in doing so. Morten Sorensen, VP at Verizon Enterprise Solutions, explains: 'To free up capacity and become a good and respected leader, one must first master the basic and fundamental aspects and techniques. One must learn to anticipate activity and events rather than become a permanent victim of them'.

Junior project managers sometimes ignore proven practices, or follow a process for the sake of compliance without attaching much *meaning* to it. Project leaders, on the other hand, implement only the techniques and processes that add value. They know that value-add doesn't come from ticking boxes but from the meaningful application of a process. Risk management, for instance, has little value if all you do is log the risks and assign ownership and mitigating actions, but subsequently don't follow up and don't take these risks into consideration when planning, estimating and executing the project. Similarly the project charter and the project plan have little value if they haven't been produced in collaboration with the team and if the stakeholders aren't fully bought into them.

As you read through this chapter, keep in mind that processes should not take over and dictate the project, but rather support it. Andy Taylor says 'when a client wants to deliver more projects for less resource, faster and with more distinctive outcomes, I advise them to strip away process to a minimum. Keep process simple, plain English and just enough to get the job done. After that it's about people. Seventy per cent accuracy at pace is way preferable to a pedestrian ninety per cent, where no blame can be laid'.

If a process, tool or technique doesn't add value it should not be used. So question the processes on your project and tailor them to best suit the size, culture and context. A multiyear project with several external stakeholder groups, unknown technology and a large global team will have a very different set of challenges and requirements to a four-month project with few stakeholders, known technology and a small colocated team. The same can be said about greenfield and experiential projects. They are harder to pin down and plan – and with good reason. When you are dealing with something that has never been done before, you have to be careful that process and unnecessary ceremony don't stifle innovation. There is no one-size-fits-all and therefore no 'best' practices.

Having said that, there are techniques that have been proved to work when applied correctly and when tailored specifically to the project's circumstances. It is some of these techniques and practices that we will examine in this chapter. What we will *not* do is list out everything you must do to effectively manage a project. Other, more detailed, process-oriented books do a much better job of that. The purpose of this chapter is to highlight the methods that cause most project managers to slip up and ensure that you avoid making those same mistakes.

Project management mistakes

Below is a short list outlining the ways in which project managers often disregard proven practices. Please don't take offence from the manner in which

I describe these mistakes. I have deliberately generalized and exaggerated to make it obvious what the mistakes are that you should avoid.

- Not producing a business case: failure to see the bigger commercial picture and assuming that the sponsor or someone more senior has already produced a strong and viable business case and that costs and benefits stack up.

- Compromising the planning stage: succumbing to pressure from senior stakeholders who believe that the project can be delivered quicker if the planning stage is reduced.

- Producing a poor project initiation document: leaving out important detail about *what* will be delivered and *how* it will be delivered, such as scope, requirements, risks and issues, success criteria, roles and responsibilities, quality, costs, resourcing, communication and the actual schedule.

- Unclear scope: producing too vague a scope description and not clearly specifying what is out of scope.

- Poor requirements management: documenting requirements at too high a level and omitting to track, assess and incorporate changes into the project in a structured manner.

- Omitting to make use of product breakdown structures, product flow diagrams, milestones, phases and iterations with clear deliverables and outcomes.

- Planning in isolation without involving other team members in the process.

- Failure to get proper buy-in for specifications and planning documents from key stakeholders: treating the sign-off stage as a tick-box exercise instead of ensuring that stakeholders have actually understood the contents and meaning of the documents.

- Underestimating the project's effort: being too optimistic when providing estimates by accounting only for the sunny-case scenarios and leaving out contingency to cater for uncertainties.

- Mechanical risk management process: failure to turn analysis into action, with risk registers and risk reports being produced and filed, but with these having little or no effect on how the project is actually undertaken.

- Poor governance: not having a clear escalation process or a well-established steering committee that is summoned on a regular basis.
- Failure to effectively review and learn from project mistakes.

You may feel that the preceding list is heavily exaggerated, but unfortunately it's the harsh reality that many projects suffer from one or more of these process-related mistakes. Many of the mistakes are concerned with lack of planning and not ensuring that a solid foundation is in place for the project to be executed. Projects need to be properly defined before they are committed to, and risks, issues and change requests must be formally assessed and managed. Accurate estimation, requirements gathering, quality control and a solid business case are prerequisites for a successful outcome and for delivering as much value as possible with the least amount of resources. The use of key performance indicators and a clear governance structure are further practices that will help do so.

What's interesting is that many project managers know what needs to get done, but are still not doing it. They procrastinate and operate at a surface level and are too busy putting out fires elsewhere.

Mismanagement of scope is very often the demise of project managers – by Morten Sorensen

One of the most commonly overlooked areas on larger projects is proper scope management, which often ends up being the demise of the project manager. Too often project managers do too many favors and over time try to absorb an unsustainable amount of scope changes (ex: gold plating or slippage), which in the end results in delays and cost overruns. Project leaders know how to politely and professionally set the expectations up front and stick to the change management processes.

– Morten Sorensen, Area VP, Global Client Services at
Verizon Enterprise Solutions

Anticipation is key – by Patrick Yengo

Project managers often go wrong early on in the project, simply because they don't take the time to identify and manage risks. This quickly becomes an issue, and in some instances a fatal one. I recently witnessed an important project being stopped because no risk analysis had been done and risks weren't factored into the plans or continuously monitored. As a result, delivery milestones weren't met, costs increased and confidence in the project team was lost. In the end the company decided to completely stop the project. In this case the project manager was an experienced professional with good interpersonal relationships, but he gradually lost control of the project as unidentified risks became large issues. Anticipation is the key! Strong risk analysis and continuous risks management are imperative to project leadership.

– Patrick Yengo, Head of PMO and Program Manager

Project information is not mined for intelligence – by Liz Pearce

While not every project manager has decision-making control, most have the data to facilitate decision-making. The problem is getting that data and turning it into something actionable. Who on my team is overloaded? Do we need to hire more people? Why were our estimates on the last project so far off? Project plans represent a wealth of information, but that information is all too often not mined for intelligence. Part of the problem is the tool being used to manage a project – how easy does a given tool make it to extract dimensions of data so it can be analyzed? The point is that decision-makers don't want more unfiltered data – they crave intelligence that can be used to justify important strategic business decisions. The mistake many project managers make is not realizing that there's gold in their project plans that's just waiting to be mined.

– Liz Pearce, LiquidPlanner CEO

EXERCISE   Which project management mistakes are you guilty of?

Take some time to reflect on the process-related mistakes highlighted above.

- How many of them have you seen other project managers make?

- How many of them have you personally fallen victim of, and what was the reason?

- In which ways can you become a role model and help others avoid making these mistakes?

It's important that you use the insights you are gaining, not just to improve the project you are currently running, but also to help your colleagues get better. Look at what you can contribute to the wider organization and maybe even to the industry. We all have an obligation to spread our knowledge and to improve the world around us. Be determined to set a good example and to do the right thing.

Project definition

In their research, Dov Dvir and Aaron J Shenhar found that one of the most significant characteristics of highly successful projects was that they begin with a long period of project definition that is dedicated to defining a powerful vision and a clear need. They write that this extended time is needed to select the best execution approach and to obtain buy-in from all stakeholders.[1]

Project leaders understand that taking time out to properly define the project is an essential practice that should not be omitted. They don't succumb to pressure from senior stakeholders who want them to press the start button as quickly as possible because they want to start doing things and seeing things. Even when more time is spent up front, the project is likely to deliver quicker because effort is invested in making people talk to one another and in understanding what they are committing to and how to go about delivering it. This doesn't mean that project leaders are complacent about the time it takes to define, plan and gain buy-in for the project. On the contrary, they act with urgency and only spend as much time planning as is absolutely necessary. It also doesn't mean that project leaders favour a rigid waterfall methodology where everything is set in stone – certainly not on more innovative and greenfield projects. They simply want to understand what they are dealing with so that they can be better prepared and are better able to deal with eventualities.

Professor Knut Fredrik Samset writes that it's essential for project success to spend time up front reducing the project's uncertainty and risk.[2] This can be done by challenging initial ideas, extracting and making use of previous experience and by consulting with stakeholders. Where projects fail strategically, it's often due to a problem that can be traced back to decisions in the earliest phases when the initial idea was conceived and developed. The key concern when a project is initiated is therefore to shed sufficient light on the underlying problem that provides the justification for the project, and the needs that the project is meant to satisfy. Samset also writes that creativity, imagination and intuition can be more valuable at this stage than large amounts of data, as the priority is to establish an overall perspective and to analyze the problem in its context in order to come up with a sensible strategy. Therefore, lack of information in the early phase of a project isn't necessarily a problem; it can even be a strength.

In order to properly initiate the project, project leaders begin with the end in mind. They partner with the client and engage the team as they uncover the project's main idea and justification and visualize the end state when all changes have taken place and all benefits have been realized. They challenge assumptions and ask the right set of questions – including the hard ones. The most simple and straightforward enquiries are often the most powerful, and the hardest to ask. We sometimes feel that questions that relate to the client's business, the project idea or the technologies we are planning to use are too basic to be asked, but if we don't ask, we won't be able to understand how to create added value. In the beginning of a project we are surrounded by people who know more than we do, but we have to push ahead until we fully comprehend the context. That's the only way to establish a solid foundation for delivery.

FIGURE 3.6.2   The most simple and straightforward enquiries are often the most powerful

Be strong enough to show weakness and ask the dumb questions – by Paul Chapman

It is not easy to show weakness, but if you are strong enough to admit you don't know something you will come across as being honest, open and trustworthy. It is a good habit that pays off hugely over time. One of my standing interview questions is what I call the 'Kobayashi Maru' question – I keep asking someone questions on a complex subject, until we reach a level of detail where they don't know the answer. I don't hire anyone who doesn't very plainly tell me that they don't know. Admitting that you don't know something is also the general principle behind the ability to ask 'dumb' questions. Project managers have a tendency to defer to subject matter experts without voicing obvious concerns or asking enough questions – not a good thing given that it's part of their role to flush out risks and issues. To beat this tendency, consider that even subject matter experts don't always know what others are talking about. On average, the higher the total subject IQ in the room, the more likely it is that multiple people are feigning a better understanding of the subject than they actually have. Dumb questions have enormous value by forcing the jargon to be abandoned and by ensuring that there is a clear joint understanding. It's of such high value that if you aren't there to ask the dumb questions, you'd have to employ someone else to do it!

– Paul Chapman, Programme Manager, Financial Services

Project leaders also set themselves apart by querying the project's business case and by ensuring that it describes and justifies the reasons and economic incentives for the project. They typically don't wait for senior managers to complete the business case, but work with them to clarify where the business is currently at and where it needs to be in the future. They drill down into the detail of *why* the project is needed, what it is that drives business value, and how/when they can measure that each benefit has been realized.

Some of the questions that should be asked, answered and documented during the initiation and planning phase are:

Why/who/what questions

- *Why is this project important?*
- *What is it intending to achieve, broadly and specifically?*
- *Which problems are we trying to find a resolution to?*
- *In which ways will the project enable the users to operate more effectively?*
- *What are the project's tactical constraints and success criteria? (Time, cost and quality)*
- *What are the project's strategic measures? (Effect, relevance and sustainability)*
- *In which ways does the project align with corporate strategy?*
- *Who are the beneficiaries and stakeholders?*
- *Who is likely to be opposed to the change?*
- *Which dependencies are there on internal and external factors?*
- *In which ways will this project have an impact on people's day-to-day activities?*
- *What is in scope and out of scope?*
- *What are the requirements and their acceptance criteria?*
- *What are the proposed and alternative solutions?*
- *In which ways can we make use of previous experience from similar undertakings?*

FIGURE 3.6.3 Considerations when kicking off a project

PROJECT DEFINITION	Take time to properly define the project
	Push back against unrealistic expectations
	Challenge ideas and the underlying business problems
	Be comfortable asking the hard questions
	Query the project's business case
	Scrutinize alternative concepts
	Collaborate with stakeholders and engage the team
	Make use of previous experience
	Draw on people's creativity, imagination and intuition

How/when/what questions

- *How will we get from here to the end?*
- *What is required in order to deliver the project? (People, technology, materials, vendors, etc.)*
- *What are the major phases and milestones of the project?*
- *Which risks, issues and dependencies surround the project? (Including people-related matters)*
- *How will the project be staffed, governed, executed and controlled?*
- *How will we best engage, retain and motivate human resources?*
- *How are we going to keep all stakeholders informed and engaged?*
- *Which regular meetings and communications will be undertaken?*
- *How much is the project likely to cost?*
- *When are the different phases of the project likely to be delivered by?*
- *Which deliverables will be produced and handed over after each major phase?*
- *How will the products and outcomes be quality checked?*
- *Which project methodologies will we make use of? (Agile, waterfall, etc.)*
- *How will the product(s) be transitioned to the client's environment and subsequently supported?*
- *When will the project be closed down and what will the process be for doing so?*

How many of the above questions have you elaborated on when you defined and initiated your project and how many of them have you discussed and agreed upon with the project's team members and key stakeholders? Remember that it's not up to you to come up with all the answers. Defining the project is a team effort.

Uncovering the project's core requirements, analyzing business processes, designing the solution, producing the technical specifications and creating the product breakdown structure and the project plans are also a team effort. Working together on these fundamental aspects means that everyone understands what is to be delivered and feels ownership for producing a quality product. A team that understands the customer's needs and that is fully involved in the design and planning phase is far more motivated and likely to pick up on inconsistencies and suggest meaningful improvements. For this reason project leaders insist that team members are directly exposed to the client and that they help verify the requirements and the emerging solution through workshops, walkthroughs, mock-ups and prototypes.

Project leaders set the bar high and demand that requirements and design documents are clearly described and illustrated by use of common-sense language and diagrams. They also insist that each requirement is associated with a set of acceptance criteria to make them specific and measurable. A popular artifact is a *requirements traceability matrix* that can be created in a simple Excel sheet. Its purpose is to show the linkage among individual business objectives, business requirements, technical requirements and testing and verification, and to track the status of each requirement as it progresses through the project. The requirements traceability matrix also serves as a baseline scope document and is an ideal place to track and control changes that happen during the course of the project.

Project leaders are aware that one of the biggest reasons for disputes and project failure relates to changes to scope and objectives. But they also know that these changes have the potential to add significant value, as long as they are carefully assessed against their impact on tactical drivers (time, cost and quality) as well as strategic drivers (effect, relevance and sustainability). It is too narrow to assess a change only against time, cost and quality criteria. The wider strategic impact of the change must also be considered. In a world where new information and opportunities come to light at a faster and faster rate, it is increasingly important to be able to adapt and change course if it serves the client or the organization as a whole. True leadership is being

FIGURE 3.6.4 Change requests must be assessed against tactical as well as strategic drivers

Up-scoping is not necessarily a bad thing – by Rich Maltzman

Up-scoping is the process of including more products, services and features into the project at the request of your client. This is not necessarily a bad thing if it's done under change control and if the customer allows extra time and budget for it. As disciplined project managers, we tend to think of scope growth as a bad thing, when in fact it's OK if the customer wants it – as long as the project is properly rebaselined. When running a project, you are often the front person, not just of the project, but also of your organization. That means you need to have your 'antennae' up for possible increases to the project's scope – and increased revenue for the organization. The advantages aren't just more sales and more value to your customer, but also that you hone your sales skills that are useful in so many project situations. So the work you do as you up-scope your project is also earning you valuable weaponry for your own personal project management arsenal.

– Rich Maltzman, co-author of *Green Project Management* and *The Sustainability Wheel*

flexible enough to respond and if necessary to change direction without fear or apology. But we have to keep the objectives and benefits in mind. By defining a set of measurable objectives up front, we are able to steer the project's decision-making and to assess if a change is worth implementing or not.

How do you ensure that the plans and processes you have created during the definition and initiation phases are flexible enough to take advantage of new information and opportunities that present themselves? If need be, are you willing to change direction without fear or apology?

Risk management

Project leaders are excellent at proactively identifying and dealing with risks that could impede the success of the project. They don't sit back and assume that the road to project delivery will be straightforward, nor do they treat risk management as a mechanical process to be carried out in isolation behind their desk. Risk management is a fundamental part of successful project delivery, which works best when all team members collaborate and share their knowledge and insight. When risks are analyzed, planned and assigned in collaboration, not only does it improve the process, it also reinforces accountability and ownership. Project managers sometimes assign themselves to most of the items in the risk register. But that doesn't leverage the team or create a shared sense of responsibility. It's important to have the courage to assign the right owners and to gain their buy-in and acceptance for fully managing a risk.

When project leaders identify potential issues, they consider different scenarios and viewpoints, and they examine each part of the project. They also include risks that relate to strategy and interpersonal conflict that more inexperienced managers may miss. Examples of such risks are changes to the client's strategy, the possibility that client and supplier will interpret the requirements or the contract differently, the risk that trust breaks down between delivery partners, the personality and character of the key players and their ability to collaborate, or the risk that one or more stakeholder groups will be opposed to the change.

Project leaders plan for the assumption that people problems will occur and mitigate them ahead of time by putting in place techniques to manage relationships and communication. They are prepared for the unexpected and involve the team in the process. They set up meetings with the sole purpose of identifying and dealing with risks and they ask people what they worry about and what could prevent them from delivering on their promises. They do this not just with the purpose of mitigating risks in the short term, but also so that they can create a risk-awareness culture that enables the team to better spot risks in the future.

But risk management isn't just about avoiding potential roadblocks. Risks can also be positive and come in the form of opportunities. Positive risks are as important to handle well as negative risks because they represent opportunities to deliver even more value to the client. It is when we challenge the status quo and find ways to continuously improve and innovate that we exploit opportunities. But these positive risks may not always stare us in the face – especially not if we are too concerned with following the plan we have laid out. More often than not we have to train ourselves – and others – to spot these opportunities, and we have to deliberately take time out to analyze how things could be done differently.

Another aspect that project leaders are good at is assessing the overall risk profile of the project. Risk is not just a label to be added to each individual threat, as the overall risk of a project may well be greater than all risks added up. David Hillson, aka the Risk Doctor, sums it up in this way:

> Another conceptual limitation that is common in the understanding of project risk is to think only about detailed events or conditions within the project

when considering risk. This ignores the fact that the project itself poses a risk to the organization, at a higher level, perhaps within a programme or portfolio, or perhaps in terms of delivering strategic value. The distinction between 'overall project risk' and 'individual risk' is important, leading to a recognition that risk exists at various levels, reflecting the context of the projects. It is therefore necessary to manage overall project risk (risk of the project) as well as addressing individual risk events and conditions (risks in the project). [3]

According to Elmar Kutsch, lecturer at Cranfield University, there are two further problems when it comes to how we manage risk. Kutsch explains that firstly project managers don't properly deal with *expected* risks – ie, the *known unknowns*. These are the risks we understand and that we can identify and predict. According to Kutsch, project managers are often overly optimistic and delay dealing with these expected risks simply because it's easier to do nothing. His research shows that people shy away from committing to risk-mitigating actions and instead *wait and see* how the risk develops before doing something about it.[4]

The second issue, according to Kutsch, is that project managers are paying very little attention – if any – to the *unexpected* risks, ie, the *unknown unknowns*. It seems there is a tendency to focus on familiar and measurable risks as opposed to those that the project team cannot predict. One of the ways in which we can get around this is to involve people in the risk identification process from outside the project. People who think in unconventional ways and have a different viewpoint may be able to spot the unknowns that we cannot spot ourselves. Some risks, however, cannot be spotted either by the team or by outsiders, as they are inherently unknown. All we can do in those cases is to build in resilience and flexibility so that we can cope with the impact of the unexpected, wherever it comes from.

To get better at managing risks, consider these practices:

- Set up risk meetings with key team members and stakeholders with the sole purpose of jointly identifying and dealing with risks and creating a shared sense of responsibility.

- Ask people what they worry about and what could prevent them from delivering their assignments.

- Involve people from outside the project to help you spot the unknown unknowns.

- Include risks that relate to change in client strategy, breakdown of trust and interpersonal relationships.

- Determine how to best mitigate risks that have a medium to high impact and probability. Decide what you can do to lower the probability of negative risks and increase the probability of positive risks.

- Explore the root cause of each major risk by asking why, why, why.

- Take a step back and assess the overall risk of the project. It may be greater than all risks added up.

- Use risk maps to understand feedback loops and relationships among individual risks.

- Assign the most appropriate owner to each risk (not just yourself) and gain the person's acceptance.

- Encourage people to also watch out for positive risks and exploiting opportunities.

- Encourage a discussion around the project's main risks at the monthly steering committee meeting – especially those that impact the project's success criteria or where you need additional funding or time to implement the risk response.

- Always communicate important risks to senior stakeholders in person before they see it in writing.

Estimating effort and measuring value

Poor estimation is a major cause of project failure – at least when measured tactically – and something that many project managers have personally experienced. Maybe you have too. Project leaders are acutely aware of this risk and don't want to deliver an outstanding product or service that ends up being labeled as a failure because it was underestimated, or because it no longer makes good business sense in light of cost overruns. If the project has been underestimated, it changes the business case and it may be that the project should never have been undertaken.

In order to produce an accurate estimate, project leaders put a lot of energy into understanding what needs to be delivered – and hence estimated. Together with the team they analyze problems and needs, scrutinize alternative concepts, split the product into its constituent parts and quantify uncertainty and risk. They don't, however, analyze *everything* up front in immense detail, but just enough that the team has uncovered the risky areas and that a robust solution is emerging. In many cases, detailed analysis is best done gradually as the project progresses.

FIGURE 3.6.5   Good estimates are realistic; neither too
optimistic nor too pessimistic

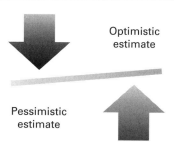

A large part of good estimation comes down to how honest and realistic
we are in our outlook. We have to be careful not to be overly optimistic, but
we also cannot be too pessimistic, as that will overinflate the estimate and
undermine the process. Many teams look at the sunny-case scenario and
provide only best-case estimates. They fail to consider the full spectrum of
activities that need to be carried out and often leave out contingency to cater
for risks and uncertainty.

Project leaders are skilled at balancing out pessimistic and optimistic
views, ensuring that what they end up with is both realistic and achievable. How do they do that? They create an environment where people can
be honest with one another and where skewed estimates are unacceptable.
They make use of estimation tools and common sense, and also apply their
gut instinct to the estimates given to them. If something doesn't feel right,
they will question it and dig into the detail about how the estimate was put
together.

To get better at estimating your projects, consider the following:

- Spend a reasonable amount of time analyzing the users' needs and
  ensure that everyone is in agreement about what needs to be
  delivered and estimated.

- Break the effort into as many constituent parts and detailed tasks as
  you can.

- Research and experiment with different estimation tools and
  techniques.

- Draw in as many experienced people as is practical, and take on
  board their expert advice.

- Have different groups of people estimate the same thing and compare
  the outcomes.

- Seek to prototype the solution before you provide a binding estimate.

- Examine past projects of similar size and complexity for guidance.

- Provide both best-case and worst-case estimates for each feature.

- Make use of the PERT method (Programme Evaluation and Review Technique). The PERT calculation is (P+4M+O)/6. P is the Pessimistic estimate, M is the Most likely estimate and O is the Optimistic estimate. This gives a weighted average toward the Most likely estimate and circumvents overly optimistic estimation.

- Factor in *all* project phases and activities, including management, documentation and training.

- Account for uncertainty. You can quantify known unknowns by assessing the cost of a risk if it were to occur (i.e., its impact) times its likelihood.

- Add contingency to every part of the estimate, particularly to account for unknown unknowns.

- Step back from the detail and apply your gut instinct to the overall estimate. Does it make sense?

- Be aware that estimating duration and effort are two different things. Estimate your project's effort in points of labor hours as opposed to calendar time and then apply a separate conversion factor to translate your effort into calendar time. This helps you cater to the fact that your team is never 100 per cent effective and that a person rarely works on a task for eight hours a day.

- Present your estimate as a range instead of just one single number.

- Re-estimate the project at regular intervals and keep the steering committee informed.

- Feed your estimates into the project's business case to ensure that the justification for undertaking the project remains realistic and compelling.

When an estimate has been produced, project leaders don't just see this as a project task that has been completed. Instead, they take a step back and look at the *meaning* of the estimate. They grasp the bigger picture and put the estimate into context of the business case and the justification for undertaking the project. They ask: *In which ways does the estimate impact the viability of the project? Is there still a strong economic incentive for completing the project? By how much can the estimate overrun before it makes the business case invalid?*

FIGURE 3.6.6 How to account for the unknown (risks) versus the known (requirements)

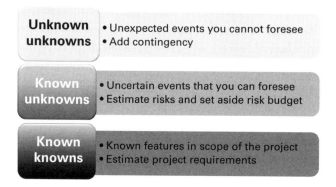

Project leaders think like an owner and consider what they would do if their own money were on the line. Try that for a minute! Imagine that you are the personal sponsor of the project. How does that make you think and feel differently about the investment and the benefits? Would you still press ahead with the project? It is in everybody's interest that you think and act like an owner and that you take joint responsibility for the business case. If someone else has already written it, ask to see it and query anything you don't understand. If it has not yet been written, take action and pull it together. If you don't know how to compose it and how to quantify benefits and calculate the payback period, decide to study it. Don't let anything hold you back. Behave like a project leader and take action to learn about the aspects that you don't yet master.

A good business case focuses on business value – by Ben Hughes

A good business case should be the foundation on which all subsequent work is built. Often business cases are written in a way to acquire funding, as opposed to demonstrating value to the business for the change. A good business case should include the following:

1. Business value – This phrase is often bandied around organizations without any real understanding of what business value is. Given that a business is a commercial structure, it's useful to state

business value in commercial terms. Business Value = Revenue
Increased + Revenue Protected + Cost Reduced + Cost Avoided.

2. Feedback – The business case must contain some mechanism by
which we can provide feedback on the progress and success of the
project. Often projects are given budgets and allowed to disappear
into the black hole of delivery, without any real feedback occurring.
The business case should contain the mechanism by which the project
will feed back to the business on progress so that the business can
regularly decide if the project or change is a wise investment.

3. Mechanism for prioritization – The business case should contain
some means by which prioritization can be done between projects or
discrete pieces of work. A common way to do this is by using 'Cost
of Delay' divided by 'Duration', which is a variation of the weighted
'shortest job first' scheduling policy. This takes business value into
consideration and allows for prioritization regardless of the nature of
the changes or the projects being prioritized.

4. Finally, a business case should be short and accessible, with
a clearly defined goal. Often business cases are tomes of complex
financials and completely inaccessible (in terms of a physical and an
academic nature). Business cases should be easy to share and to
communicate.

– Ben Hughes, Owner of Action Agile – Innovative Agile Coaching

Governance and communication

Although project leaders often have a significant amount of influence over
their projects, there is still a limit to their authority – and if something
exceeds it they will have to escalate. The better their access and relationships with senior decision-makers, the quicker they will gain a resolution in
the form of a decision. Cutting down the execution time and ensuring that
decisions are made quickly enables project leaders to move forward without
holdups and time waste.

In order for the escalation and decision-making process to work as
smoothly as possible, project leaders work closely with the executive sponsor to ensure that the project's steering committee (or project board) is
established early on and that people with the right level of experience and

authority are chosen as members. In addition to the executive sponsor, the steering committee will normally consist of a *senior supplier(s)* who represents those responsible for producing the end products, and a *senior user(s)* who represents the various groups who will be using the end products and who are responsible for providing the requirements.

It can be a good idea to invite allies as well as opponents to join the board. Skeptical stakeholders – or opponents – can be a blessing in disguise, as they influence the group to address concerns that end up producing a better outcome and reduce opposition.

FIGURE 3.6.7 Project organization chart

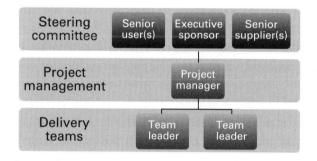

EXERCISE: How can you speed up decision-making on your project?

Take a step back and examine how the escalation and decision-making process takes place on your project.

- Is it clear when you need to escalate and whom to?

- Is it easy for you to access senior decision-makers, and do they tend to make prompt and consistent decisions?

- Are people's roles and responsibilities clear?

- Is the steering committee well established and does it meet on a regular basis to discuss the project's overall direction and progress, risks and issues?

- Is the information that you present and escalate clear and precise and does it enable the steering committee to make informed decisions?

Look at where the most time is consumed on your project in making decisions and setting the direction. Now take a step back and consider the options. What action can you take to improve the process?

Project leaders understand the importance of having an engaged steering group. They ensure that each committee member understands their specific responsibilities and that he or she is fully bought into the project. Even though the executive sponsor is the ultimate decision-maker, it doesn't mean that they are accustomed to steering a change programme and that they understand the importance of their role. Project leaders mitigate this risk by spending time with them up front explaining what is required from them – that they are expected to provide strategic direction and adhoc decision-making when an issue is escalated.

Project leaders also organize the practicalities of summoning the committee on a monthly basis and will seek to chair the steering meeting with confidence, ease and clarity. They can comfortably do so because they have the trust and buy-in from the committee members and because they have cleared any contentious issues in advance of the meeting by liaising with each person individually. Having said that, the aim is not for the steering committee meeting to be a pro forma tick-boxing exercise, but to facilitate rich and meaningful conversation around the project's status, risks and issues and major decisions. During the steering committee meeting itself, project leaders endeavor to:

- Provide an update and a RAG status (Red/Amber/Green) for the overall project.
- Provide a timeline with major phases and milestones and visually illustrate where the project is.
- Showcase achievements since the last meeting (preferably in a very tangible way) and highlight the team's good work.
- Address any actions from past steering committee meetings.
- Inform the committee about the upcoming milestones of the project.
- Provide an overview and discussion around the project's top 10 risks and issues.
- Clarify which decisions the steering committee needs to take (if any) and provide the background information for it to do so.
- Provide an overview of proposed scope changes for approval (if any) and their impact.

- Provide a financial overview in the form of actual spend compared with budget as well as remaining spend compared with estimate to completion.

As we have previously discussed, project leaders communicate with clarity and simplicity and don't overload senior executives with unnecessary detail. On many projects the governance process doesn't work optimally, either because of information overload, poor transparency of progress and risks or because of poor-quality metrics and lack of indicators. Project leaders try to circumvent this by providing good, quality information, summarizing the status and by clearly indicating when they need advice and decision-making. The same is true for the weekly status reports. They convey the project's status with clarity and make use of plain English and simple graphs that are easy to read. If the project is on track and the report is for information only, they will make that known. If, on the other hand, something is not going to plan, or if a significant risk or issue has come to light, project leaders will highlight it – and preferably address it in person rather than simply document it in a report.

Project reviews

Most project managers know that it is good practice to carry out post-project reviews after the project has finished, to conclude on what worked well, what didn't work so well and what should be done differently next time. This process certainly has merit, but the problem is that organizations often fail to learn from these post-project reviews, as many reports are never read after they are produced. What would be more effective is to review, learn and course-correct halfway through the project instead of waiting until the end. But why not take it one step further? Why not review the project with the team after each phase or iteration so that the team can learn the lessons, adapt and improve straight away? There is no time to waste and no reason to.

Susan Pritchard says that we must learn through rapid cycles of action and reflection in the moment and that it's all about learning *in* the experience rather than *from* it.[5] Tim Banfield also argues that lessons-learnt papers have limited value. He says that it's far better to get people to talk and share their experiences across projects by giving them the space and opportunity to learn from each other as the project progresses. He emphasizes the importance of asking people outside the project for input in order to continuously learn and improve.

In conclusion, there is no one-size-fits-all when it comes to project management processes, but some techniques and practices are so instrumental to success that they must be tailored and applied to any project. It is true that people deliver projects, but processes support them in doing so. These processes, however, must add value and be produced in collaboration with stakeholders and team members in order to be justified.

Top 10 project management artifacts

Below is a list of the top 10 artifacts that you might consider making use of. Some of them may be included in the PID (Project Initiation Document) or project plan. Go to www.powerofprojectleadership.com to download the templates.

1 Business case

2 Project Initiation Document (PID)

3 Product breakdown structure

4 Project schedule or milestone plan

5 Requirements traceability matrix

6 Weekly project report

7 Monthly steering committee pack

8 Risks and issues register

9 Financial tracking sheet

10 Resource tracking sheet

How to embed the new behaviour

This key described the most prevalent process-related mistakes that project managers make, including poor planning, underestimation, lack of governance and mechanical risk management. Putting in place a solid foundation is all about taking a step back and ensuring that the processes we implement make sense and add value. It's about making them human, asking the right questions and involving other people in the process.

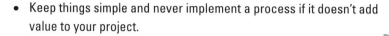

How to embed the learning

- Keep things simple and never implement a process if it doesn't add value to your project.

- Spend time gaining a thorough understanding of the project and its scope before you start to execute it and commit to timelines.

- Remember that although you are the project manager, it's not for you to come up with all the answers or to plan the project in isolation. Involve the team as much as you can.

- Share the responsibility for the business case with the project's executive sponsor and document it if it has not already been done.

- Use a traceability matrix to track requirements and verify the requirements with the users through demos, walkthroughs, illustrations and prototypes.

- Continuously look for positive as well as negative risks in collaboration with the team and involve people from outside the project to help you identify unknown unknowns.

- Involve different groups of people in the estimation process and use techniques that help you come up with a realistic estimate and not an overly optimistic one.

- Clarify all roles and responsibilities and summon the steering committee on a regular basis, e.g. every month.

- Review the project with all key players after each phase or iteration so that you can learn *in* the experience.

- Go to www.powerofprojectleadership.com to download the most important project management templates, such as the business case, PID, budget tracking sheet and a steering committee presentation template.

Checklist: Do you master the learning?

- According to your client and team members, the project's processes are conducive and fit for purpose. They are neither too rigid nor too flexible. You are using just enough process to get the job done.

- You have produced a thorough Project Initiation Document (PID) or project plan that describes the project's rationale, the business case, scope, approach, risks, issues, dependencies, milestone plan, governance, controls, quality assurance, communication strategy, costs, resourcing and suppliers. You have walked all major stakeholders through the PID and addressed their concerns in order to gain their buy-in.

- You have put in place a process for tracking, assessing and approving changes to scope. You know exactly how scope has changed since the project was initiated and what the impact has been.

- You work in collaboration with the team to plan the project and to identify and mitigate risks. You rarely have major issues crop up that either you or someone else had not foreseen.

- You regularly track the project's expenditure and include the information in the weekly report and in steering committee packs. You use simple graphs to help illustrate the message wherever possible.

- If you are running an experiential project, you have ensured that project documentation and processes are not standing in the way of innovation.

- You report on project progress at regular intervals and include information that your stakeholders have told you that they find relevant.

- Your steering committee is effective and is summoned monthly to review the project's progress, risks and issues and to provide advice and guidance.

- You have a method for regularly reviewing the project so that you can learn *in* the experience and course-correct as and when needed. You encourage your team to exchange ideas and lessons with other groups.

Write down at least three insights you have gained from this section along with three actions you will take to embed this key into your daily work.

Notes

1 Dov D and Shenhar, A (2011) What Great Projects Have in Common. *MIT Sloan Management Review* [Online] http://sloanreview.mit.edu/article/what-great-projects-have-in-common/

2 Samset, K F, Projects, their quality at entry – and challenges in the front-end phase, [Online] http://www.concept.ntnu.no/attachments/058_Samset%20-%20quality%20at%20entry.pdf

3 Hilson, D (2010) Managing Risks in Projects: What's New? *The Risk Doctor*, *www.TheProjectManager.co.za* [Online] http://www.risk-doctor.com/pdf-files/mar10a.pdf

4 Elmar Kutsch spoke at "Building the Bridge" conference at the University of Westminster in October 2013

5 Susan Pritchard, Research Fellow, Ashridge Centre for Action Research, spoke at ICCPM's Fourth Annual Research and Innovation Seminar, London, October 2013

Key #7
Work with intent

FIGURE 3.7.1

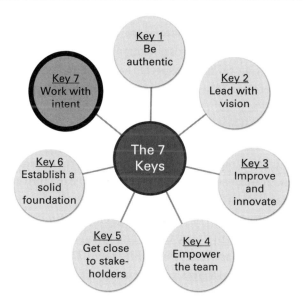

IN THIS KEY YOU WILL LEARN

- What it takes to stop firefighting and instead spend your time on high-value and proactive activities
- Why delegation is crucial to project leadership and what it takes to get it right
- How you can overcome procrastination and limit time wasting
- How Pareto's principle and frog-eating can make us better project managers

The Time Management Triangle™

In the preceding chapters we have examined certain attitudes, behaviours and activities that have the potential to transform you from project *manager* to project *leader* – that is, if you make time and space to implement them. In this key, *Work with Intent*, we look at how you can do that by freeing up time to attend to the most important and proactive activities. If you want to get to the next level, it is not enough to act like a project leader, say, 30 per cent of the time. Your entire day, and week, should be made up of actions that add outstanding value and that help you deliver strategic benefit.

Project leaders know that time is of the essence, and they do everything they can to utilize it in the best possible manner. They are excellent at prioritizing and at focusing on those aspects that yield the biggest results. They have learnt to overcome procrastination and consistently put the important over the urgent. They use delegation and collaboration as effective tools to train and grow others, which in turn frees them up to provide leadership. They don't let excuses, fear or self-doubt hold them back. They have a healthy way of training their mind so that they don't waver and go off course. The aim of this key is to show you how you can cultivate those same habits and forge the way to sustained success.

Let's begin by observing *The Time Management Triangle™* (figure 3.7.2). What you will see is that there are three fundamental ways in which you can spend your time: 1) Proactive, 2) Firefighting and 3) Time Wasting.

In the *Proactive* category you find the activities that relate to the 7 keys. This is about planning for the future, leading with vision, improving and innovating, empowering the team, applying the right processes and building relationships of trust with your stakeholders.

Firefighting is where you deal with crisis situations, urgent issues, queries, defects and deadlines. When you operate from that space, you may get a lot done, but your activities aren't necessarily contributing to the underlying drivers of project success. When you fix an issue, for example, it's true that it helps your project in the short term, but if you are not being proactive and also fixing the underlying *cause* of the problem you may be contributing to even more issues being raised in the future.

The last category is *Time Wasting*. This is where your activities don't contribute to either the short-term or the long-term results of the project. This could include unimportant conference calls, superfluous meetings, interruptions, indecision and unimportant water cooler conversations. Sometimes we are so exhausted putting out fires that when there is no fire to put out we strike up an unimportant conversation just to get a break.

FIGURE 3.7.2 The Time Management Triangle™

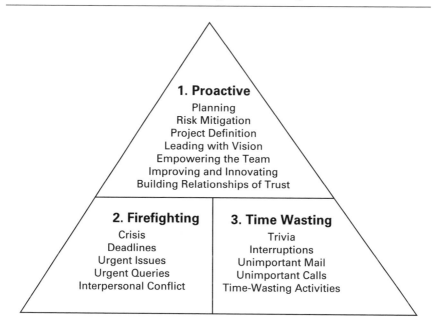

In order to get results, at least 80 per cent of our time should be spent in the top part of the triangle. Take a moment to consider how this relates to your average working day or working week. What percentage of your working time is spent in each of these three categories? In which situations do you firefight, and which activities tend to waste your time?

The issue many project managers face is that although they want to generate results, they have difficulties finding time to carry out the proactive activities. They start out with good intentions but soon get caught up in the flood of urgent requests and let the influx of queries define their day. Meetings have to be attended, issues resolved and fires put out, and before they know it the day has passed. They completed a lot of work and responded to a lot of e-mails, but it wasn't necessarily the work they had hoped for. As Steven Covey wrote: 'It is incredibly easy to get caught up in the activity trap, in the busyness of life, to work harder and harder at climbing the ladder of success only to discover it's leaning against the wrong wall. It is possible to be busy – very busy – without being very effective'.[1]

Operating in a reactive mode quickly becomes a vicious circle. There is no time to be proactive, looking ahead and building a strong foundation for the future, meaning that more issues crop up that require our urgent attention. There are many reasons why we end up in this pattern. We want to be seen as being responsive and being able to turn things around. It can feel very rewarding when people depend on our skills and knowledge and when we immediately see the result of our actions. In addition, we live in a time when we are constantly accessible via phone, e-mail and social media, and where it is expected that we instantly respond and get back to people. It takes a great deal of courage to go against the flow, to sometimes switch off the e-mail, find a quiet space to work from and decline a meeting request if our time is better spent elsewhere. But sometimes that is exactly what is needed. Remember that project leadership is not about being popular in the short term, but about doing the right thing and delivering the most value to your project and your client. If *you* don't take time out to concentrate on the big picture and on leading the team, who will?

It's only when we consistently attend to the important rather than the urgent that we get the kind of results that lift us to the next level. This is not to say that we should stop attending to urgent matters from one day to the next. The trick is to gradually change the flow of events, address the root causes of the fires and start to take control of time. Problems crop up in any job that need to be dealt with, but it is *how* we deal with them that determines if the response is effective. There will normally be at least two ways in which we can respond: a tactical way that produces a short-term result and a more strategic way that produces long-term results.

If, for instance, a client unexpectedly changes an important requirement, or if there is a flaw in the design, we have to look at *why* this is happening. In addition to dealing with the short-term impact of the change, we have to find out what we could do to better verify the requirements and the design. Has the solution been properly prototyped? Have storyboards been created that help the client visualize what the end product or service looks like? What else could be done to prove the viability of the product we are planning to build? We have to deliberately work to minimize issues by building a strong foundation, asking the right questions and taking the right action.

If we don't seek to put out the fires for good, not only will we get mediocre results, but we may also end up being highly stressed and more likely to burn out. Constantly being on high alert requires a lot of energy and wears us out, physically and mentally. It is much more rewarding to carve out time for the important and to deliberately grow and empower the team to help us create a successful outcome for everyone involved. So be determined to take control of the flow of events; free up time to be proactive and help your team do the same. In which ways could you help the members of your team to operate from the top part of the Time Management Triangle™ and to be more proactive?

To increase your effectiveness, not only do you need to limit firefighting, but you also have to reduce distractions and time-wasting activities to a minimum. What are the activities, events or circumstances that tend to be the least productive for you? Which regular meetings or conference calls serve neither you nor your client? Who has a tendency to interrupt you, and which events break your flow or steal your time? Dealing with these time wasters may require you to get better at saying no, for instance, to extra assignments, meetings or people. As we touched upon previously, you can do that in a soft way by saying 'I can't do A, but I can do B', where B is less of a commitment. You may also find that people are usually OK to be told no if you explain the reason and tell them that there is a bigger yes some-where else. It is not always *what* you say that matters but *how* you say it. So practise saying no in a way that doesn't seem like a no. Maybe you can suggest an alternative solution that could work for both of you.

Breaking the vicious circle

EXERCISE   Overcoming roadblocks to working with intent

Let's examine some of the roadblocks that might be preventing you from working in a proactive manner.

- You are dealing with the fallout of a poorly planned project and simply don't have time for the big-picture and proactive activities.

- You work for an organization where meetings and requests come up at short notice and where you're expected to immediately reprioritize your other commitments to fit them in.

- You work for a senior manager who has a habit of involving you in many of the problems that land on his or her desk. Your manager often expects you to drop your own projects to help out.

- You run a lot of smaller projects and your workload just seems to be growing and growing. More projects are being assigned to you, and you feel that it's affecting how well you are able to deal with each project in a proactive manner.

- You easily get distracted by incoming e-mails and by people who interrupt you or who sit next to you. It's hard to find a quiet moment to focus on the big, important pieces, especially as people expect you to respond almost instantly to their requests.

- You have a habit of procrastinating when it comes to certain activities that you find boring or hard to deal with. You know they are important, but you still tend to delay them.

- You work with a relatively junior team that you have difficulties delegating to. As a result you have to be involved in all the detailed discussions and rarely find time to be more proactive or think about innovation or how to build better interpersonal relationships.

Which of the preceding roadblocks do you recognize, if any, and in which ways can you start to address them? We all have a choice and we all have influence over how we work. If you want to generate better results and increase your effectiveness, you have to change your habits and those of your team members too. Anything is possible if you put your deliberate attention to it.

Prioritize the important

The first step in breaking the vicious circle is to acknowledge that you are in control of your own time and to decide that you want to make a change. If you feel victimized by a reactive company culture or a boss who always gives you assignments in the last minute, or because you have been assigned a project with lots of issues, it will be hard to break the flow. You need to own up to the fact that *you* are in control and that no matter what the circumstances, there will always be ways for you to turn the tide, slowly but surely. So make that decision now. Decide that as a first step you will set the intention every single day to focus on the important rather than the urgent. Find a system that works for you, but make sure that you take time out on a daily basis to capture and review the activities you absolutely need to focus on.

Once you understand what your top priorities are, the second step is to make time for the important. If you start your day answering e-mails and clearing smaller jobs, you may never get to the big, important parts. Maybe you end up postponing them, as you feel you don't have enough time to start a big, important activity. Consider for a moment the image shown in figure 3.7.3. On the left side you see a jar, which is first filled with water and sand at the bottom, then small stones and lastly the rocks on top. As you can see, some of the rocks don't fit into the jar.

FIGURE 3.7.3   Rocks, stones, sand and water. Always start with the big rocks.

Now consider the image on the right. First you put in the rocks – your big, important activities – and then you add some smaller stones. Now the jar looks full, but somehow there is still space for the sand, and finally also the water. Only now is the jar completely full. If you try out the experiment at home you will find that this is in fact true. If you begin with the smaller pieces, you may end up with no space for the larger ones.

You can use the same approach when planning your daily activities. The key is to begin your day with the big rocks so that you are sure they will get done. It is the big rocks that get you your results. They represent those tasks that only you can deal with, and that will make a real difference to the success of your project if you do them well. One way of doing it is to set aside 90 minutes each morning of uninterrupted time to get your head down and get some solid work done. Don't use this time to clear small items and answer e-mails; it's to be used on the big items, such as writing the business case, planning for the future, taking a step back and observing the project from afar or having that difficult conversation you have been procrastinating on. Imagine how quickly your productivity and results might increase by using the first 90 minutes of your day to complete your most important and process-intensive activities whilst you have a fresh and alert mind.

In the beginning it may not be easy to carve out 90 minutes of uninterrupted time each morning. But it is entirely possible to gradually create this habit and to make it work wonders for you. It will require you to manage the expectations of those around you so that they understand what you are doing. It may also require you to switch off your e-mail or to go to a meeting room on your own where you will not be disrupted. Many people feel that it won't be possible for them to check e-mail less frequently than they do, but I have met many leaders who have made it a habit to check their e-mail only at set times during the day. Some have even encouraged their teams to do the same. They all claim that it dramatically improved their productivity and that if something truly urgent – and important – comes along, people will call them anyway.

Whatever it takes, find a way to gradually introduce this 90 minutes of focus time into your daily routine. At least give it a try and see what happens. Test it for the next 10 days and then judge the results. Every morning, when you have a fresh and alert mind, set aside 90 minutes of uninterrupted time and focus on your most attention-rich and highest-value tasks. Make a commitment to yourself and keep it. That's how you begin to establish inner stamina, strength of character and basic habits of effectiveness.

Eat that frog!

Another way of looking at this is that you should eat the biggest *frog* as early in the morning as possible. This is a well-known metaphor coined by Brian Tracy in his best-selling book, *Eat That Frog!* The frog represents the biggest and the most important task that you are procrastinating on. It is also the task that can have the greatest positive impact on your project and on the value you are adding. Tracy writes, 'The ability to concentrate single-mindedly on your most important task, to do it well and to finish it completely, is the key to great success, achievement, respect, status, and happiness in life'. And Mark Twain said, 'If the first thing you do each morning is to eat a live frog, you can go through the day with the satisfaction of knowing that that is probably the worst thing that is going to happen to you all day long'.

FIGURE 3.7.4 Do not procrastinate. Eat your biggest and ugliest frogs first thing in the morning.

Many people procrastinate and come up with excuses for not doing something. They busy themselves with smaller and less important activities in spite of knowing that something bigger requires their attention. Project leaders rarely procrastinate. They know what needs to get done, and they have built a habit of completing the highest-value items at the first opportunity. Not only does it yield great results, but it also frees up their energy, as it saves them from worrying about all the tasks they aren't getting around to.

Which frogs are currently waiting for you to get eaten? Which important tasks or activities do you need to complete but have been procrastinating on? This could be a challenging conversation you need to have with someone, a difficult decision you have to make, or a certain report you have been putting off and that only you can do. Write down what these frogs are and be determined to clear them.

If you need a small incentive to get started, use the five-minute rule. It simply states that you should spend just five minutes on the activity you have been procrastinating on. This will help you complete the task, as it's human nature to want to finish something we have started – even if it's only for five minutes. Professor Richard Wiseman says, 'When people give something just five minutes of their time, a really interesting psychological mechanism kicks in, which is that we don't like unfinished business. As soon as that happens you are motivated to do more. By using the five-minute rule, people are motivated to get tasks finished and increase the likelihood of doing so by around 30 percent'.[2]

If ever you are in doubt whether you are eating enough frogs during your working day, stop and ask yourself the following questions: *Am I inventing things to do to avoid the important? Am I being productive or just active?* In fact you can add these questions to your electronic diary and schedule them so that they pop up at a specific or random time every day. Try it and see what happens. It is an excellent way to remind you of where you should put your attention.

FIGURE 3.7.5   To increase your productivity, ask yourself these important questions every single day

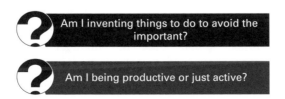

Limit multitasking

Another consideration that can help you increase your focus is to limit multitasking. Multitasking is a symptom of trying to do too much at once and is often something we revert to when we are being reactive and firefight. Multitasking gives us the illusion that we are being more productive because we are more active, but in reality the opposite is true. Research shows that when people carry out two cognitive tasks at once, their cognitive capacity can drop by up to 50 per cent.[3] It's a phenomenon called dual-task interference.

Our brains simply aren't wired to multitask. While it may seem as if we are juggling many balls simultaneously, what we are really doing is switching our concentration rapidly between tasks and frequently dropping something in the process. As we switch between multiple tasks, we lose significant amounts of focus and time and we lose even more as the tasks become increasingly complex.[4] As our brain can't process two simultaneous, separate streams of information and encode them fully into short-term memory, it also means that they can't be transferred into long-term memory for later use.

Take a moment and think about some of the things you are doing right now as you are reading this book. Perhaps you are also listening to music, texting a friend or having a conversation with a family member. And what about work-related situations? Do you sometimes multitask by checking your e-mail whilst in conversation with a team member? To optimize your effectiveness and retain information, it's important that you focus singlemindedly on one task at a time. As the brain's ability to process items and make great decisions is limited, you have to conserve this resource and use it well. If accuracy and depth of thinking is important, don't divide your attention among multiple tasks. This is particularly important when you have your 90 minutes of dedicated frog-eating time in the morning.

Pareto's principle

Another powerful practice to observe is Pareto's principle, or the 80-20 rule. Pareto was an Italian economist who proved that 80 per cent of the effects stem from 20 per cent of the causes. He observed that 80 per cent of the land in Italy was owned by 20 per cent of the population and that 20 per cent of the pea pods in his garden contained 80 per cent of the peas. Pareto's principle can be applied in many different contexts; it may, for instance, be that 80 per cent of the faults in your product relate to only 20 per cent of the features or that 80 per cent of the results from your team are produced by

FIGURE 3.7.6 Applying the 80-20 rule

80-20 RULE	What are the 20 per cent of activities you do during your day or week that generate 80 per cent of your results?
	What is it that you do really well and that always works wonders for you?
	What would happen if you were to pay more attention to these 20 per cent? In which ways would it benefit you?
	How can you start to focus more on these 20 per cent?

20 per cent of the team members. It is an interesting principle to play with and that can help us focus on the highest-yielding areas.

The key question is *what are the 20 per cent of activities that generate 80 per cent of your successes?* What is it that you do really well and that always works wonders for you? Is it a certain meeting you hold, a certain person you ask for advice, a certain way you involve your team, a certain technique you use? Have a think. These 20 per cent of activities are part of your blueprint for success. Make sure you never compromise on those activities, but that you amplify them where you can.

When I originally asked myself this question, I found that it was the weekly user group meetings and the monthly steering committee meetings that produced most of my results. The weekly user group meeting was a regular gathering of all key stakeholders and team leaders. This was the forum where strategic decisions were made and where questions about scope and priorities and ad hoc queries would be answered. The meeting took place at the same time each week and consisted of the same group of team leaders and key stakeholders. I chaired the meeting myself so that I could ensure that all major topics were discussed and that actions were agreed to. After I realized exactly how important this meeting was, I made sure it always happened, that I was exceptionally well prepared and that I recorded all decisions in the most detailed and accurate manner possible.

The art of delegation

One of the most significant changes you can make, which will instantly help you to free up time and to focus on the big picture, is to delegate more to your team. The biggest stumbling blocks project managers face when it comes to delegation is that they either don't feel they have anyone to delegate to or that they believe they have to know it all and do it all by themselves. They want to be in control of the detail and therefore have little faith that someone else can carry out the task as well as they can. But delegation is essential if you want to get to the next level and produce as much value as possible for your client. I repeat: it is *essential* that you learn to delegate and build up other people's ability to handle the detail if you want to operate as a project leader. Controlling the detail is a symptom of micromanagement, not that of an enabling leader. Your role is not to know it all and do it all but to enable your team to operate to the best of its ability.

The question you need to ask is '*how?*' How can you start to delegate more of the day-to-day activities and thereby free yourself up to attend to your leadership role? There is always a way to do it, but you must be prepared that things will be done differently – and maybe even better – than if *you* did them. You also need to accept that delegating to others will require some up-front investment of your time because you will have to train people. You can't expect others to pick up a new task and to run with it without first having been supervised, trained or mentored.

When you begin to pass on tasks to your team, make sure that you don't delegate the 20 per cent of activities that generate 80 per cent of your successes. Those tasks should remain with you. The most obvious activities to start delegating are administrative tasks, of which there are many on a project: time sheet tracking, financial tracking, keeping the document repository up to date, taking minutes, creating newsletters, etc. It is essential that these activities are done, but it is not essential that *you* do them. Someone else is likely to be better skilled – and eager – to do this than you. So get a project administrator on board, or ask the project management office (PMO) – if you have one – for help. If not, you may have to create a business case for why a project administrator – or a more junior project manager – should be added to the team or department. Take a minute to ponder that thought. Is it possible that the person you need to delegate to is not yet part of your team and that you need to create a case for it?

The other areas you can consider delegating are detailed planning, decision-making and execution of specific work streams. Initially you may not feel that your team leaders are fully qualified to do this, but by gradually handing over the work, and supporting them in the process, you will find that they quickly rise to the challenge. Many managers make the mistake of handing over a task too quickly without making it clear what kind of outcomes they expect and without regularly supporting or checking in with the person they have delegated to. When they later find that the task wasn't done to the standard they expected, they quickly take back control of the assignment.

When you delegate a task – or an entire job role – take time to think through what you expect to be done and what results you want. Then give people the support they need to succeed. Think back to the *yin and yang of project leadership* that we discussed on page 140. Project leaders use a lot of supporting yin as well as challenging yang when leading a team. The same is true when it comes to delegation. You have to make your expectations clear and set the standards high so that the assignment stretches people. Agree on a deadline and make the outcome as measurable as possible. At the same token you need to provide people with all the support they need to meet the expectations. Ask them what they need from you in terms of guidance and training and check in with them regularly to find out how they are getting on.

It is this strategy of making the outcome as SMART as possible – whilst providing the team member with as much support as needed – that is the essential ingredient of effective delegation. Can you see how this approach will enable you to keep an overview of the job you are delegating whilst not getting lost in the detail? Can you also see how it will make it easier for you to gradually let go of the detail? If the answer is no and you are still reluctant to delegate part of your job, you may want to examine why that is. Could it be that your need for *certainty* is having a negative impact on your ability to empower, trust and delegate to others? Could it be that this need is leading you to exercise control over people, information and decisions on your project? If you have a high need for certainty, why not look at other ways in which you can satisfy it. Could you, for instance, increase the level of certainty by improving people's skills, by only delegating smaller jobs, by setting shorter time frames, etc? Remember that delegation is essential to project leadership, so start to challenge yourself and experiment with how you can make it work for you.

If you are delegating to someone who is already very competent but who lacks confidence, chances are that the person will need your moral support and praise more than anything. If, however, you are delegating to someone who doesn't have all the knowledge required, you may initially have to show the individual how to do the work and only gradually take a step back when you see that he or she masters the task. Deliberately set people up for success by assessing what they need from you and then providing them with it.

The beauty of delegation is that not only does it free you up to attend to the strategic and proactive leadership activities, but it also develops and empowers your team when done correctly. The best way to delegate is to match a task with a real interest from your team member's point of view.

If one of your team leaders is keen to become a better planner or better at estimating effort, what an excellent opportunity for both of you. You help the member align personal interests and purpose to that of the project. Try to see the situation from your team members' point of view. What is in it for them? Which of *their* needs and desires do they get fulfilled by taking on one of the tasks you want to delegate?

Project managers believe they have to be involved in all the detail – by Peter Taylor

The most common mistake that I see inexperienced project managers make is that they believe, as I did when I was learning the skill, that they have to be involved in all the detail, that absence from a meeting will have a negative impact on the project success, that not being on that call will mean that they will miss something really important. In fact this generally slows things down, and good project leaders will identify when and where they need to be involved, where they need to be part of the decision-making process and when the project team is more than capable of getting it right. Mature project managers will not commit all of their time but will move to where the project (and project team) needs them most, to encourage, to guide, to advise and to motivate – sometimes proactively and sometimes reactively (as issues arise) but always with enough time to prioritize as the project requires.

– Peter Taylor, author of The Lazy Project Manager

Don't panic – by Benoit Jolin

At some point, the pressure, demands or deadlines mount and it becomes easy to give in to emotional reactions. Don't. When overwhelmed, take a step back and pause. Be aware that stress will affect your leadership style. Assess what circumstances are under your control and ignore the ones that are not. Divide complexity into small, bite-sized tasks and ask yourself: 'What would happen if we didn't do X, Y, Z?' Then focus only on the areas that would severely impact the outcome of the project. By tackling the discrete areas that matter most, you stand the chance of identifying and resolving the root causes that are contributing to the urgency. Your sense of cool will also calm others and increase odds of a favourable outcome in periods of stress.

— Benoit Jolin, Head of Global Supplier Experience, Expedia Inc

How to embed the new behaviour

This key was all about how you can become better at optimizing your time and consistently put the important over the urgent. It requires you to limit time waste, reduce multitasking, focus on the 20 per cent that generates 80 per cent of your results and to not let excuses, fear or self-doubt get in your way. But most of all, it requires you to get better at delegating and to set aside 90 minutes of focused time to eat the biggest frogs first thing in the morning when you have a fresh and alert mind.

How to embed the learning

- Carve out 90 minutes of uninterrupted time each morning to focus on the important. Find a quiet space and switch off your e-mail.

- Beat procrastination by identifying your most unpleasant, yet important, tasks and clear them as early in the day as possible. 'Eat that frog!'

- Pay special attention to the 20 per cent of activities that generate 80 per cent of your results. Seek to amplify that 20 per cent as it represents the things you do really well.

- Perform an analysis of the activities that tend to waste your time and seek to minimize them. Limit multitasking and practise saying 'no' if there is a bigger 'yes' somewhere else.

- Delegate administrative tasks to a project administrator and make a case for why you need them. Demonstrate that it will produce better overall value to your client.

- Let go of the detail by delegating planning, work streams and entire roles to someone who has the potential to do just as well – or better – than you.

- Make it clear what you expect from the assignment you are delegating and create a stretch for the team member you are delegating to. At the same token, provide team members with all the support and guidance they need to succeed.

Checklist: Do you master the learning?

- You start your day with a clear focus and you almost always accomplish the activities that you set out to.

- At least 80 per cent of your day and week is spent on proactive activities that add significant value to your client.

- At times an urgent issue crops up that requires your attention, but it's the exception rather than the rule. When that happens you always seek to provide a short- as well as a long-term solution, which addresses the underlying cause of the issue.

- You take a step back at the beginning of the week and assess which important tasks and activities you need to attend to. You rarely procrastinate or waste your time.

- You prioritize relationship-building activities along with other important tasks.

- You delegate anything that someone else could do just as well as you, and that will provide a stretch and a growth opportunity for the other person.

- Your team is fully capable of handling detailed work streams and decision-making, which has freed you up to provide leadership and direction and to build outstanding interpersonal relationships.

Write down at least three insights you have gained from this section along with three actions you will take to embed this key into your daily work.

_____

_____

_____

_____

Notes

1   Covey, S R (1989, 2004) *The 7 Habits of Highly Effective People*, Pocket Books

2   Wiseman, R (2013) *Project Magazine*, no 266, 11, 2013

3   Rock, D (2009) *Your Brain at Work*, Harper Business

4   Cherry, K [accessed May 2014] Multitasking: The Cognitive Costs of Multitasking, *About.com Psychology* [Online] http://psychology.about.com/od/cognitivepsychology/a/costs-of-multitasking.htm

Making the transition happen

IN THIS CHAPTER YOU WILL LEARN

- What you can do to step up and implement the 7 keys to project leadership
- How you can expand your comfort zone and break free from old ways that are no longer serving you
- How you can feel more confident, determined and driven in designing your own career
- What you can do to contribute with all that you have and become a role model for others to follow

Acknowledge your achievements

Welcome to this last part of the book where I will show you how to implement the knowledge you have gained and assist your transformation. I will help you let go of the old ways that are no longer serving you and embrace the 7 keys so that you can achieve your ambition and start to deliver better projects. But first I would like you to acknowledge everything you have learnt from the book up until this point. I would also like you to glance back over the challenges you identified earlier when you first began reading. As you look at the list, cross off all the challenges you have found a resolution to and put a tick next to the ones you know exactly how to address. Doesn't it feel great to know that you have already progressed leaps and bounds?

At a bigger scale, I would also like you to be reminded of everything you have achieved in your career to date. In the years that have passed you have learnt and experienced an enormous amount, which makes up who you are today. You have worked in teams, managed projects, dealt with conflict, built relationships, developed new skills and received recognition, and you have learnt that some ways work better than others. Take a moment to consider your biggest successes in the past couple of years. Recall the moments you are most proud of and what your biggest achievements were. Maybe you overcame certain fears or limitations, delivered a difficult project, mastered a new skill or situation or moved into a new area. Pause for a second and recognize the role you played.

We rarely stop and acknowledge our past achievements, pat ourselves on the back or examine the factors that drove us to achieving them. We just rush off to the next big thing. But it is worth contemplating what brought us to where we are, and what we have learnt along the way. Consider for a moment what it was that drove you to accomplish some of your biggest successes, and in which ways they are linked to the six human needs that we discussed. Are you mainly motivated by certainty, variety, significance, connection, growth or contribution? Be specific about the ways in which you have met these needs throughout your career. What have you learnt about yourself along the way and the manner in which you approach new situations and overcome challenges? Do you tend to dive in headfirst, or are you more cautious and considerate when faced with something new?

It is important to ponder these questions, as whatever worked for you in the past is likely to work well for you going forward. So pause and remind yourself of what your biggest drivers and motivators are and how you can use them to move you forward and into project leadership.

Whatever your achievements in the past, big or small, they all came about due to *your* commitment and your active participation. They happened because you wanted them to happen and because you put your energy into them – consciously or subconsciously. You studied hard, obtained qualifications, got your first job, worked on your first project, managed your first team, attended your first steering committee, etc. All of these steps were unfamiliar the first time, but you still persisted with them. You got on with it. You learned and progressed to the next level.

Now you have reached a place where the next step is leadership. It is no longer about your technical competencies, the knowledge you hold or your ability to instruct others. This time it is about enabling others to shine and inspiring them to innovate and contribute to the project's overall vision. At that level it is about your attitudes and behaviours and your ability to stand

FIGURE 4.1 Review your past achievements

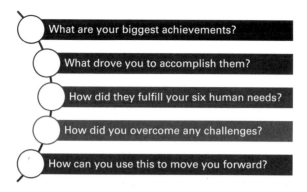

- What are your biggest achievements?
- What drove you to accomplish them?
- How did they fulfill your six human needs?
- How did you overcome any challenges?
- How can you use this to move you forward?

out and lead by example. The 7 keys can help you to achieve that. But you will become a project leader only if you continue to progress, if you dare to challenge yourself yet again and overcome the discomfort of standing up and leading the way.

If you didn't achieve the things you wanted in the past – or at the speed you wanted – it is most likely because you weren't determined enough. The determination, focus and grit we put into something is directly proportionate to the results we get. Sometimes we are very aware of what we want to achieve and we focus all of our energy on a specific goal – and quickly get results. At other times we are less determined; we drift and simply go where the flow is taking us. The better you are at directing your energy and taking action, the quicker you will achieve the things you aspire to and serve others in the process. There is no time to play it small and there is no reason to settle for less than excellence. You deserve to be the best version of you and to unleash your full leadership potential. Judging by the many failing projects, it is clear that the world needs your leadership and that we need more role models who can show the way. All you have to do is to be honest about the kind of leader you want to become, raise your standards and make the decision to give it your all.

Be honest about your ambitions

In order to facilitate your transformation from *manager* to *leader* you have to be conscious about what you want to achieve. At this stage, you understand the needs that drive you and what it takes to become a project leader. Now it is time to take a step back and make meaning from it all. Becoming a leader is not about copying other people or taking everything you have read about the 7 keys on board in raw form. It's about making up your own mind about what works for you and acting accordingly. Take all the learning and knowledge that you have acquired in this book into consideration and integrate it with your own wisdom. Simply look at the 7 keys and consult your own intuition. What does that throw up for you? What does your intuition and wisdom tell you about how far you would like to take this? What kind of project leader would *you* like to become? What does that future look and feel like for you? And what is the first step in getting there?

Answering these questions requires you to listen to yourself and to your intuition – and to be truthful. You don't have to mirror anyone else. All you have to do is be honest about the direction that feels right to you. What would you most like to achieve in your career, say two or three years from now? Where do you see yourself working and with what types of projects and people? More important, what is the *impact* you would like to have on other people, on projects and on the industry? In which ways would you like to be a role model and a thought leader and how would you like to make the world a better place to live?

Grab a piece of paper and write down whatever comes to you. Capture your thoughts and your vision on paper, either with words or in pictures – or speak it into a Dictaphone. See yourself as the project manager and leader you would like to become and imagine that you are taking steps every single day to get there. Feel certain in your body that you will reach your goals and be committed to doing whatever it takes. Decide to raise your standards, expect more of yourself and be prepared to make mistakes along the

FIGURE 4.2   What is your project leadership vision?

Your vision	What type of project leader would you like to become?
	What would you like to achieve two or three years from now?
	Where do you see yourself working, and with what types of projects?
	How would you like to impact your clients and your industry?
	In which ways would you like to be a role model and a thought leader?
	How can the 7 keys help you become that project leader?

way. No one ever got to where they are without making mistakes. Besides, it is not the mistakes themselves that matter, but how quickly you learn from them and move on. So press on. Maintain momentum and know that the universe will support you as long as you take action and do what can reasonably be expected of you. The rest will fall into place. Just keep taking action, little by little, to move yourself forward.

Determine your actions

To firm up what actions you need to take on your leadership journey, and what your first steps are, flick back through the book and remind yourself of the capabilities, attitudes and behaviours that characterize project leaders. Look at the last box of each of the 7 keys, called *how to embed this learning*, along with the *insights and intentions* you wrote down. Then determine the ways in which you can start to integrate the 7 keys into your daily work in a way that resonates with you. How can you start to be more authentic, lead with vision, improve and innovate, empower the team, get close to your stakeholders, put in place a solid foundation and work with intent in everything that you do? Which of the 7 keys stand out as needing your immediate attention?

Write down your thoughts and make your first action step as concrete as possible. Be specific about what you *will* do and by when you will do it. Keep it simple and make it achievable. It is important that you set yourself up for success by setting small goals that can easily be achieved. As you gain confidence you can start to stretch yourself and take on bigger challenges. But in the first instance, you just need to get moving. So identify the very first step you need to take, and then do it. You can develop your detailed plans later as momentum builds.

EXERCISE   Determine your action steps

Stepping up and becoming a project leader will happen only if you begin to implement those aspects of the 7 keys that are most relevant to you. So determine what your most immediate priorities are and decide to take action.

1   Which of the 7 keys stand out to you as needing your immediate attention?

- Be authentic

- Lead with vision

- Improve and innovate

- Empower the team

- Get close to your stakeholders

- Establish a solid foundation

- Work with intent

2   Which of the behaviours and strategies of the 7 keys would have the biggest impact on your performance and development as a leader if you were to implement them straight away?

3   List five specific behaviours and strategies that you are committed to implementing and exactly how you will make use of them.

4   What are the very first action steps you need to take for each of these strategies, and by when will you do so?

EXERCISE   Overcoming roadblocks to transformation

Many people start off with high spirits after having attended a talk or read a book like this one, but their motivation doesn't always sustain. They start off with good intentions and with lots of good action steps, but after a while they get caught up in the urgent, forget about the important, and before they know it they are back to where they started. So let's look at some of the possible roadblocks that may get in your way so that you can prepare for them in advance.

- You don't feel that you have enough time to try out new strategies, get a mentor or take a step back and observe where you are and where you want to go.

- You are unsure what you want in your career or if project leadership is for you.

- You are very busy outside of work looking after your family, and you feel guilty about spending too much time on your own personal and professional development.

- You feel that you are not currently in a job where you can utilize the strategies you have read about so you are finding it hard to keep up the spirits.

- You feel that there is some form of resistance from your boss, your colleagues or your spouse to see you change. As a result you are not playing full out.

- You are currently doing other types of professional development and can't commit to several tracks at one time.

- You struggle to keep up the momentum of professional development on your own. You work best when you're in a group with other people who help you stay focused and committed.

- You are unsure about the reasons, but you tend to quickly slip back into the old ways of working.

From experience, which of the above roadblocks are most likely to come into play and interfere with your plans? What has typically derailed your good intentions in the past and how might they impact you again? Take a minute to consider how you can get to the root of these threats and pacify them in advance. Is there anyone – either yourself or someone else – you need to have an honest conversation with? Or maybe you need to engage a coach, or team up with a good friend who also wants to grow professionally so that you can support each other. Make a decision now that you will set yourself up for success and address the roadblocks you have identified.

Act your way into thinking

Virtually everyone is able to identify goals they want to accomplish, but many fail to put their plans into action. I want you to be part of those who accomplish what they set out to. I want you to carry through with your good intentions and fulfil your leadership potential. Psychologist Albert Bandura carried out studies that showed that people who were good at approaching and achieving their goals had a strong sense of *self-efficacy*. These people perceive challenges as tasks that need to be mastered and they develop a deep interest in the activities in which they participate. They also

FIGURE 4.3 Mastery leads to efficacy and goal achievement

form a strong sense of commitment and recover quickly from setbacks and disappointments. Bandura's studies showed that the most effective way of developing a strong sense of efficacy is through mastery of experiences, which means that as we perform a task successfully we strengthen our sense of self-efficacy, and thereby our likelihood of following through.[1]

So the best way to achieve your project leadership goals is simply to get out there and continually take small steps forward that build your confidence. Don't procrastinate. Just take action and build stepping stones for success. Action and momentum fuel motivation, while procrastination kills it. So act without hesitation and you will soon reach a point where you know that you will never quit. There is nothing stronger than a made-up mind, so make up your mind now! Decide that you will do whatever it takes to honour your project leadership ambition and that you will continually take action that gradually moves you forward.

If you have a habit of procrastinating, a good solution may be to hire a coach. There are thousands of powerful stories and testimonials for coaching, and people who have ever worked with a coach know that it would have taken them much longer to achieve their ambitions on their own. Note that a coach is different from a mentor. A coach is someone who is professionally trained to help you increase your self-awareness, performance and well-being – or whatever your goals are – irrespective of domain and industry. A coach will normally not tell you what to do, but will help you gain clarity over a situation so that you can get to your destination faster. A mentor, on the other hand, is typically someone who works within your company or industry. This is someone who has already done what you would like to do and who can guide you. Mentors are not trained to coach you, but will give you advice and direct you based on their own experiences.

Before you decide if you need a mentor or a coach – or both – examine what your development needs are and what you would like to get from the relationship. If you decide to hire a coach, choose someone who is fully qualified. If you decide that you need a mentor, choose someone who has already managed the kinds of projects you would like to manage, and who is well connected within the firm or industry.

But be careful never to get blinded by your role models and mentors or feel that you have to mirror them. It is important that you follow the path that feels right for *you*. Become an authentic project leader *in your way*! Not in my way and not in your mentor's way. In fact, there is no other way than your way. Whilst leaders do the right thing and are excellent at collaborating and coming up with win-win solutions, they are never afraid of standing out and being true to themselves. There are enough people in the world who are good at following and copying others. What we need more of are authentic, honest and outstanding project leaders. We need project leaders who make sense of the world in their unique way, who can navigate

Aim for continuous small change – by Paul Chapman

We have an instinct as humans to look for big, sweeping changes, but smaller improvements are more likely to stick. If you work on a Kaizen process of continuous small change, it will usually have a larger cumulative benefit than trying to make a big improvement and failing. It's important to build a general positive momentum in everything you do rather than swinging between big wins and demoralizing failures.

– Paul Chapman, Programme Manager, Financial Services

Practise continuous improvement – by Harlan Bridges

I advocate that as a project manager you attend formal leadership training as well as find a mentor with proven leadership skills. Solicit feedback from team members, stakeholders, peers and other appropriate individuals regarding leadership skills. Seek to continually increase business, leadership and project management knowledge, skills and experience. Continually seek out assignments that are beyond your comfort zone, ones that 'stretch' you. In other words, practise continuous improvement.

– Harlan Bridges, PMP, BOT International

Action leads to transformation – by Kevin Ciccotti

Stepping up as a leader is one of those areas that can stretch us and challenge us beyond our expectations or perceived limits. It strikes at the heart of many of our deepest fears – the fear of failure, fear of rejection, fear of not being enough, and so on. So how do we truly transform? Growing as a leader requires us to make the decision to do it. And, once the decision is made, we must take action to drive us in the direction of our decision. As Anthony Robbins says, 'It's in your moments of decision that your destiny is shaped'.

You see, many people spend a lifetime learning about leadership, taking courses and joining programmes that promise to elevate their leadership skills. And, the only thing that will truly lead to transformation is to take new actions. Quite simply – it's action that leads to transformation. And, once we take action it's important that we monitor the results we're getting, and when necessary make changes in our approach. Too many times, when we begin to take new actions, we bump up against our fears again, because it's uncomfortable and unfamiliar, and we're not very good at it. It's critical that we take an objective view of the results we're getting and rather than judging ourselves for 'doing it wrong' we simply adjust.

Think about the first time you learned some new skill like tennis or golf. Were you skilled at it right from the start? If you're like most, then the answer is no. And, if it was important enough to you, you stuck with it, made adjustments and continued to take action towards achieving your goal of becoming a better player. It's the same with transforming your project leadership. Take action, monitor your results, make adjustments and take more action. A simple concept, yes. Just not an easy one.

– Kevin Ciccotti, Certified Professional Coach, Owner,
Human Factor Formula Inc

complexity and who are extremely skilled at unleashing other people's brilliance and at focusing on that which really matters. I have said it before, and I will say it again: the world needs your genius, and it needs your leadership. There is no playing small. Go for it and make it yours!

Expand your comfort zone

As you start to take action and move towards your project leadership goals, it is likely that you will come across situations where you feel uncomfortable and out of your depth. That is entirely normal, as you will be stretching yourself in new ways and covering grounds where you have not been before. In fact, if you *don't* feel uncomfortable as you step into the leadership space it may mean that you are not stretching yourself enough. So don't worry about treading unfamiliar grounds. Challenge yourself to new heights, as that is what it's all about. The key is to keep going in spite of feeling uncomfortable.

One of the ways of picturing this is that you are currently standing on a shore, but you would like to get to the island off shore. The only way to get there is to swim. You know that it will be a cold and wet journey and that you will not be able to feel the ground until you have safely arrived on the island. But it will be worth it. What's important is that you don't expect it to be an easy swim – and that you don't turn around when you start to tire. Just keep going, accept that it will feel uncomfortable at times, and trust that you are doing the right thing.

Stepping up and becoming an authentic project leader is not necessarily going to be an easy journey. But before you know it, you will have reached your first destination and you will have your eye on the next one. Don't hesitate! Magical things happen when you have the courage to step outside of your comfort zone. If you don't take the lead, out of fear of discomfort or failure, everything will stay the same and you will not progress. You will not become a great project leader by reading about it or hearing about it. You have to get out there, into the line of fire, push yourself and stretch yourself.

FIGURE 4.4 Growth happens only if you expand your comfort zone

Stepping up requires risk-taking and being prepared to make mistakes – by Julia Strain

Getting to the next level isn't going to be easy, because people have to be prepared to take risks and get out of their comfort zone. It is going to be uncomfortable and people will stuff up and make wrong decisions along the way. But what's important is how they handle those mistakes. Handling a mistake well is much more important than never making a mistake. Good leaders understand that if they fail there is an impact, and they manage that. They are prepared to take risks and to take responsibility. For those who do want to make the leap, there are great rewards, but it does mean that they have to start trusting their instinct, as that's the only thing they can really rely on. The way to do that is to just try it and to not be afraid to fail. Failing isn't the worst thing in the world. The more you get used to operating outside of your comfort zone, the easier it is going to be. The first time you do something new it's always going to be scary, but it becomes easier the more you do it. I have actually found that many people operate very well when they are slightly outside of their comfort zone. It gives them a bit of an edge.

– Julia Strain, CIO, Standard Bank

Manage your mind

To sustain your journey towards leadership, you have to master your mind and control any negative mind chatter. Even the most resilient leaders encounter situations that make them feel unsure or in doubt about their abilities, but they manage these negative thoughts before they spiral out of control. Feeling unsure about something can be a good sign – a sign that we are being stretched and that there is a facet that we don't yet master and that we need to explore. But managing our mind can be easier said than done. Sometimes we inadvertently end up in situations that cause us to seriously doubt ourselves. Our confidence is failing us and we feel overwhelmed and are close to giving up.

In those situations, the first thing you need to do is to *stop* whatever you are doing. Find a place where you can be on your own and where you can quiet your mind. Ten minutes will be enough. Just stand still and take a deep breath. You also need to pay attention to how you are sitting or standing. The quickest way to change your state of mind is to change your physiology. If you are slouching, looking down or curling inward, do the opposite! Look up. Straighten your body and roll your shoulders back. It is incredible how quickly a change in posture can affect the way we think and feel. Try it now. Pay attention to your body and raise your chest until you feel a powerful energy inside you. Stand or sit up straight and feel the power in your body.

Another great way to manage your mind, and to put a stop to a negative downward spiral, is to pay attention to all the things you have to contribute in the particular area. We often have a tendency to focus only on the negatives, so force yourself to also see the positives and arrive at a balanced view. If, for instance, you have just had a proposal or great new idea turned down by your boss, or if you have received negative feedback, be careful not to think that you are all of a sudden useless at everything. Find at least 10 items that you are good at or contributions you have made in the recent past. Consider all the good work you have done and what you have achieved. Bring to mind some of the moments that made you proud and remind yourself of the bigger reason for why you are doing this. Own where you are and where you want to go. Say to yourself that everyone has setbacks once in a while and that it is part of the learning process.

FIGURE 4.5   Coach yourself to success

Goal-setting	Be honest about your ambition
	Determine your project leadership goals
	Assess past successes
	Clarify your drivers and motivators
Action-taking	Expand your comfort zone
	Take small steps each day
	Act without hesitation
	Manage negative mind chatter
Self-coaching	Write down your goals
	Do a power meditation every morning
	Get a daily dose of inspiration
	Mentor others
	Ask for feedback

You are not in this game of project leadership to do what everybody else is doing. You're in this because you want to learn and progress. You want to do the right thing, add value, deliver great projects and be a role model for others. Sometimes that means getting bruised and feeling hurt. But all you need to focus on is the end goal. Dare to be different and dare to be you! Trust your inner guidance system and listen to yourself. You *are* good enough. You have a lot to offer and you are making a difference. Trust that you are on this path for a reason, that you are in this job for a reason and that you are having this moment of doubt for a reason. Now step up and step into the shoes of a leader. Do whatever you need to do, and feel comfortable leading the way. There will be moments of doubt on your journey, but that is OK. Just take a minute to center yourself and remember your big 'why'.

Coach yourself to success

In addition to taking lots of action, implementing the 7 keys and gradually expanding your comfort zone, there are a few other techniques that will help you break free from the old ways of working and transform you into a project leader. The more you embrace these techniques, and the more energy you channel into your professional development, the quicker the transformation. The choice is yours, but I urge you to fully embrace them and to commit to doing whatever it takes to step up and apply yourself fully.

Write down your goals

Be as specific as you can about your project leadership goals and write them down in a notebook that is dedicated to your professional development. Begin with the end in mind and create an overall vision and description of the project leader you want to become. Also determine how you will incorporate each of the 7 keys into your daily work. You can capture your leadership goals in an inspiring vision and mission statement or maybe in a more expressive passion poster, i.e. a collage that expresses your ambition in a visual manner. What's important is that you feel inspired and energized by the statement, image or poster you create, and that it helps you to focus your mind.

Once you are clear on the big-picture goal, work backwards and decide what the first action steps are and by when you will take them. Be specific, both in terms of what you will do and by when you will do it. It's important that you keep things simple and that you don't overcommit yourself. Make your actions positive and clear and just focus on the very first step. Then allocate time for this first action step by writing into your diary when you will actually do it. There is a very big difference between *thinking* about contacting a mentor or *considering* learning about your client's business and physically setting time aside in your diary for doing it. Start small with goals you know you can achieve and then gradually stretch yourself as you start to feel confident about your progress.

Another good way to stimulate you to take action is to set *minimum, target* and *outrageous* goals. For instance, if you have decided that you want to set up one-to-one meetings with all your team members to better understand their strengths, needs and drivers, your minimum goal could be to meet with one person this week. Your target is to meet with three people this week, and your outrageous stretch goal is to have connected with everyone on the team by Monday next week. Can you see how that sets you up for success? It will get you moving – as the minimum goal is easily achieved – but at the back of your mind you will try to reach for the stretch goal. If you fall short, however, it is not a failure, as you may have reached your minimum, and even your target. Try it and see how it goes. Write down your goals, determine the very first action step and agree to minimum, target and outrageous measures for each of them. Keep going and keep refining your methods as you find what works best for you.

Improving your leadership capabilities is an iterative process that requires continuous planning, action taking, monitoring and refining – just like any other project. Set time aside in your diary now for planning and reviewing your project leadership progress on a weekly or fortnightly basis. Be disciplined and take time out to attend to your own professional development. Treat your leadership progression as a high-profile project – albeit an ongoing one. Schedule in helicopter time at least once every two weeks where you take a step back, fly up high and look at what you have accomplished and where you are heading next.

Power meditation

Every day, before you leave the house to go to work, imagine yourself as the project leader you want to become. Be reminded of the key attributes and behaviours you would like to embrace and the *impact* you would like to have on other people and the world. Find a moment of stillness and concentrate on that image, even if it is just for two minutes. Don't move or open your eyes until you can fully identify and resonate with who you want to be. Focus on the values and beliefs you would like to embrace, and on the positive mental attitude you would like to have. Identify empowering words or phrases that you can say to yourself that put you in the right frame of mind.

In the beginning this may seem a bit strange or unusual, but little by little it becomes a ritual that is second nature to you. Before you know it, you will start to resonate with the project leader you aspire to.

The use of strong, resounding images and words during a power meditation is one of the most impactful techniques that can help you transform. The subconscious mind cannot differentiate between real and imaginary situations, so if you feed it with images of how you would ideally like to think and behave, it will start to believe it. When the belief becomes strong enough, you will begin to change your reality through your choices, behaviours and actions. Albert Einstein said it in a different way. He said that we 'cannot solve a problem with the same mentality that created it', meaning that if we want to change our circumstances, we have to embrace a new set of thoughts that help us react in new ways. So create a daily ritual, or power meditation, where you feed your mind with the right kinds of words, feelings and images. Use whatever works for you, but make it strong and real and don't leave the house until you fully resonate with the new attitudes and feelings you would like to hold.

Be inspired and inspire others

To keep your spirits high and continue on your leadership journey, read inspirational books, listen to podcasts and connect with inspirational people, either in person or online. Feeding your mind with empowering information, for at least 15 minutes each day, is one of the best sources for recharging your batteries and cultivating desire. There is a lot out there in terms of good leadership books, goal-setting programmes, mind training and stimulating videos. It's also great to network and mingle with like-minded people. Choose people who are positive and proactive and who are already getting the results you want, or are on their way there. As Napoleon Hill famously said, 'If you want to be rich, be in the company of rich men'.

You can also join LinkedIn groups relating to project management and leadership and any other subject that interests you. Twitter is another great place to be inspired and learn from some of the greatest thought leaders. We certainly should not underestimate the power of social media. There are people all over the world who are in a similar situation to you and who appreciate where you are. I cannot stress enough how positively surprised I have been at all the support and encouragement I have received from people I have never even met in person. We live in a truly magnificent time where we have access to the greatest and kindest minds at our fingertips. All you have to do is to get out there and start connecting.

And remember that you need to do more than learn from others. One of the most transformational experiences is to start sharing your insights with those around you. We sometimes feel that we don't have anything unique to contribute, but nothing could be further from the truth. We are all unique and we all have special talents and valuable experiences that others can learn from. So set up a website, start a LinkedIn group or start blogging about your particular interests. Maybe you know a lot about a specific project management technique, a certain industry or project management challenges such as how to implement agile on a global scale within the oil and gas industry. Or maybe you are really good with people and have found a certain way to quickly build rapport, deal with conflict or have difficult conversations. Irrespective of topic, write down your top 10 tips and share them.

You should also consider the ways in which you can start to mentor others who are junior to you. No matter where you are on your professional journey, there will be people who can benefit from your knowledge and insight. We all have a responsibility to help others be the best version they can be, so take time out to share your wisdom. Sometimes a focused 10-minute conversation can be enough to make someone's day because you brought about a meaningful and different perspective. Maybe you helped someone reframe a situation, or you helped increase the person's confidence or assisted him or her with a particular technique. Reach out, even if people don't formally report to you. Not only will it have a big impact on the person you are assisting, it will also hone your listening skills and help you fulfil your need for connection and contribution. Give it a go. Start to mentor others and you will be amazed by how much you personally grow in the process.

Ask for feedback

The last transformational technique I will encourage you to embrace is that of asking for feedback. It is often uncomfortable for us to ask other people about their opinions of us, but it is one of the most powerful actions we can take. We are much better off knowing how others perceive us so that we can do something about it. Consider how much of what others can see of you that can you see. Only a small piece! Other people can see you from all angles, but without the use of a mirror you can see only a limited part of yourself. You need feedback in order to ascertain how you look and how you come across. But in asking for feedback you have to choose the right people to ask, people whose opinion you respect and admire.

The simplest way to request feedback is to ask the following three questions: *What should I stop doing? What should I start doing? What should I continue to do?* When you ask these three questions, you give people a chance to balance their feedback between positive and less positive aspects. They are likely to highlight the things you do really well – something you may or may not be aware of – as well as areas where there is room for improvement. Asking for feedback is not about being criticized. It's about understanding what you could be doing better in the eyes of your close colleagues, team members and clients. You can overcome the discomfort of asking by starting with a person whose opinion you trust. You may come away feeling enlightened and positive. And as with everything, make up your own mind about the feedback you receive. Apply your own wisdom and decide what feedback to seriously take on board and what to leave behind.

FIGURE 4.6 Use these three powerful questions when asking for feedback

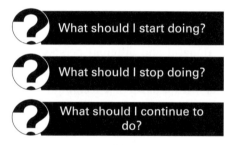

Design your own career – by Eileen Strider

To develop into a leader, pick the ways that fit your personal development. Rather than letting it happen to you, design your own career by picking jobs, assignments and training, reading and finding coaches and mentors. Once I realized I could do this, I started making decisions that moved me in the direction I wanted to develop next. For example, I knew that I wanted to eventually be a consultant to executives and CIOs, so I wanted to have the experience of being a CIO, so I would know what it was like. To get this experience, I left a company and an industry that I'd been with for 24 years and took a CIO job in a totally different industry. I was a CIO for four years before leaving to become a full-time consultant.

– Eileen Strider, co-founder and President of Strider & Cline Inc

Find a mentor or role model – by Hala Saleh

Identify what it is that motivates you the most about your role, or about project management. Is it figuring out challenges and how to rally people around a solution for those challenges? Is it motivating teams to feel invested enough that they want to get things done to the best of their ability? Is it the satisfaction of completing projects within a set of constraints? Or is it figuring out how things can get done better? Identifying what it is that motivates you is an important step in understanding what your strengths and focus areas are, but also the areas you need to invest a bit more time in.

You should also find a mentor or role model who is doing things the way you want to do them, and either emulate that person's behaviour or work with him or her to identify areas where you can improve. Improvement should be constant, and we should all have self-improvement goals that we set and track. Having an outside opinion from someone who has been successful is a great way to gain perspective and get 'outside' of our own heads.

– Hala Saleh, Director of Projects and Agile Coach

Project managers need to become bold – by Robert Kelly

As a project manager you need to become bold. Your teams may have patented engineers, senior executives and other specialists, but you are the project manager. Be bold, drive your meetings and challenge assumptions/dates/dollars. I know that is easier said than done, but if you take time to understand your company and the market it plays in, this will be easier. Also, consider brushing up on some finance classes to understand some basic accounting and balance sheets. In addition, you should understand the basics of marketing and sales, as these are the revenue generators of most companies and if you understand their space, then you will better be able to speak out and challenge folks.

I also encourage you to take on projects outside of your core industry, as it will open your eyes to different industries and how project management is applied differently. Mix it up and move from government to private or pharma to manufacturing and get into product development if all you have done is software development. There is a reason companies strive for diversity. There is real value in being able to view challenges and share your personal 'case studies' from that diverse perspective.

– Robert Kelly, Managing Partner, Kelly Project Solutions

Summary

We have come to the end of the book, where it is time to summarize what we have learnt and what we will do with it.

In Chapter 1 we looked at the reasons why the old project management regime of authority, control and task focus is no longer enough. The world is increasingly complex, competitive, interconnected and fast-moving, and to help navigate we need better leadership. We discussed the differences between management and leadership – how managers are authority-based and believe they have to know it all and tell others what to do, whilst leaders acknowledge the unknown and empower their teams to make better decisions, take risks, innovate and fill in the blanks. We also discussed the three basic mistakes that most project managers make and established that to get results project managers must be proactive, focus on the project's long-term strategy and maintain the right balance between tasks and people.

In Chapter 2 I asked you to look inwards, to assess your values and beliefs and the working patterns that may be holding you back. We discussed how you can take control of the thoughts and habits that limit you by adopting a more empowering mindset. We also examined your sources of motivation and what your big 'why' is. In that respect we looked at the six human needs (certainty, variety, significance, connection, growth and contribution) and the ways in which you seek to satisfy them. In order to sustain your growth as a leader, it's important to fully understand what your needs and desires are and how a move into project leadership can help fulfil them.

In Chapter 3 we discussed each of the 7 keys. The first key, *Be authentic*, is about being who you are, trusting your instincts and standing up for what you believe is right. It is also about creating harmony among what you think, feel, say and do and fostering the right attitudes of honesty and integrity.

The second key, *Lead with vision*, is about partnering with your client and taking joint responsibility for delivering the project's ultimate goals and objectives. We talked about the importance of considering the project's strategic as well as the tactical success factors and how you can best overcome resistance to change.

In the third key, *Improve and innovate*, we discussed the importance of assessing how you can challenge the status quo and encourage your team to think unconventionally. We looked at how questions and diverse points of view can help people think in new and innovative ways that better satisfy the client's needs.

In key number four, *Empower your team*, we looked at how you can increase motivation and collaboration by tapping into people's strengths and desires and by understanding what makes each person tick. This key is about building rapport, listening, supporting (yin), challenging (yang) and acting as an inspirational mentor and guide.

Key number five, *Get close to your stakeholders*, talked about about how to build excellent relationships with your clients, partners and customers. We looked at the components that build trust (competence, connection, honesty and clear communication), how to win over opponents and how to cater to people's communication preferences and different personality types.

The sixth key, *Establish a solid foundation*, focused on the most prevalent process-related mistakes that project managers make and how you can avoid making those same mistakes. We discussed what it takes to effectively define a project, manage risks, estimate and govern a project, and how you can best learn in the experience.

The last of the 7 keys, *Work with intent*, talked about how you can become better at prioritizing and at optimizing your time. We discussed what it takes to consistently put the important over the urgent and how to limit time waste, reduce multitasking, delegate and not let excuses, fear or self-doubt get in your way.

This brings us back to Chapter 4, which is all about the action you will take to embed the 7 keys and sustain your transformation from project manager to project leader. We have talked about what kind of project leader you would like to become and which of the 7 keys – and specific strategies – are most relevant to you. Becoming a leader is not about compliance and uncritically following a specific set of rules. It is about taking something in the external world and applying your own wisdom to it. The fundamental question I asked in the last part of the book was how you will apply your own wisdom to what you have read and what specific action you will take. We also discussed that even if it feels uncomfortable to try out new strategies, it's important that you do so, that you challenge yourself, expand your comfort zone, ask for feedback and keep refining your approach as you go along. The best way to achieve your project leadership goals is to continually take small steps forward that build your abilities and confidence.

I wish you all the best as you step up and unleash your project leadership potential. The world needs your genius and it needs your leadership.

How to embed the new behaviour

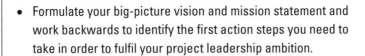 How to embed the learning

- Formulate your big-picture vision and mission statement and work backwards to identify the first action steps you need to take in order to fulfil your project leadership ambition.

- Ponder all the things you have achieved in the past and what drove you to achieve them. Feel proud of everything you have accomplished and pat yourself on the back.

- Examine the techniques you used to achieve your ambitions in the past. Utilize those same techniques for stepping into the leadership space.

- Become conscious of the items that tend to derail you and put in place methods to overcome these roadblocks in advance of their occurrence.

- Spend between 2 and 10 minutes on a power meditation every morning where you visualize what you want for yourself and what type of project leader you would like to become. Feel it, see it and hear it. Really home in on your authentic desires, skills and strengths.

- Take small steps every day that bring you closer to your goals and that stretch and challenge you.

- Practise listening to your intuition and designing the career path that best matches your desires.

- Work with a mentor, coach or accountability buddy – or all of them.

- Take out helicopter time at least once every two weeks to assess your progress and plan your next action steps.

- Ask for feedback from people you respect and admire to uncover your blind spots.

- Do whatever it takes to develop your leadership potential. Be determined, step up and decide to be outstanding.

- Take action and be a role model for others.

- Go to www.powerofprojectleadership.com for inspirational material, videos, worksheets and more transformational stories.

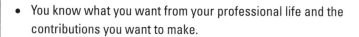

Checklist: Do you master the learning?

- You know what you want from your professional life and the contributions you want to make.

- You take actions on a daily basis that stretch and challenge you, and you are okay to operate at the edge of your comfort zone.

- You are aware of your strengths and weaknesses and actively seek to hone them.

- You achieve great results on the projects you lead, and your clients have expressed that without you and your team they would have never achieved those outcomes.

- You take your role as a mentor and role model seriously and you actively contribute to the growth of other people as well as the wider project management community.

Notes

1 Cherry, K [accessed February 2014] What Is Self-Efficacy? *About.com Psychology* [Online] http://psychology.about.com/od/theoriesofpersonality/a/self_efficacy.htm

REFERENCES

Bandura, A (1994) Self-efficacy, *Encyclopedia of Human Behavior*, New York,
Academic Press (Reprinted in H Friedman [Ed], *Encyclopedia of Mental Health*.
San Diego, Academic Press, 1998) [Online] http://www.uky.edu/~eushe2/
Bandura/BanEncy.html

Brown, R (2013) *The Influential Leader: Using the Technology of Our Minds to
Create Excellence in Yourself and Your Teams*

BusinessBalls.com [accessed February 2014] *Frederick Herzberg's motivation and
hygiene factors* [Online] http://www.businessballs.com/herzberg.htm

Camila Batmanghelidjh CBE, founder of Kids Company. APM conference
2014, New Frontiers, London. [Online] https://www.youtube.com/watch?v=
y57ZC0xzLDc&list=PLQzq_ylfBVzJpc3u_Inr2owS1v1pS8izo&feature=share&
index=2

Cherry, K [accessed May 2014] Multitasking: The Cognitive Costs of
Multitasking, *About.com, Psychology* [Online] http://psychology.about.com/od/
cognitivepsychology/a/costs-of-multitasking.htm

Cherry, K [accessed February 2014] What Is Self-Determination Theory? *About.
com Psychology* [Online] http://psychology.about.com/od/motivation/f/self-
determination-theory.htm

Cherry, K [accessed February 2014] What Is Self-Efficacy? *About.com Psychology*
[Online] http://psychology.about.com/od/theoriesofpersonality/a/self_efficacy.htm

Covey, S R (1989, 2004) *The 7 Habits of Highly Effective People*, Pocket Books

Drucker, P F (1999) Managing Oneself. *Harvard Business Review, On Point*
[Online] http://www.pitt.edu/~peterb/3005-001/managingoneself.pdf

Duckworth, Angela Lee (2013) The key to success? Grit, *TED*, [Online] http://
www.ted.com/talks/angela_lee_duckworth_the_key_to_success_grit

Duquesne University [accessed February 2014] Center for Teaching Excellence
[Online] http://www.duq.edu/about/centers-and-institutes/center-for-teaching-
excellence/teaching-and-learning/pygmalion and Paul, A M [accessed February
2014] *Time,* How to Use the 'Pygmalion' Effect [Online] http://ideas.time.
com/2013/04/01/how-to-use-the-pygmalion-effect/

Dvir, D, and Shenhar, A J (2011) What Great Projects Have in Common, *MIT
Sloan Management Review* [Online] http://sloanreview.mit.edu/article/what-
great-projects-have-in-common/

The Economist Intelligence Unit (2013) Why Good Strategies Fail: Lessons for the
C-Suite, sponsored by the Project Management Institute (PMI), [Online] http://
www.pmi.org/~/media/PDF/Publications/WhyGoodStrategiesFail_Report_EIU_
PMI.ashx and [Online] http://www.pmi.org/en/About-Us/Press-Releases/New-
Research-Why-Good-Strategies-Fail-Lessons-for-the-C-Suite.aspx

George, B [accessed April 2014] The Spirituality of Authentic Leadership [Online] http://www.billgeorge.org/page/the-spirituality-of-authentic-leadership

George, B [accessed April 2014] Truly Authentic Leadership [Online] http://www.billgeorge.org/page/truly-authentic-leadership

Gerush, M (2009) *Define, Hire and Develop Your Next-Generation Project Managers*, Forrester Research

Godin, S (2012) Stop Stealing Dreams (What is school for?) [Online] http://www.sethgodin.com/sg/docs/stopstealingdreamsscreen.pdf

Godin, S (2013) Stop Stealing Dreams, TEDxYouth@BFS [Online] http://www.youtube.com/watch?v=sXpbONjV1Jc

Hilson, D (2010) Managing risks in projects: what's new? *The Risk Doctor. www.TheProjectManager.co.za* [Online] http://www.risk-doctor.com/pdf-files/mar10a.pdf

House of Commons (2012) Assurance for major projects, Fourteenth Report of Session 2012–13, [Online] http://www.publications.parliament.uk/pa/cm201213/cmselect/cmpubacc/384/384.pdf

http://www.pmi.org/~/media/PDF/Business-Solutions/Navigating_Complexity.ashx

http://www.projectleaders.com – see the psychometric report

ICCPM (2013) *Hitting a Moving Target: Complex Project and Programme Delivery in an Uncertain World*, International Centre for Complex Project Management (ICCPM)

Jensen, D G (2013) How Leaders Should Think about Leadership Models [Online] http://www.pmhut.com/how-leaders-should-think-about-leadership-models

Kaplan, R E, and Kaiser, R B (2013) The Yin and Yang of Leadership, American Management Association (AMA) [Online] http://www.amanet.org/training/articles/The-Yin-Yang-of-Leadership.aspx

Kouzes, J M, and Posner, B Z (2009) To Lead, Create a Shared Vision, *Harvard Business Review* [Online] http://hbr.org/2009/01/to-lead-create-a-shared-vision/ar/1

Levinson, M (2009) Top 10 skills you need to succeed as a project manager @ *itbusinessca* [Online] http://www.itbusiness.ca/news/top-10-skills-you-need-to-succeed-as-a-project-manager/14232

Madanes, C (2009) *Relationship Breakthrough: How to Create Outstanding Relationships in Every Area of Your Life*, Rodale Books

Marano, H E [accessed February 2014] *Psychology Today* [Online] http://www.psychologytoday.com/articles/200308/depression-doing-the-thinking

Pentland, A (2012) The New Science of Building Great Teams [Online] http://hbr.org/2012/04/the-new-science-of-building-great-teams/ar/2

Pink, D (2009) The puzzle of motivation, *TED* [Online] http://www.youtube.com/watch?v=rrkrvAUbU9Y&list=TLubtQgNESVgeg4S-PDiwGT6RwEf-r2BBC

PMI (2013) *PMI's Pulse of the Profession In-depth Report, The High Cost of Low Performance: The Essential Role of Communications*. Project Management Institute (PMI) [Online] http://www.pmi.org/Knowledge-Center/Pulse/~/media/

PDF/Business-Solutions/The-High-Cost-Low-Performance-The-Essential-Role-of-Communications.ashx

PMI (2014) *PMI's Pulse of the Profession In-depth Report: Navigating Complexity*, Project Management Institute (PMI)

PMI (2014) *PMI's Pulse of the Profession: The High Cost of Low Performance 2014*, Project Management Institute (PMI)

Professor Eddie Obeng at APM conference, 2014, New Frontiers, Closing speech, London

Robbins, A (2006) Why we do what we do, *TED,* [Online] http://www.ted.com/talks/tony_robbins_asks_why_we_do_what_we_do#t-221391

Robinson, K (2006), How schools kill creativity, *TED* [Online] http://www.ted.com/talks/ken_robinson_says_schools_kill_creativity

Rock, D (2009) *Your Brain at Work*, Harper Business

Samset, K F, Projects, their quality at entry – and challenges in the front-end phase, [Online] http://www.concept.ntnu.no/attachments/058_Samset%20-%20quality%20at%20entry.pdf

Scharmer, C O, and Kaufer, K (2013) *Leading from the Emerging Future: From Ego-System to Eco-System Economies* (p 287), San Francisco: Berret-Koehler Publishers

Seekri, B (2012) How Perceptions Shape Realities, *ChangeThis*, Issue 97-05 [Online] http://changethis.com/manifesto/97.05.ShapingRealities/pdf/97.05.ShapingRealities.pdf

Strider, W (2002) *Powerful Project Leadership*, Management Concepts

Susan Pritchard, Research Fellow, Ashridge Centre for Action Research, spoke at ICCPMs Fourth Annual Research and Innovation Seminar, London, October 2013

Taylor, B (2013) Playing It Safe Is Riskier Than You Think, *Harvard Business Review* [Online] http://blogs.hbr.org/2013/09/playing-it-safe-is-riskier-than-you-think/?utm_source=Socialflow&utm_medium=Tweet&utm_campaign=Socialflow

Tim Banfield spoke at the Fourth Annual Research and Innovation Seminar in London in October 2013. At the time he was the Director of the National Audit Office.

Ulrika Berg, project manager at BAE systems, spoke at the Fourth Annual Research and Innovation Seminar in London in October 2013

Williams, T, Samset, K, and Sunnevaag, K (2009) *Making Essential Choices with Scant Information: Front-end Decision Making in Major Projects*, Palgrave Macmillan, ISBN 978-0230205864, [Online] Chapter: Projects, their quality at entry – and challenges in the front-end phase, http://www.concept.ntnu.no/attachments/058_Samset%20-%20quality%20at%20entry.pdf

Willis, Roderick Clarke (2014) What Drives Resistance to Change? A Leader's Perspective, *Academia.edu,* [Online] http://goo.gl/7msEvQ

Wiseman, L (2010) *Multipliers: How the Best Leaders Make Everyone Smarter*, Harper Business

Wiseman, R (2013) *Project Magazine*, no 266, 11, 2013

INDEX